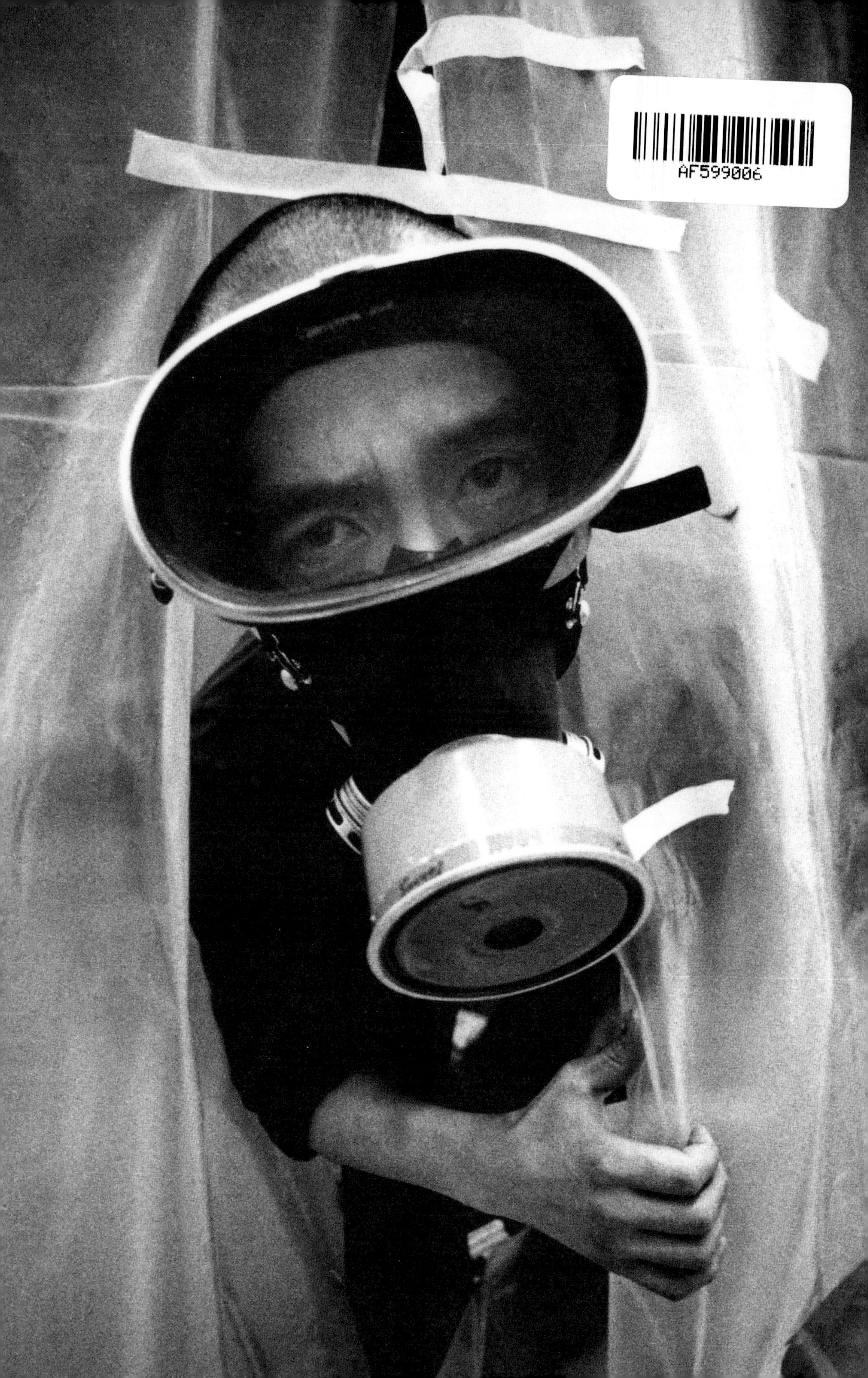

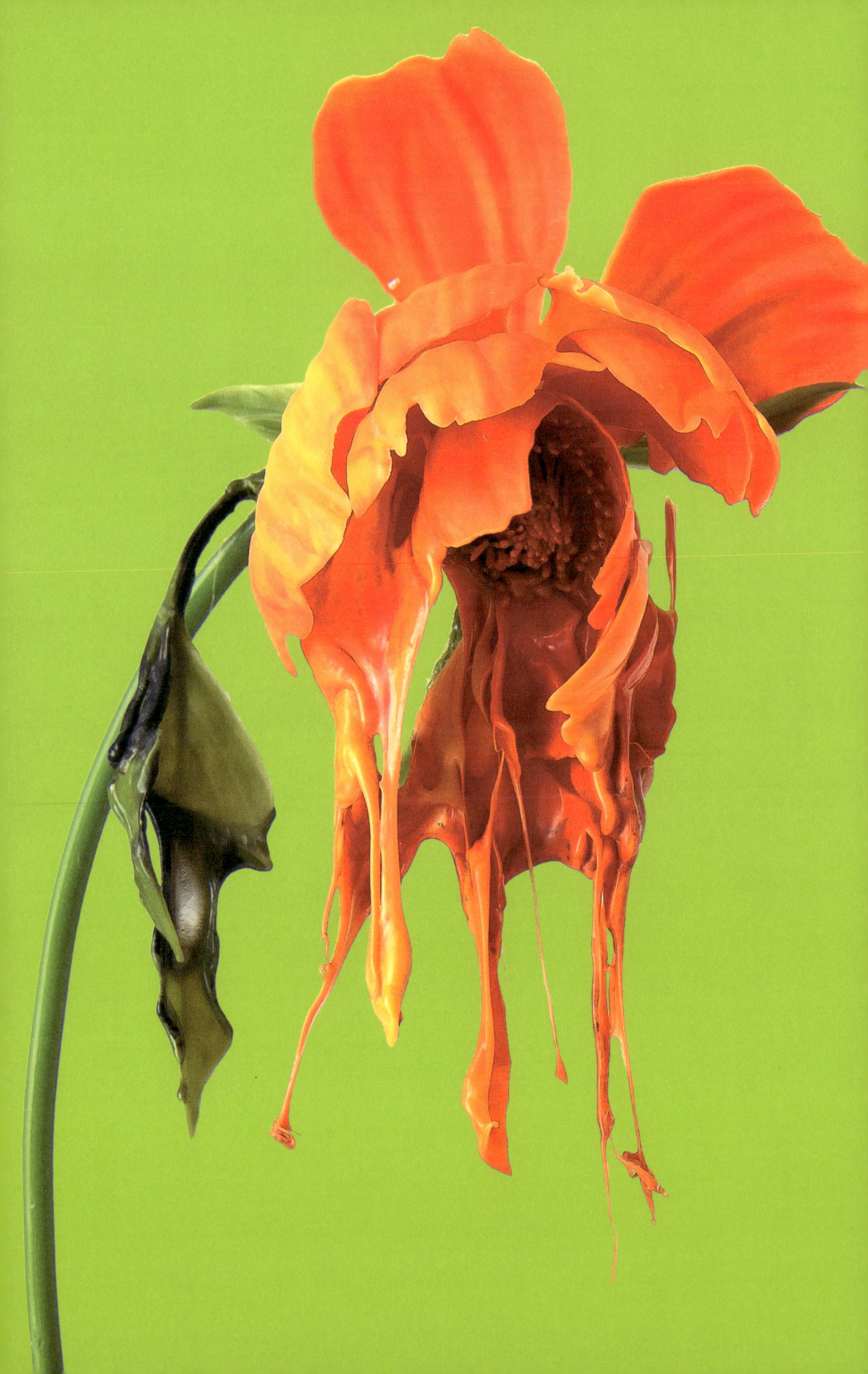

# TETSUMI KUDO

# CULTIVATION

5 Foreword
By Tine Colstrup and Poul Erik Tøjner

7 Cultivation
Introduction to Tetsumi Kudo
By Tine Colstrup

32 Pollution – Cultivation – New Ecology
By Tetsumi Kudo

36 Conversation with Kudo, Paris, 1974
Questions and Answers by Kudo

39 Biography
By Joshua Mack

48 List of Works

52 Works

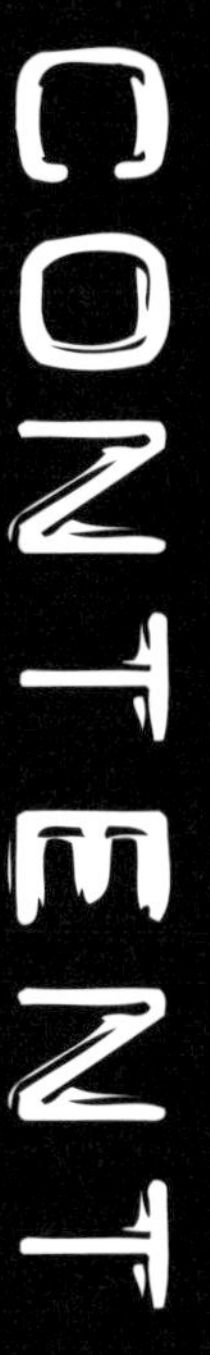

## Acknowledgments

First and foremost, we thank Hiroko Kudo for her encouragement and support in realizing this exhibition, and for invaluable and friendly assistance along the way.

Thanks to Kudo specialist Joshua Mack for graciously and generously sharing his comprehensive knowledge of the artist's work, as consultant to the exhibition, and for his contribution to this publication.

Thanks to Andrea Rosen and the Andrea Rosen Gallery team, in particular Andrew Kachel, for their solid support from the early conception of this exhibition.

Thanks to Hauser & Wirth in New York and Zürich, in particular Marc Payot, Yuta Nakajima and Maria Brassel, for their crucial assistance.

For great help with the image material, we thank Takashi Fukumoto, Assistant Curator at the National Museum of Art, Osaka.

Thanks as well to Akiko Tobu for facilitating the communication between Japan and Humlebæk.

Special thanks to all the lenders for their trust and generosity in making essential loans:

Andrea Rosen Gallery
Agnes & Frits Becht Collection, Netherlands
CNAP – Centre national des arts plastiques, France
Collection Antoine de Galbert, Paris
Collection Fabre
Stedelijk Museum Amsterdam
Galerie Christopher Gaillard and Galerie 1900-2000
Loevenbruck, Paris
Gothenburg Museum of Art
Hauser & Wirth
Kunsten – Museum of Modern Art Aalborg
mumok – Museum moderner Kunst Stiftung Ludwig Wien

and private collectors and lenders who wish to remain anonymous.

Sincere thanks to the C. L. David Foundation and Collection for its support, which made this exhibition possible.

# Foreword

This exhibition presents a selection of works from the 1960s and 1970s by Japanese artist Tetsumi Kudo (1935-90) that boldly articulate key topics in today's debates about the global ecosystem.

The old days – when humanity and culture were one thing, nature another, and the climate was just the climate – are over. The boundaries have blurred as our own role in the global ecological equation has become increasingly clear. Understanding and handling the various existential and practical issues in the human-influenced climate is no longer a concern for the few but has moved to the top of the agenda everywhere in recent years – in politics and science, even schoolyards. It is also a hot topic in contemporary art, with one work after another scrutinizing the balance between humanity and polluted nature, the relationships between the body and technology, and the habits and power balances that have shaped the current state of affairs. All these were already key subjects in Kudo's art in the 1960s and 1970s.

Kudo is at once an old and a new acquaintance at the Louisiana. The museum collection holds two outstanding works by the artist, acquired after the comprehensive exhibition *Japan at Louisiana* in 1974. Kudo featured prominently, with nine works installed in a gallery of their own in the contemporary art section. While the two works were not reactivated again until 2013, they have since played a significant part in different presentations of the collection, including a look at contemporary nature images and, most recently, in 2018, an exhibition examining men and masculinity in art from the postwar period to the present.

The museum's history provides a solid backdrop for the current exhibition. Japanese postwar and contemporary art has been a focus since the museum's opening in 1958. The collection includes a number of works by Japanese artists of Kudo's generation, notably his fellow avant-gardists Yoko Ono and Yayoi Kusama, who have both been presented in solo exhibitions at the Louisiana in recent years. Just as relevant as his Japanese compatriots in the collection are postwar movements, such as Nouveau réalisme and Fluxus, and works by artists like Joseph Beuys, Jean Tinguely, Niki de Saint Phalle and Ed and Nancy Kienholz. Kudo is often linked with these movements and artists, even if his work does not click perfectly with the main currents of the 1960s and 1970s.

For decades, before his recent rediscovery and the large, international presentations of his work, Kudo was mainly an artists' artist. American artists like Paul McCarthy and Mike Kelley name him as a source of inspiration. The thematic presentation at the Louisiana follows major museum retrospectives over the last decade in Europe, the US and Japan – at La Maison Rouge in Paris, the Walker Art Center in Minneapolis, the National Museum of Art in Osaka, the National Museum of Art in Tokyo, the Aomori Museum of Art and the Fridericianum in Kassel. Even so, the artist will be new to most people. Accordingly, this exhibition dovetails with the museum's continued commitment to nuancing the modern canon by exploring and spotlighting under-exposed movements and oeuvres in 20th-century art and bringing them into current conversations.

Tine Colstrup
Exhibition curator

Poul Erik Tøjner
Director of the Louisiana Museum of Modern Art

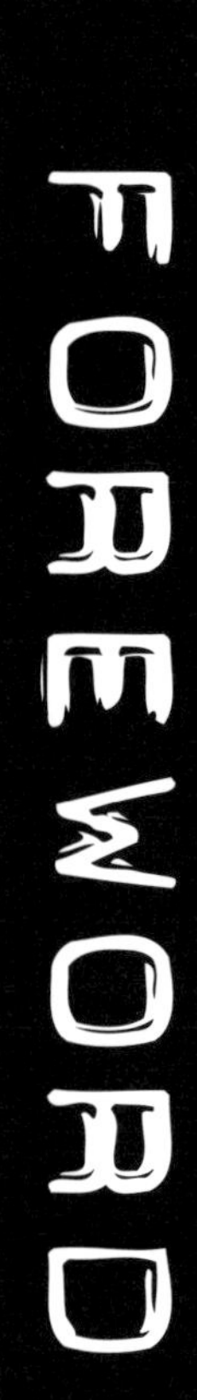

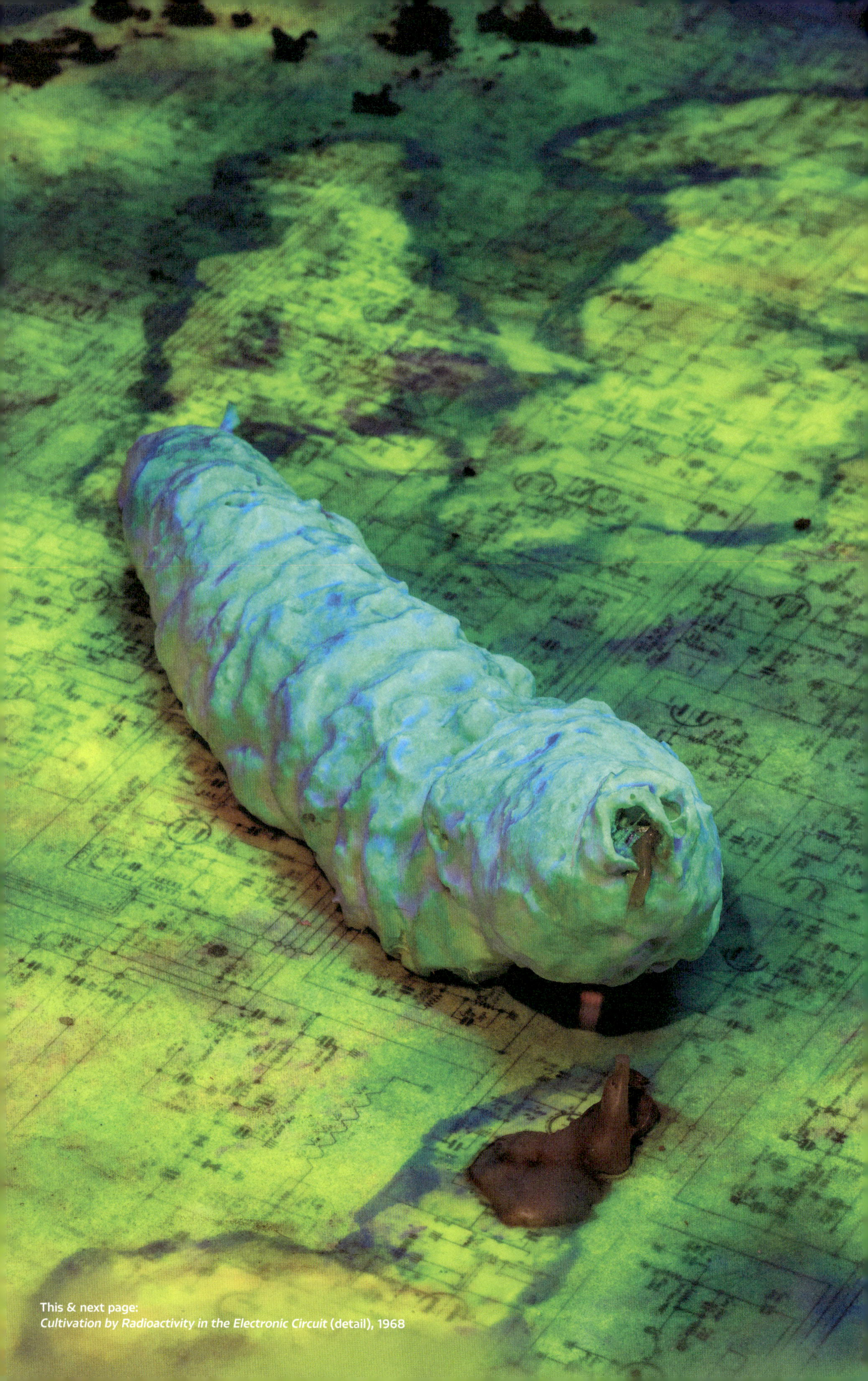

This & next page:
*Cultivation by Radioactivity in the Electronic Circuit* (detail), 1968

# ʌn introduction to Tetsumi Kudo

## 3y Tine Colstrup

**It's not a dream world, it's your current situation. :'s your portrait decomposing amid polluted nature nd the tide of technology. This decomposition of umanity does not signal its death; in reality, we are eing decomposed, we are being metamorphosed, nd we are being kept alive. My work consists in naking you cognizant of this situation in the form of visual maquette."**

**Tetsumi Kudo, 1974.**[1]

. brightly coloured terrarium inhabited by hairy noses, rawling penises and pink brains. A plexiglass dome with pallid male head, a plastic flower, a penis, cactuses and lectronic components – all growing in soil like strange otted plants. These two startling works by Tetsumi udo (1935-90), from 1968 and 1970-71 respectively, vere astonishing rediscoveries in Louisiana's storage in 013 during the preparations for an exhibition of works rom the museum's collection. They looked like they had nded from another planet. The works stood among reyish-brown sculptures of bronze, wood and iron – rom Giacometti and Germaine Richier to Minimalism - and some suddenly almost equally prosaic greyish-rown Nouveau réalisme and Fluxus assemblages and arbage sculptures by Arman, Jean Tinguely and Arthur öpcke. Finding an extension cable and switching on the lack light in one of the Kudos – the original tube still vorked – only intensified the synthetically colourful and riginal impact of the artist's works in this collection f postwar art. Even the Pop art on other shelves now ooked paler and less kapow. Could Kudo's works really e from way back in 1968-1971? I had to double-check.

No one could remember when the two works by udo had last been shown, probably not since the 1970s vhen they were acquired.[2] This has since proved quite ypical. Kudo's works are being rediscovered today and ave long been out of sight in many places.[3] It is by no neans rare for artworks to sit in storage for decades, vhich can happen for various reasons. But surely the ollowing factors could have played a role in Kudo's ase: his work has been difficult to place neatly in the uccession of isms and movements that have defined raditional art history. Perhaps, it has been considered oo outrageous, kitschy, perverse and absurd. Or, his rt has not seemed suitably relevant, with its themes nd provocative depictions of cultivation experiments nvolving body parts and nature.

While for some time it has apparently been difficult o get a handle on Kudo's work, his statements stand ut with striking topicality today. Both formally and hematically, his work seems to pointedly articulate rends in today's contemporary art, where we often ncounter intensely colourful assemblages of artificial

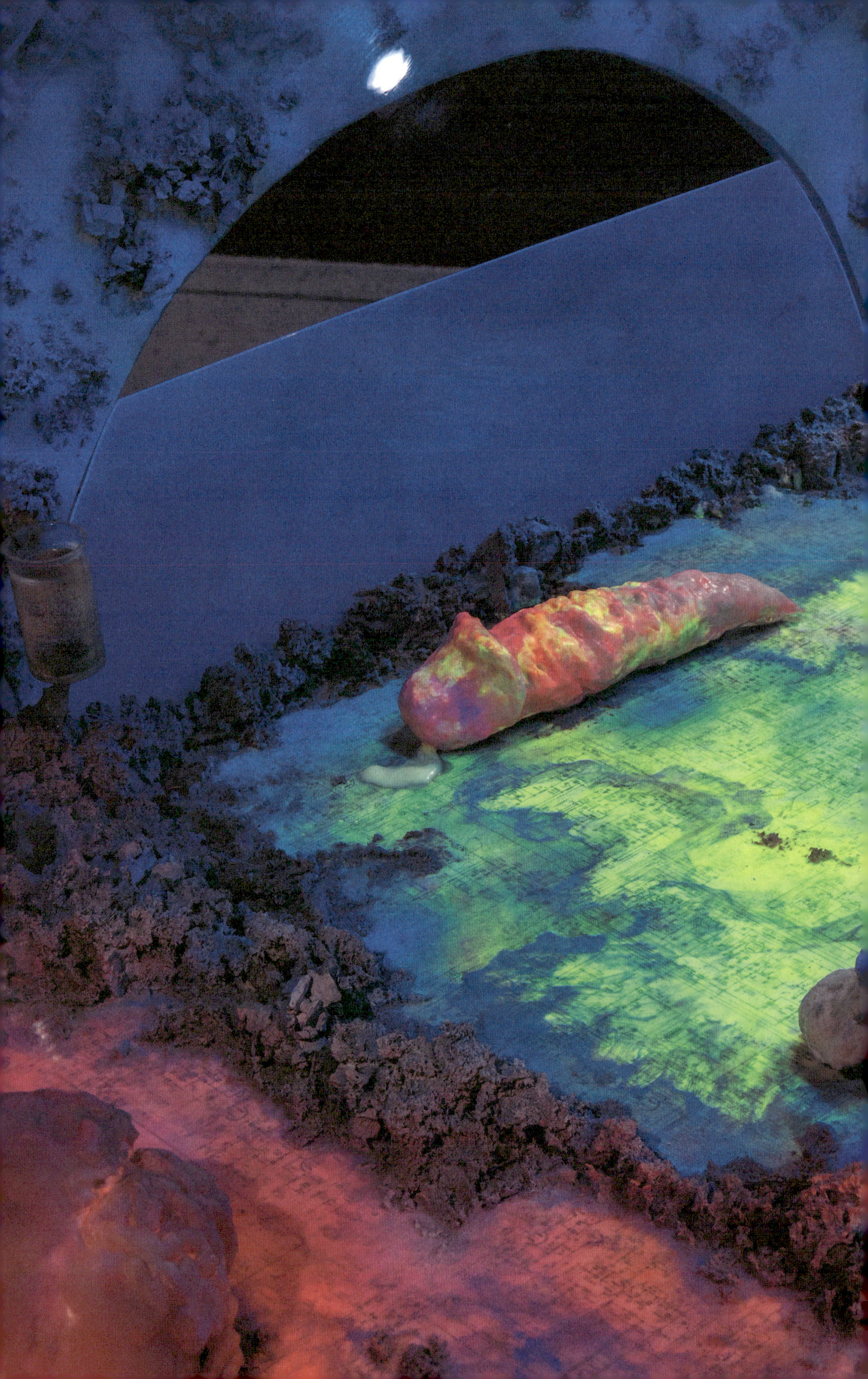

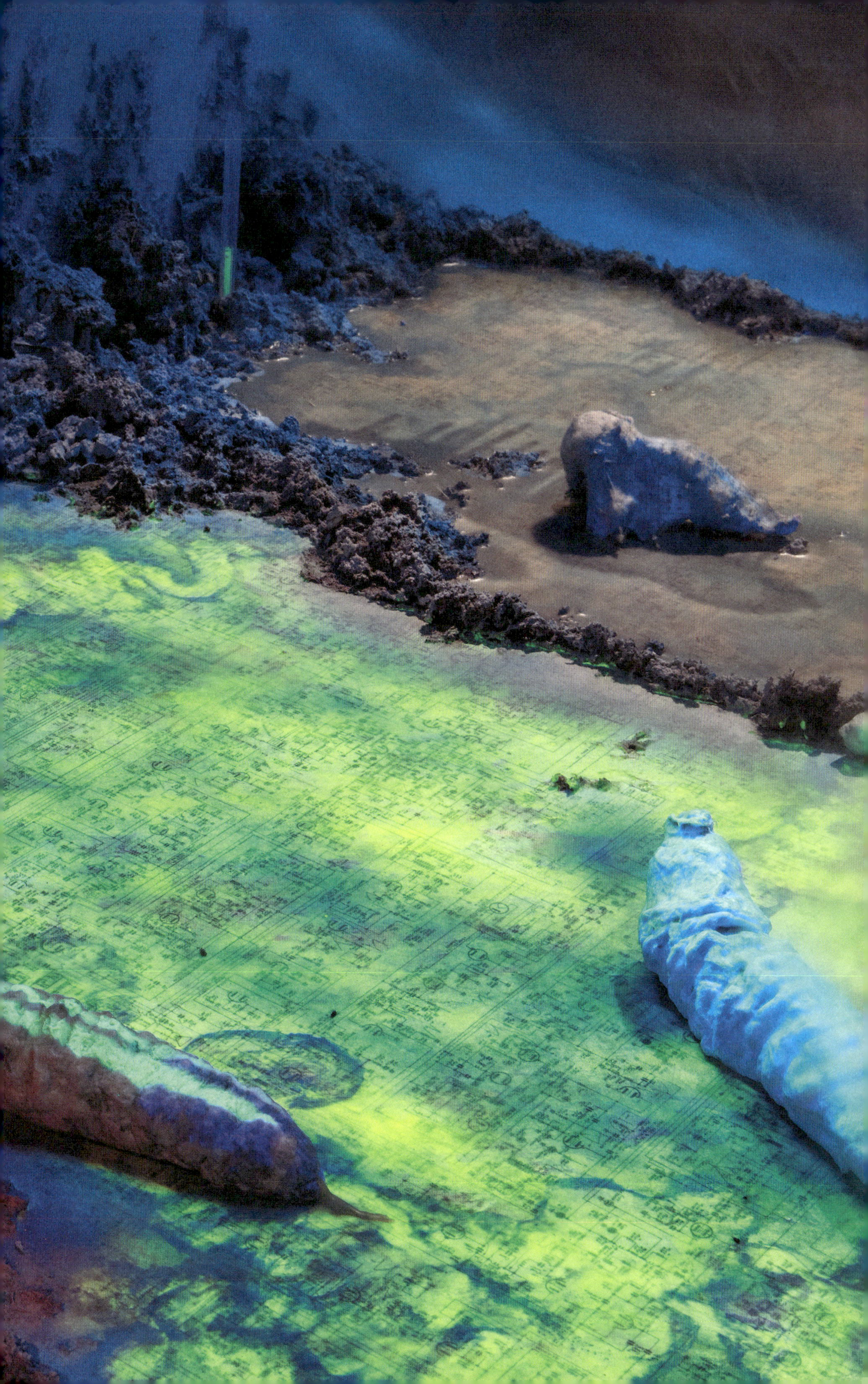

materials, small environments arranged in vitrines, powerful currents of surrealism and science fiction, and critical analyses of relations between cultures and genders. Above all, across all art forms, we currently see intense scrutiny of the relations between humanity, nature and technology, reflecting today's acute awareness of humanity's influence on the climate and the environment and the raging debate about finding our place in this new skein of geo-/bio-/eco-/techno-logy.

Kudo precisely articulates a new balance and new circuitry connecting mankind, nature and technology. We find ourselves in a self-dug "septic pit" of polluted nature and technology, Kudo says. With oil, toxins, chemicals and gas we have contaminated birds, fish and ourselves, he writes. "So, after having experimented with this comic process, we notice that we have lost our lover, nature."[4] But Kudo (cf. the introductory quote) sees scope for new biological collectivities. In his many small "cultivation environments", we find human limbs, plants and electronics growing together in new, symbiotic relationships.

These small worlds are Kudo's distilled images of the greater world. He describes his works as "visual maquettes" or "models" of the situation that he calls our "new ecology". The exhibition and this catalogue presents a selection of these maquettes from the 1960s and 1970s.[5]

## Kudo's Background

Kudo began his artistic career in Tokyo as part of a tradition-critical and wildly experimental avant-garde scene marked by Neo-Dada and Anti-Art, extending the Gutai group's radical experiments with materials and happenings.[6] In 1962, after a few short, but productive and successful years on the Tokyo art scene, Kudo won a grant to study for six months in Paris. He ended up staying, making the French capital his base for a good 20 years, along with his wife, Hiroko, and, from 1972, their daughter, Koei. Over the course of the 1980s, he gradually returned to Japan, where he died of cancer in 1990 at the age of 55.

Soon after his arrival in Paris, Kudo became active on the Parisian and wider European art scenes. He made happenings and showed in solo and group exhibitions with artists like the Nouveau réaliste group, whose members, besides the group's founder, Pierre Restany, among others included Yves Klein (who died the same year Kudo arrived in Paris), Arman, Martial Raysse, Daniel Spoerri, Raymond Hains, Jean Tinguely and Niki de Saint Phalle.

After his move to France, Kudo's work took a new turn. The abstract, informal tendencies in his early paintings and sculptural works disappeared. He perfected an assemblage practice combining elements sourced from the world of rampant modern mass-production with modelled elements, in carefully staged, richly detailed environments. Among the first works he made in Paris was a series of cubes painted like dice – symbolizing the vagaries of chance – and filled with various sculpted elements and store-bought objects that can be seen by opening one side of the cube. The dice works were followed by assemblages placed in other small compartments, and this format became central to Kudo's work over the next decades. In additio to these small environments, he also created larger, freestanding works, with deck chairs and baby strollers as receptacles for deformed body elements, as well as a few big installations. Alongside his object-based works, Kudo throughout his career stuck to his performative practice, carrying out a great number of happenings and ceremonies with various degrees of audience participation, provocation and self-orchestration.

## Cultivation by Radioactivity

Kudo's work contains rich, symbolic layers of meaning ir all their meticulously planned details. In the following, a number of Kudo's key themes will be unpacked based o concrete observation of the works themselves.

First a closer look at one of the two works in the Louisiana's collection, *Cultivation by Radioactivity in the Electronic Circuit,* 1968. The first part of the title is written in large, stencilled letters on the outside of the work, almost like a warning. As is often the case with Kudo's titles, it clearly indicates what is going on: something is being cultivated with the aid of radioactivity in an electronic circuit. The process takes place inside a small plexiglass hothouse atop a simple, blue-painted wooden structure. This contained space recalls a reptile terrarium or a small greenhouse for germinating plants, while the openings in either side suggest laboratory environments and various kinds of protective incubators.

The small environment is divided into three zones containing different "species": a muddy green zone with noses, a yellow-green one with penises and a pink one with brains. The zones are separated by small strips of soil laid out over the diagram of a large electronic circuit Inside the terrarium, we also find a small container for water and a thermometer for checking the temperatur of the cultivation environment. All in all, this is clearly a meticulously planned and controlled environment which it must be assumed, ensures optimal conditions for the species cultivated there. The built-in black light makes the fluorescent colours in the little ecosystem glow, as Kudo visualizes the otherwise invisible radiation of the title.

Kudo was 10 years old in 1945 when the atomic bombs were dropped on Hiroshima and Nagasaki. While his family did not live in either bomb zone, growing up i an irradiated, traumatized Japan of the post-war age is clearly a foundational experience for his art. Preoccupie by new theories of nuclear physics, his earliest work visualized phenomena such as chain reactions and proliferation. Later, as exemplified in this work, Kudo zooms out from the concrete nuclear processes and assumes a broad culture-analytical perspective in which the atomic bomb is but one, however prominent, example of humanity's self-destructive behaviour, as seen in the radioactive contamination of humans and the environment.

The scenario inside this hothouse is insane, a toxic, post-human apocalyptic fantasy. But we also find ourselves laughing, thanks to Kudo's superb narrative

*ultivation by Radioactivity in the Electronic Circuit*, 1968

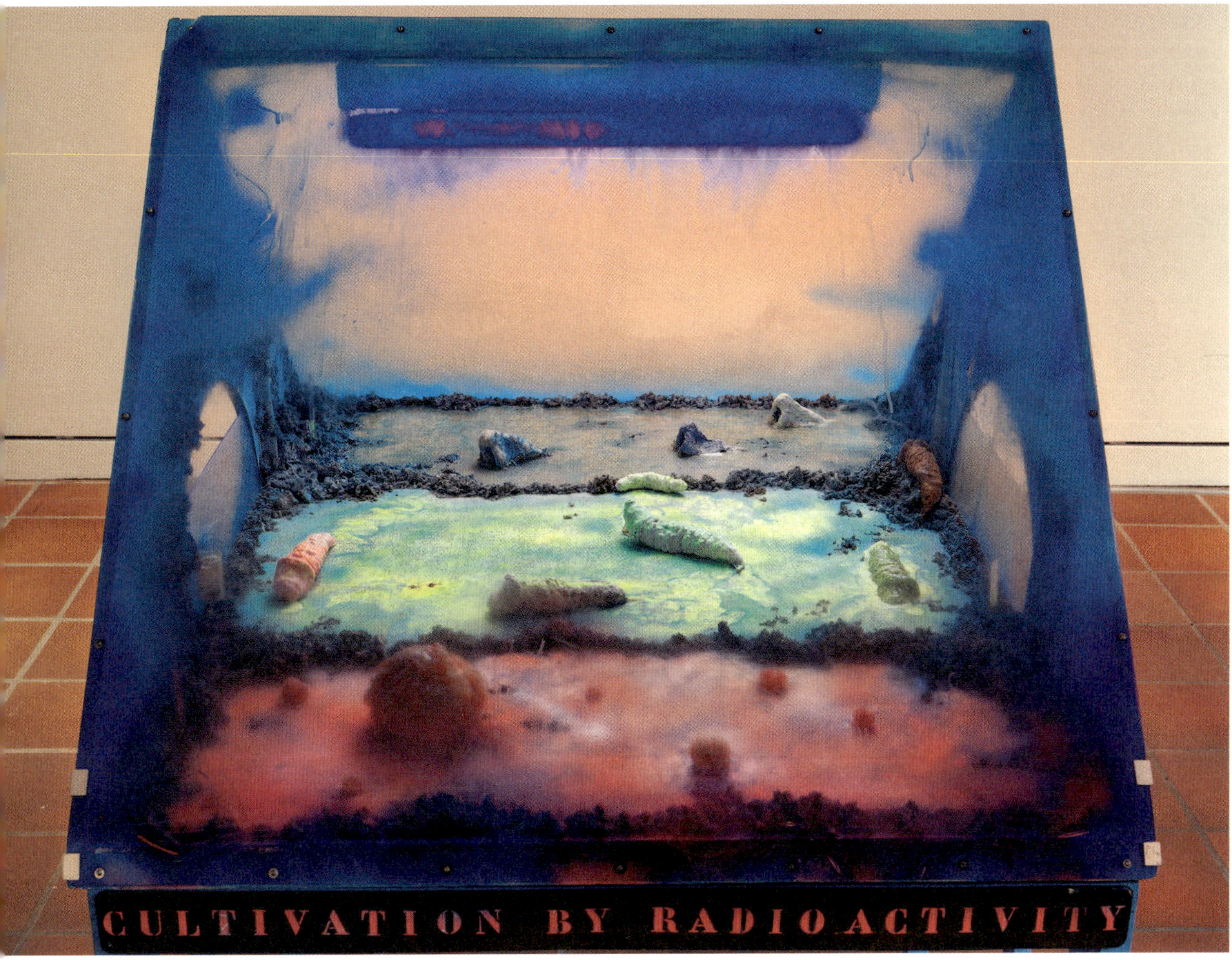

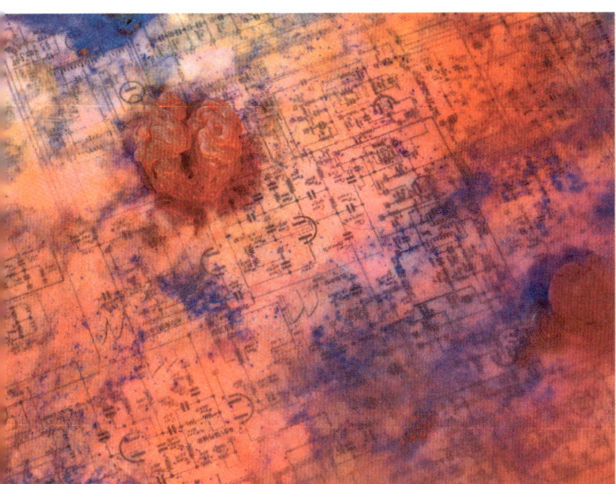

*ultivation by Radioactivity in the Electronic Circuit* (detail), 1968

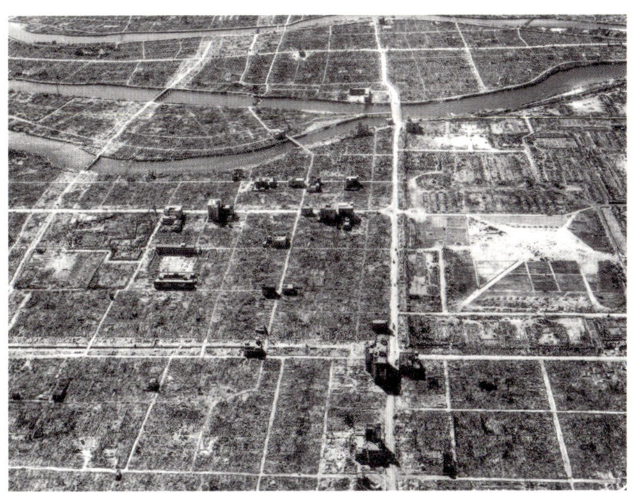

Hiroshima after the atomic bomb. Photo: Getty Images

talent and his flair for the grotesque and absurd. Isolated body parts crawl around on their own, the penises especially behaving like autonomous beings. One seems to be headed for the hairy noses (or has it fallen asleep?), while another raises its head and ... vomits?

The whole human body, of which the penises and other body fragments were once part, is missing. This is consistently the case in Kudo's work, which only shows us isolated parts – noses, penises and brains, as well as eyes, arms, legs, heads and the sloughed-off, rejected or discarded skins of hands, feet and other limbs. Kudo often uses the word "souvenir" in his titles. The fragments can be understood as reminders of something that once existed – a whole, integrated body and a whole, integrated nature.

Kudo's terrarium is a bizarre and grotesque biotechnological experiment with fresh guinea pigs thriving (more or less successfully) in a toxic, radioactive micro-environment. As mentioned above, Kudo's micro-worlds are symbolic of a general macro-condition. This particular work, however, could also be seen to have a specific Japanese reference.

We are looking into a lab experiment. But is it also a deformed, irradiated plastic version of a Japanese garden? Perhaps the gaze of a European tourist is required to hatch this idea. Nevertheless, it crops up as a meaningful reference scaling up Kudo's micro-landscape.

The traditional Japanese garden, a thoroughly cultivated symbolic landscape, is laid out as an abstract distillation of nature, a tableau serving as a vehicle for spiritual insight. Zen gardens are often arranged with large, isolated stone blocks "crawling" around on a bed of (often white) gravel, which is neatly raked, almost like a diagram.[7] The raked gravel symbolizes water, while the large stones, as islands, symbolize land. In other words, the geography of Japan, with its many islands, is reflected in the gardens. The gardens are often surrounded by walls or in other ways marked off from the outside world. Many gardens are laid out as showpieces – one does not move around in them, one simply observes these landscapes for meditation.

In Kudo's "meditation landscape", the garden's symbolic, nonfigurative rocks, lying like islands in rippling water, are replaced by very specific, recognizable body fragments. The raked gravel has become an electronic diagram, while the Japanese garden's typical monochrome calm has been replaced by a synthetic blast of neon colour. Kudo has substituted the Japanese garden's vision of serenity, beauty and spirituality with an image of a grotesque, post-nuclear world. Another iconic image comes to mind here: aerial photos taken of Hiroshima and Nagasaki after the atomic blasts show individual buildings standing like solitary islands or limbs isolated from the body of the city – on the diagram of streets and paths drawn between the pulverized remains of buildings and people.

Summing up this train of thought, Kudo's radioactive micro-environment can also be viewed as an image of the destructive power of the atomic bomb, concretely and locally in Japan. The bombs destroyed not only cities, people and healthy bodies – the glowing penises do not at present seem able to partake in reproduction – the radiation also struck at Buddhist core values in Japanese culture as embodied in Zen gardens.

## Cultivation in Different Growth Environments

In the 1960s and 1970s, Kudo develops a number of basic themes and motifs that he varies in different types of work. The cultivation environments include circular or semi-circular plexiglass domes whose contents develop in closed ecosystems. He also creates aquariums where the cultivation takes place in water, while the aforementioned miniature greenhouses or terrarium-like enclosures hold other cultivation processes. Limbs, plants and electronic components – the most basic ingredients in Kudo's vocabulary – are also planted in blue plastic buckets as a form of pre-germination. Moreover, Kudo cultivated a number of small gardens where the various elements are planted in little mounds of soil.

The most recurrent type of work in Kudo's oeuvre consists of assemblages inside cages for birds or other pets. Over 15 years, starting in 1965, Kudo worked with cages that likewise present a number of different meetings, mainly between body fragments, plants and electronic components, as well as portraits. While both the biodomes and the terrariums recall scientific experiments in clinical laboratories, the cages are a familiar cultural format from the domestic sphere. Indeed, several cages were created "for your living room" and contain "souvenirs" that we can look at with "nostalgia", to use typical words from Kudo's titles. As always, the various environments in the cages are arranged with tender care for the organisms within them. There are perches to sit on and hamster wheels to spin in. There is food in small feeding troughs – in the form of assorted pills, apparently always including aspirins – and standard thermometers for monitoring temperature. In a cage, the contents are confined, taken care of and put on display at the same time. The rich symbolism of the cage itself[8] is, of course, a crucial co-producer of meaning, particularly in the cages with a self-portrait of the artist[9] as "the artist in crisis" – trapped and displayed as a pet or a guinea pig, while hard at work knitting and transforming strings into new structures.

## The Fragrance of Plastic Nature

Kudo wallows in artificial materials. While tree roots were included in some of his sculptural works in the 1950s, there is very little organic material in his later ones, as he only kept cranking up the artificiality and synthetic colour intensity. Kudo cultivates the aesthetic properties and possibilities of plastics more consistently than most of his contemporaries, although, needless to say, many of them do dive deep into modernity's synthetic materiality – among them Ed Kienholz, Paul Thek or Niki de Saint Phalle, just to mention a few obvious figures in relation to Kudo.

Typically, Kudo makes precise aesthetic choices that do not risk sending romantic or nostalgic signals

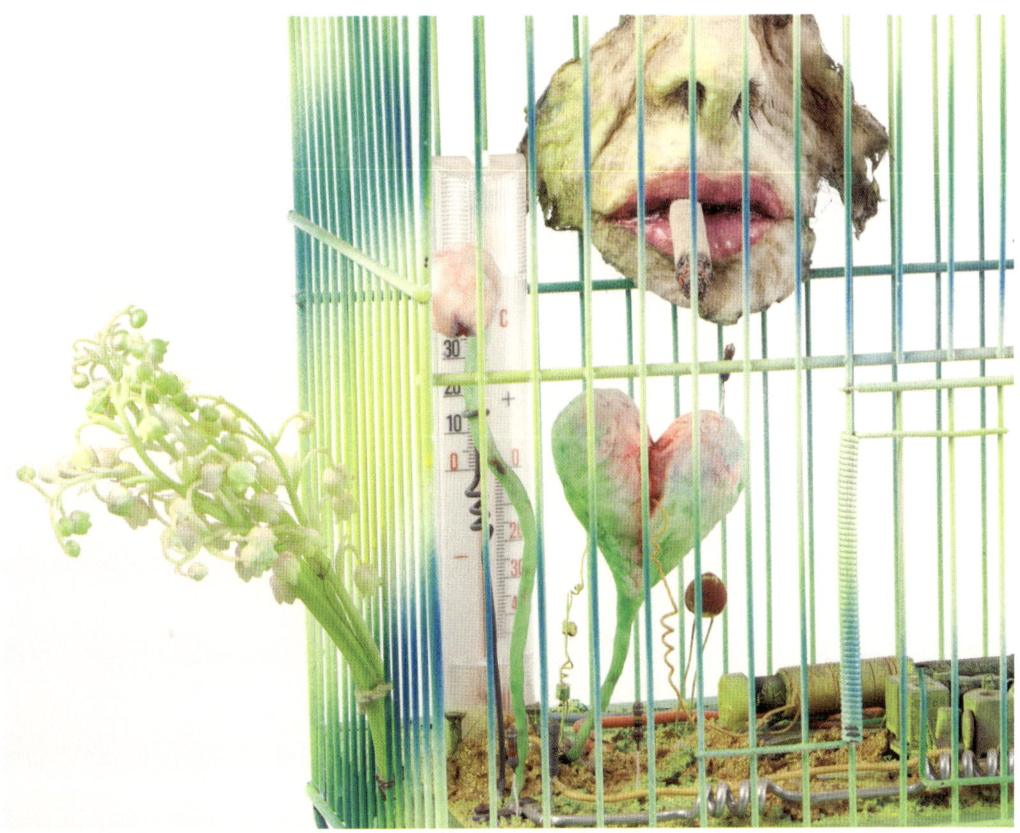

*Bonheur* (detail), 1974

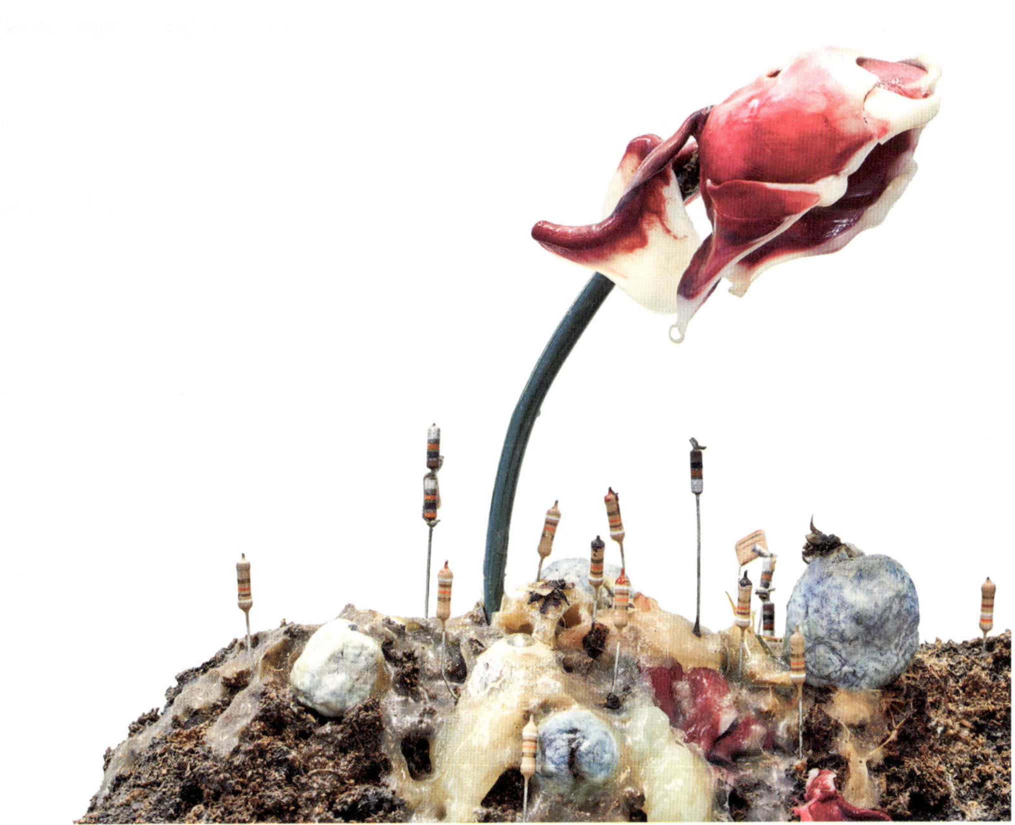

*Pollution Cultivation New Ecology (B)* (detail), 1971

harkening back to the past: if he needs a bucket, he picks a loud plastic bucket, not an old-fashioned freyish-brown one of wood or zinc. The synthetic and garishly coloured material reality of modernity and vociferous capitalism makes up Kudo's palette, to an extreme extent reflecting the boom of plastics and new materials in the postwar years and up through the 1960s. The use of plastics enables Kudo to create and sustain glistening wet, abject blotches – slime, secretions, rot – as well as sloughs of parchment-dry dead skin. The assertive and fascinating power of the works is based not least on Kudo's obvious material expertise and his detailed work with different textures. Then there are the actual motifs in plastic. Artificial plants and flowers, ready-made and store-bought, are key components in Kudo's collaged environments. Is it possible that he was the first artist to seriously introduce plastic flowers into art as a main motif? A pioneer, at least.

With the development of plastics, artificial flowers burst into new, lifelike bloom. The perversity and nostalgia that plastic flowers can be said to embody obviously excited the artist – that is, the grotesqueness of the phenomenon of "plastic nature" produced in factories and sold in shops, while wastewater is pumped into the other nature.

The flowers are important in Kudo's iconography as "plastic flowers" alone. However, it is also relevant to look at them more closely as an example of the symbolic wealth of nuances that is found in his works when examining them in detail.

Kudo uses many different species of flowers. Some of the most frequent ones are chrysanthemums (Japan's national flower – the Japanese imperial throne is called the Chrysanthemum Throne), tulips, carnations and roses. To my knowledge, Kudo has not himself described his choices of flowers and their possible symbolic meanings in Japanese or European culture. But choices were plainly made from work to work.

At first, Kudo most often used roses, sometimes growing in birdcages alongside "souvenirs" from living bodies in the form of sloughed-off skin (see *Souvenir "La Mue"*, 1967, p. 67-68). In a Western context, the rose is a common symbol of love. The flower of Venus, it is a symbol of beauty. In Christian symbolism, it represents the Virgin Mary. Several of Kudo's works from the late 1960s have noses and penises crawling up erect rose stems, as in *Cultivation by Radioactivity in the Electronic Circuit (Pink Flower)*, 1968 (p. 99). In this simple scene, a penis working its way up the stem towards the head of the rose is followed by a hairy nose hanging by its nails from the rim of the flowerpot. The scene is not only a cultivation situation in the new post-human, post-natural ecology – the rose is supported by an electronic stem – it is also a classic representation of the relationship between man and woman, carnality and spirituality. The image is both simple and complex, as so often with Kudo, and the choice of flower seems anything but incidental.

The fragrant but poisonous lily of the valley also makes frequent appearances. In France, it is a common, centuries-old tradition to present each other with small bouquets of lilies of the valley on May Day to celebrate the coming of spring. Symbolically, this little herald of spring is also a bringer of good fortune. Kudo's Paris works feature many such harbingers of the return of spring and good fortune – in cages, or in decomposed, peeling hands belonging to equally decomposed men (see *Bonheur*, 1974, p. 94-95 and *Votre Portrait*, 1970-79, p. 62-63). Best of luck, we cannot help but think, noting Kudo's sarcasm.

Let us glance once more at a widespread phenomenon in Japanese culture, the traditional art of flower arrangement known as ikebana. Rooted in the custom of flower offerings in Buddhist contexts, ikebana is found everywhere in Japan. Regarded as an art with various customs, schools and masters of carefully curated flower assemblages, it is related to the Japanese garden as an aesthetic representation of the beauty and essence of nature. Kudo's arrangements of plastic flowers are a far cry from the essence of natural beauty. The flowers may be stuck in a mess of slimy substances or oil, and the heads of the flowers are very often melting and running in long strings before our eyes. Here, Kudo exploits another aesthetic possibility of plastic materials, as melting beauty is one of the clear and impactful symbols of his iconography. The chrysanthemum, a powerful symbol of Japanese nationhood, is also represented in a state of melting, sometimes added a splash of oil (p. 83). In the 1970s, the phenomenon of global warming was not as widely recognized as it is today, when Kudo's melting flowers are hardly less dramatic symbols.

## Critique of the West

Kudo depicts polluted and deformed nature. At the same time, in equally dramatic and decidedly provocativ[e] fashion, he depicts the foundations of Western and European culture, and its degeneration. Christianity and the notion of humanism are two main targets in his line of fire.

Many of his works include small crucifixes. In the relief *Origine de la pollution*, 1972-73 (p. 92), a crucifix is dragged by a chain after a penis-snail that almost seem[s] to be corroding its way through the plastic lawn. The title echoes Gustave Courbet's iconic 1866 painting of a female pudenda, *L'Origine du monde*, suggesting a hard gender-political point we will return to later.

In *Esclavage de Conservation de l'espèce humaine*, 1972 (p. 72-73), a crucifix is held in the wrinkled skin of a hand above the cage, while in other cages a crucifix lies on the bottom in mud of some kind. In the cage *La liberté de l'étalon*, 1972-77 (p. 84), the crucifix occupies the central place in the composition, which mimics classical depictions of Christ on the cross, with mourning and worshipping figures standing or kneeling at the foot of the cross. The Virgin Mary, Mary Magdalene and othe[r] figures that may appear in traditional images have, of course, become mourning and worshipping penises in Kudo's version. The crucifix itself is mounted in an elaborate electrical system with an abundance of wires, as if to visualize that a little extra help is needed here to keep the system running.

Another striking subject in Kudo's work is the Romanian-French playwright Eugène Ionesco (1909-94

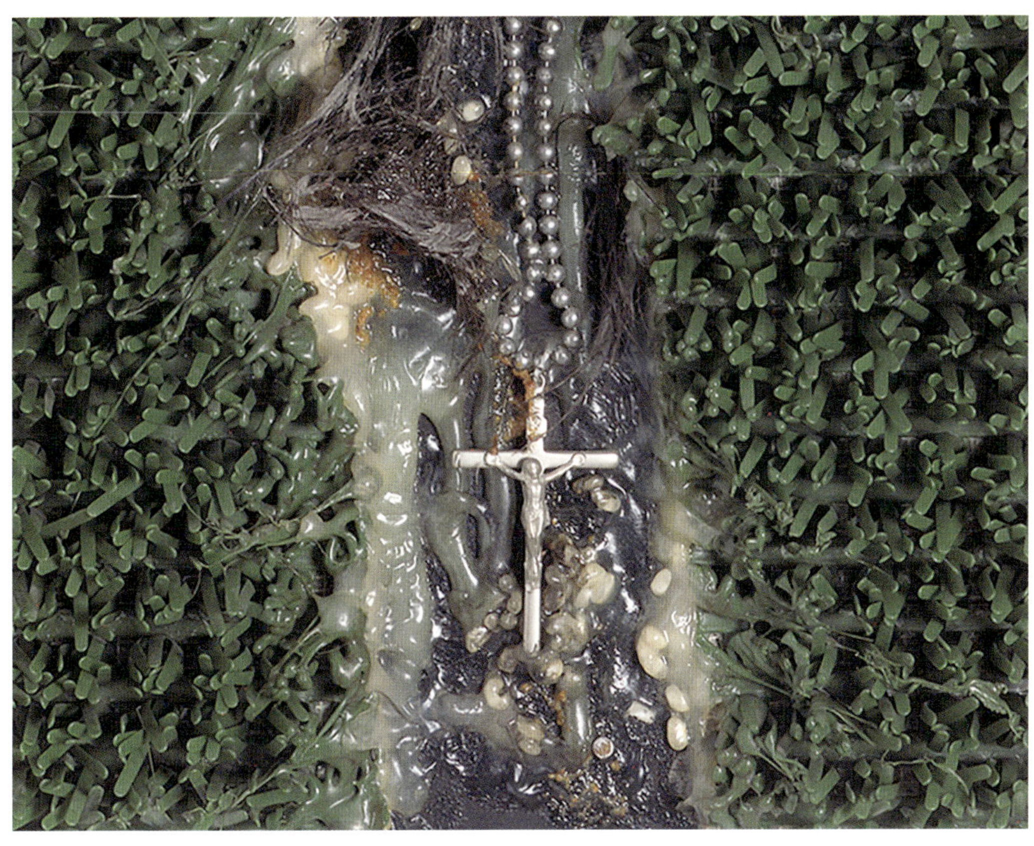

*Origine de la pollution,* (detail), 1972-1973

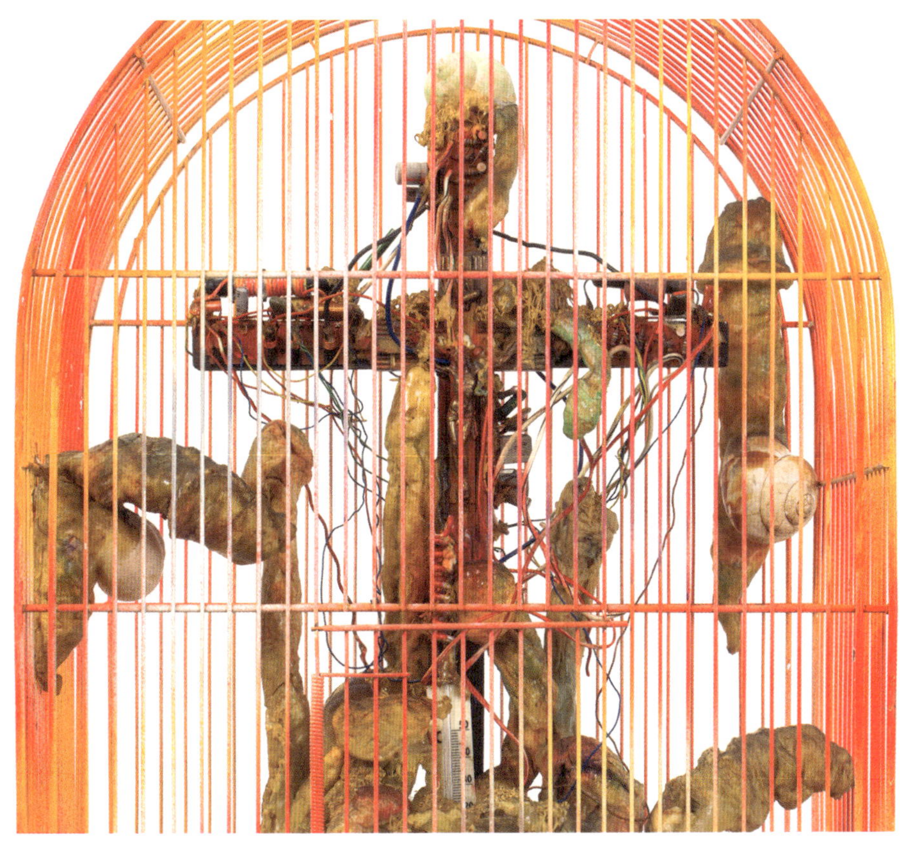

*La liberté de l'étalon,* (detail), 1972-1977

This father of the Theatre of the Absurd is absurdly included in several of Kudo's works from the 1970s. He is the only directly portrayed person in Kudo's oeuvre, apart from the artist himself. The two met during an artistic collaboration, when Kudo served an art director of sorts for Ionesco's film *La Vase* (Mud), 1970, adapting one of the writer's short stories. Kudo was hired by the film's director, Heinz von Cramer, who had visited Kudo's solo exhibition at Kunstverein für die Rheinlande und Westfalen in Düsseldorf and figured that Kudo's and Ionesco's absurd sensibilities would be a good match. However, this seems to have been mostly true on paper. According to Kudo, he and Ionesco engaged in power struggles and arguments.[10]

The film is an absurd self-portrait, with Ionesco playing himself aging, dying and decomposing. The film ends with Ionesco lying in a muddy swamp, represented by copies of his head and limbs, which Kudo had made for the film. After the film was completed, Ionesco became a prominent figure in Kudo's critical apparatus. The artist recycled some of the film's props and the theme of Ionesco decomposing in his own work, taking Ionesco's theme a step further, while ramping up the humiliation.

Rather unflatteringly, to put it mildly, the author appears in Kudo's works as a severed head or peeling portrait. In *Portrait of Ionesco and/or the End of Some Generation*, 1970 (p. 71), the head lies at the bottom of a cage beside a glass of red wine and a turd in his withered hand. A similarly withered cocoon of a penis and a pair of severed feet are hung at the top of the cage, alongside receipts for various purchases and a crucifix.

*"Pollution – Cultivation – New Ecology" (Portrait of Ionesco)*, 1970-71 (p. 54-55), one of the works in the Louisiana's collection, shows Ionesco's head planted in a blue plastic bucket. The head looks pallid, the eyes watery and red. Ionesco's hand (presumably, it is detached from the head) rests on a bucket beside it, where we again find a turd, encrusted with flies and maggots, melting and oozing out through the yellow plastic. Here the Ionesco head is part of a cultivation environment with plants and electronic components, while a cable connects the head to some vacuum tubes growing in a bowl beside it. In a flowerpot in front of Ionesco's face grows a penis – its colour presumably signalling its Caucasian race – with a runny nose. The penis drips into the potted plant next to it, where the flower, echoing the curve of the penis, is melting.

While it is unmistakably Ionesco that is seen in the works, for Kudo the author also symbolizes a wider phenomenon. In an interview, Kudo explains that it is not Ionesco personally who is being pilloried but a whole class: "The works aren't meant as a personal attack on Ionesco. I wanted to create a portrait of the European postwar intelligentsia with him on top, and I thought I would attach all kinds of dirty things to it."[11] The above title reflects this: *Portrait of Ionesco and/or the End of Some Generation* – a generation of European intellectuals who at this point were permeated by French Existentialism.

## Philosophy of Impotence

The male sexual organ is the main motif in Kudo's work. It is an original choice, as the isolated penis is not exactly a mainstream subject in art. Of course, there is a history of the male sexual organ in art, but as a rule the genitals are firmly attached to a body and often hidden from view by fig leaves, clothing or the figure's posture. If we do encounter an isolated penis, it is usually erect in peak phallic form, as in cultic fertility objects and, of course, in the explicitly erotic imagery and object culture of both ancient and modern times across the planet.

The motif has multiple facets in Kudo's poetics, and penises are seen in many variants, though never in peak phallic form. Sometimes the penises look like cocoons, sometimes they grow like strange plants or crawl in hamster wheels. Sometimes they have snail shells of the kind sold in any French supermarket to prepare classic escargots, and often they perform with a certain independent, charming and empathy-attracting personality. Kudo points to the isolated penises as a symbol of the collapse of human dignity: "I think there is nothing like the symbol of the male organ detached from the body to symbolize the decomposition of human dignity", he writes in 1974, and continues, "The female sex is so natural. Conversely, the phallus seems artificial and quite comical, in both form and function."[12]

Kudo used the subject for the first time in 1961 and exhibited an entire environment of penises the following year at the 14th Yomiuri Independent Exhibition in Tokyo. Phallic forms hung from the ceilings and walls in a lattice of strings in *Distribution Map of Impotence and the Appearance of Protective Domes at the Points of Saturation*, often abbreviated as *Philosophy of Impotence*. Compared with the detail Kudo later gives the subject, the forms in the early pieces are relatively abstract, the majority very much resembling hanging cocoons.[13]

Kudo took parts of this work with him to Paris. A few months after his arrival, when he had the chance to meet the French art world, he decided to introduce himself with a happening entitled *Philosophy of Impotence*, which used the parts from the earlier environment. Judging from the documentation of the happening, he was literally forced to the ground by the phalluses, some of which were tied to his body.[14] The work has been explained as a kind of exorcism, associated with the wish to cancel out and liberate an anthropocentric culture and humanity which, in Kudo's own words, is driven by the desire for sex and procreation, with the perpetuation of the race as its only goal.[15]

As mentioned, Kudo's penises often resemble cocoons. Thus, they are also a metamorphic motif, the most classic and standard of its kind. In 1969, Kudo chiselled the dual image of a penis cocoon into a cliff face, when he was invited to create a large work in a privately owned part of the range around Mount Nokogiri, south of Tokyo. The result is the 25-metre tall *Monument of Metamorphosis* (p. 43).

In a film about the genesis of the work,[16] Kudo discusses the metamorphic process by which a larva becomes a cocoon and one day a butterfly: "An

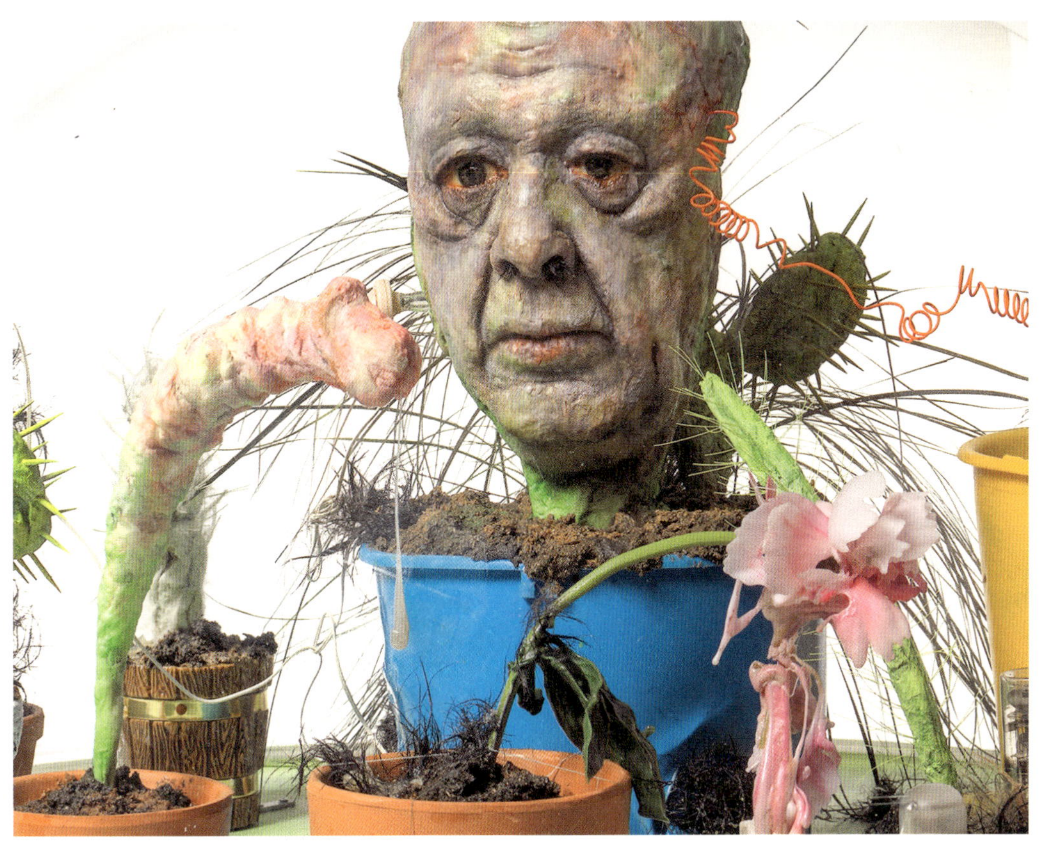

*"Pollution – Cultivation – New Ecology" (Portrait of Ionesco)* (detail), 1970-71

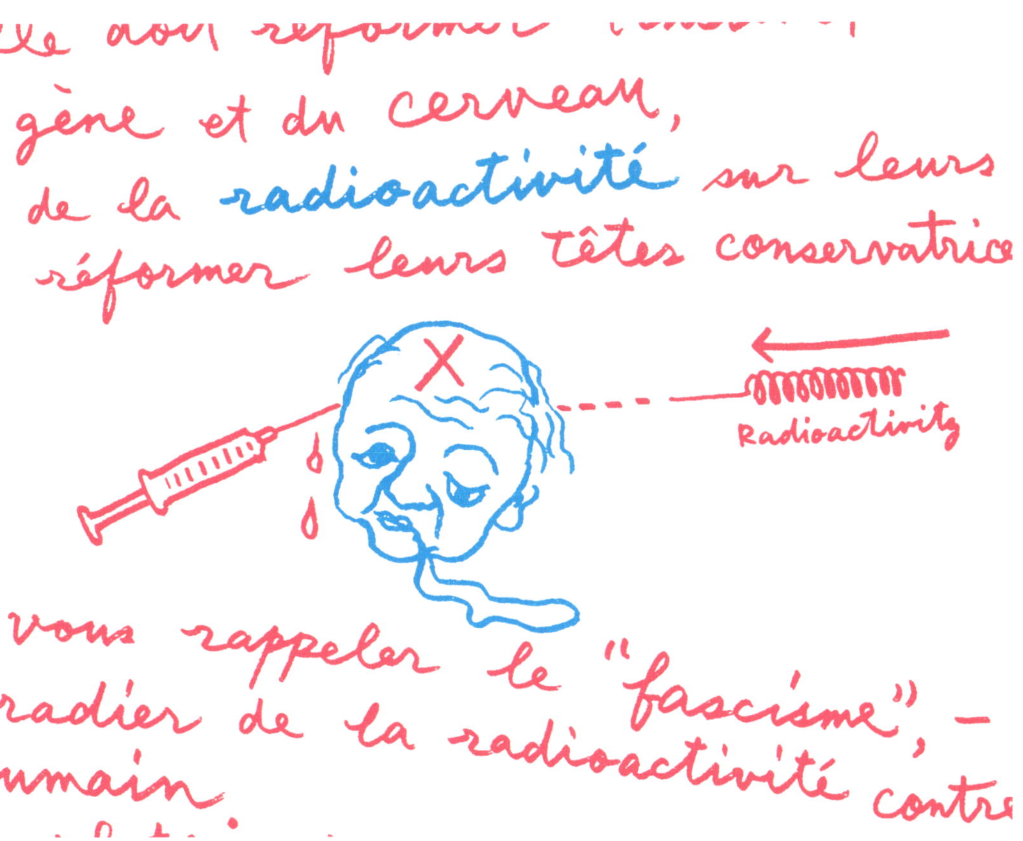


*Pollution – Cultivation – New Ecology* (detail from Kudo's manifest), 1971

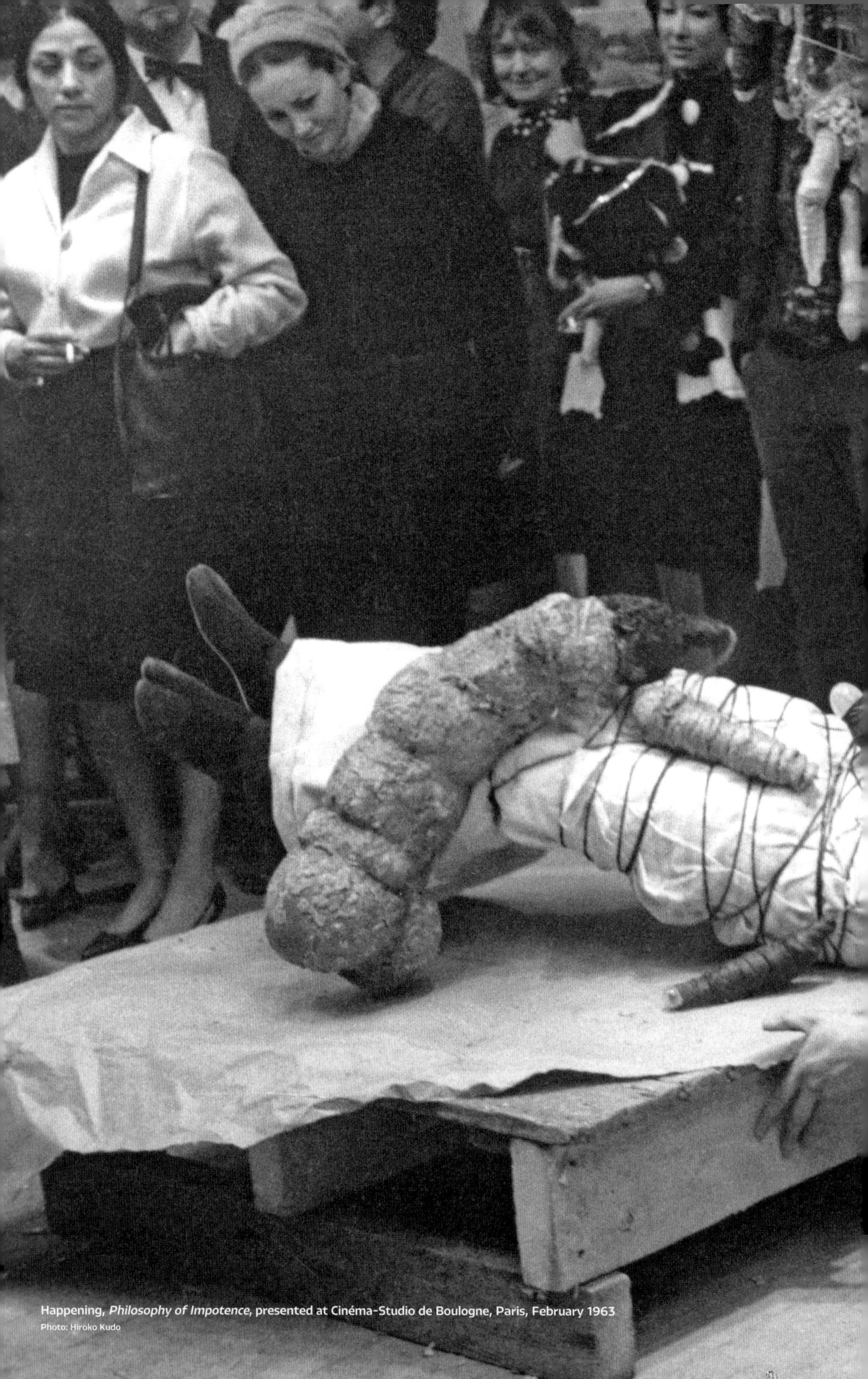

Happening, *Philosophy of Impotence*, presented at Cinéma-Studio de Boulogne, Paris, February 1963
Photo: Hiroko Kudo

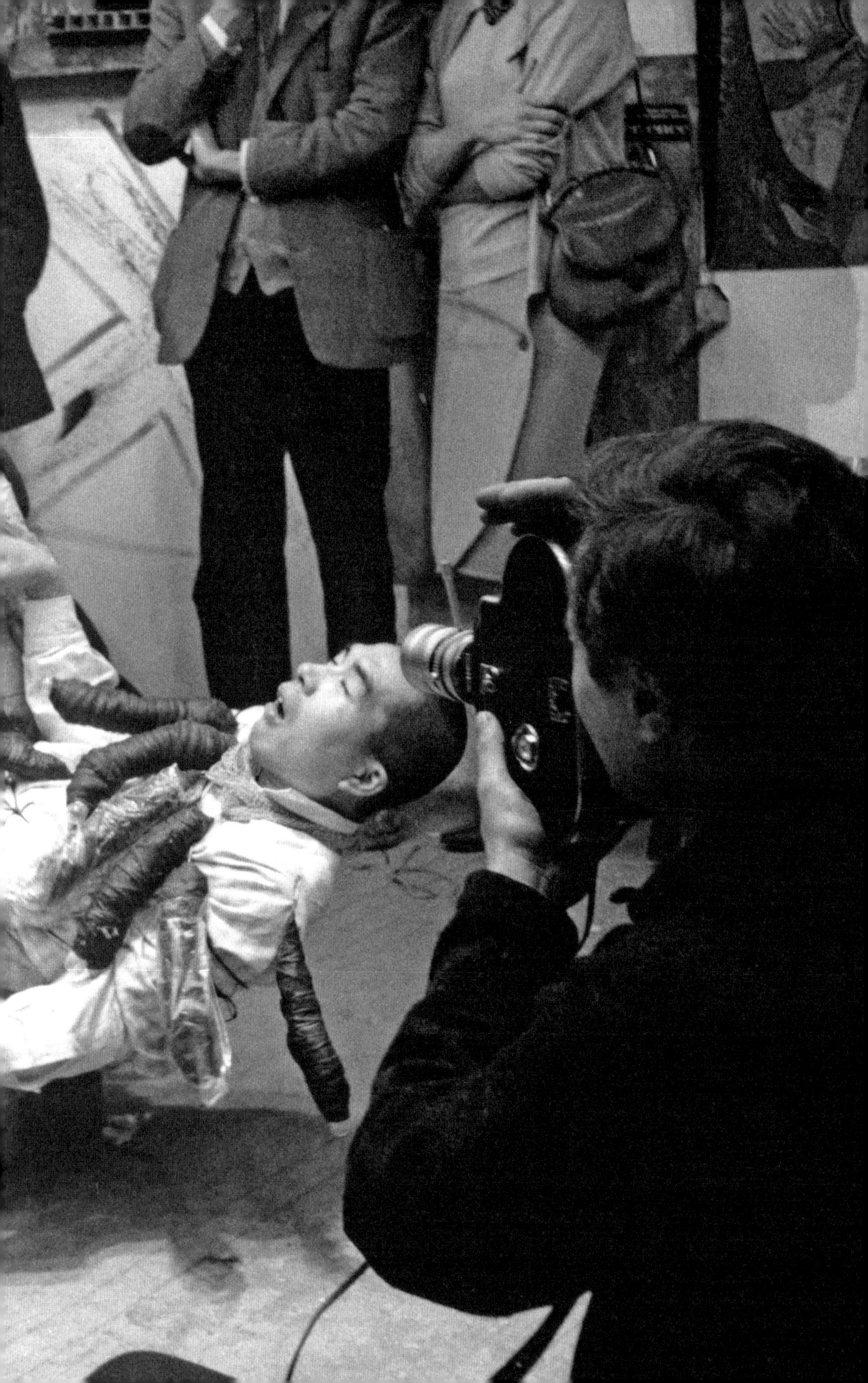

absolute state of transition prevails in the cocoon. I wanted to bring in this idea." Moreover, he speaks of the cocoon as a revolutionary force capable of breaking down the existing system. In the penis cocoons, Kudo visualizes the transformative force inherent in them. Metamorphosing, they will one day slough off their skins and, well, become butterflies. The butterfly is a symbol of the soul in most cultures and spiritual traditions, including Japan and Buddhism, where metamorphosis can be a metaphor for the constancy of the soul, no matter the bodily form in which is reincarnated.[17] On the whole, butterflies never appear in Kudo's works. Sometimes, empty cocoons remain in the cages as testimony to the radical final step of transformation and the successful emergence of the butterfly. But as a rule, he shows the cocoons while they are still in the promising process of development.

In the climate of the gender debate both then and now, Kudo's insistent and visually frank theme of castration and impotence, seemingly suggesting a "post-masculine" universe, is radical. While the male organ on the face of it *is* the subject – as well as the "origin of pollution", to reference the above work – the scope is wider, covering humanity as such, not only masculinity and the male gender. The penises symbolize the castration of egotistical, hegemonic mankind, which has lost its potency, dignity and power. In Kudo's depiction of a "new ecology", fragments of humanity are forced to form new symbioses with plants and technology in order to survive.

### A New Hierarchy

Kudo chisels out his messages, including in writing. His 1971 manifesto articulates in words what his works express in plastic nature, crucifixes, Ionescos and penis cocoons. The manifesto, "Pollution – Cultivation – New Ecology", originally handwritten in French, was published in the catalogue of Kudo's solo exhibition "Pollution – Cultivation – New Ecology – Your Portrait" at the Stedelijk Museum Amsterdam in 1972[18] (the text is reproduced in this catalogue on p. 26-31 and in English translation on p. 32-33). The text is written in synthetic pink and blue, with small diagrams illustrating its points. In the handwritten manifesto, there are important arrows between the words "Pollution → CULTIVATION → Nouvelle ecologie", as well as an arrow directly from "Pollution" to "Nouvelle ecologie". In other words, it describes a metamorphosis from pollution to cultivation to a new ecology.

Kudo begins the manifesto with a description of the dramatic desperation he sees in people's reactions to the environmental crisis: "Pollution of nature! Decomposition of humanity (humanism)! The end of the world! You declaim like tragic actors in the theatre. Besides, these exclamations are fashionable words nowadays." Kudo notes the general anxiety and confusion in the increasingly environmentally sensitive society around him. But the situation is by no means only a catastrophe, he states. Rather, it is a chance for us to change, a chance to revolutionize our primitive thinking in terms of the polar opposites of humankind and nature, humankind and animals, humankind and machinery. "This fundamental conception (primitive antagonism) was probably born out of Christianity," he continues, outlining how dualistic/antagonistic thinking has led to a "net" of slavery, colonialism, nationalism, capitalism, etc. A network that has now been broken and is in the process of shedding its worn-out skin: metamorphosis.

Conspiring with pollution and technology, nature has now turned against humanity, Kudo writes. It is all in the process of being mixed together, and this mixture will constitute the new ecology of reciprocal, not oppositional, relations between the parts. In the new situation, humankind cannot stand in a privileged and dominant position at the top of the pyramid, Kudo writes. Here, too, he fires a salvo against egoistical (his word) humanity which calls itself "humanist" and clings to old habits.

Kudo's version of a new ecosystem is far from just a new relationship between humans, nature and technology. It is also very much about new power hierarchies between peoples and cultures. As mentioned he singles out colonialism as one part of the old system that is decomposing. The ideologies and power balances that have been driving the metamorphosis into the polluted swamp in which we find ourselves are ready for recoding, Kudo proclaims. The manifesto ends by urging us to listen to the younger generation, including young artists and students. Indeed, the revolutionary spirit that preoccupied Kudo and surrounded him in Paris in 1968 an obvious context for the artist's battle cry.

### The New Ecology

There is an almost Hieronymus Bosch-like sensation, and pleasure, to be had from looking into Kudo's colourful scenes of trippy, wacky, grotesque effects. As with Bosch, in Kudo's work we are not always entirely sure whether we are glimpsing the "garden of earthly delights" or Hell itself.

Kudo does not mince words in his unsentimental and bold images of a post-human condition – a term employed here very broadly to encompass the goodbye to the traditional version of humanity as well as the ideological shift away from a "humanistic" mindset privileging humanity above nature and other beings.

Kudo's particular critique of basic Western values largely agrees with the climate of dissent that found general expression in the many political and artistic revolts of the 1960 and 1970s. At the same time, Kudo typifies the protest and frustration at the massive influence – political, economic and cultural – of the West on Japan throughout the 20th century, with renewed impact after World War II,[19] Japanese post-war art's opposition to the hegemony and high status of Western values in Japanese culture, and Japanese society's conservatism, nationalism and control, notably embodied in the Imperial system. Kudo arrived in Europe with the characteristic antiauthoritarian, anarchistic and fundamentally obstructive attitude of his generation.[20] Continuing his investigative critique inside "the enemy camp", he excoriated humanistic self-understanding, Christian morality and Western dualistic thinking.

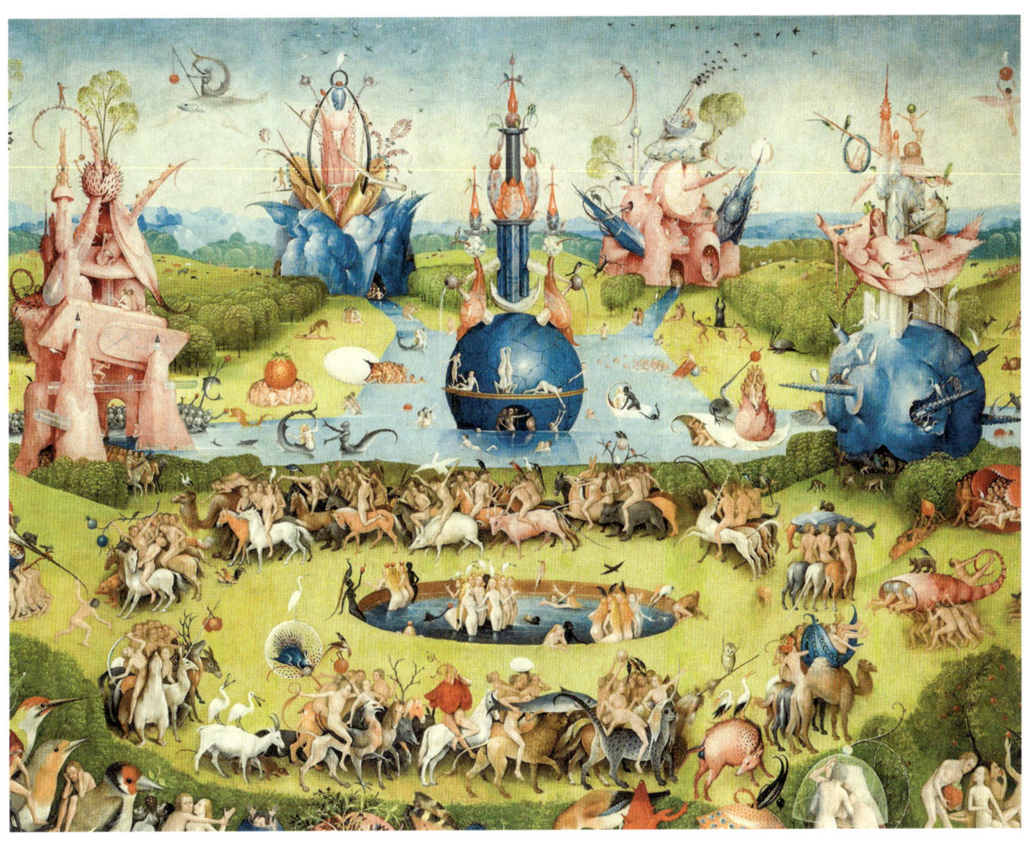

Hieronymus Bosch: *Garden of Earthly Delights* (detail), 1490-1510

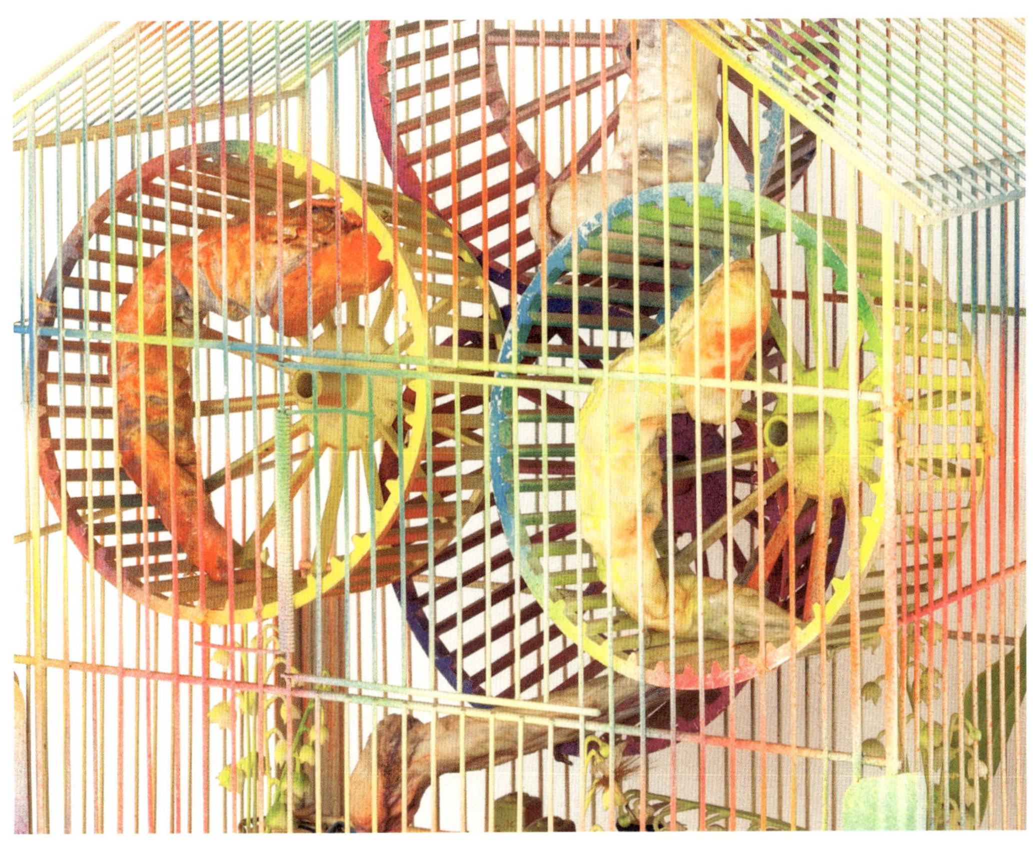

*Paradise* (detail), 1980

The fact that Kudo's works stood out so notably in the museum's storage at our first encounter naturally has to do with the radical way in which they articulate their criticism of the modern, postwar world, as compared to most European and American art of the period. Kudo clearly points ahead in his images not just of modern humanity's existential and physical scars, deformations and the body's technological dependency, but also of the deformed state of our surroundings – the ecosystem. The "natural circuit" has metamorphosed into an "electronic circuit" in Kudo's bio-technotope. Despite many points of convergence with his Western colleagues, it is obvious that the aesthetic Kudo perfects in his work, starting in the 1960s, adheres to and cultivates its deep roots in Japanese visual culture. For example, he perpetuates a Japanese tradition of creating small, carefully arranged and detailed enclosures and tableaux suggesting small temples, gardens and bonsai and ikebana arrangements. His work also seems to have strong ties to the figurative, narrative, intensely coloured and often grotesquely fantastical style abundantly found in Japanese woodcuts, including the erotic Shunga genre, and in manga. The American artist Mike Kelley draws a straight line between Kudo's work and postwar science-fiction films, especially the Japanese filmmaker Ishiro Honda's science-fiction and eco-disaster films from 1954 on, in which nature takes revenge and strange monsters are awakened by the atomic bomb, whose destructive power they also symbolize.[21] As early as 1954, the giant dinosaur-like monster Godzilla comes out of Tokyo Bay, in Honda's iconic *Godzilla, King of the Monsters*, and invades civilization with untameable destructive force.

Finally, Kudo stands out today because he succinctly articulates, as far as that is even possible, the Anthropocene. This term, which was coined in 2000, describes that we now find ourselves in a new geological epoch that is crucially affected by humankind.[22]

In recent years, the Anthropocene has become a popular buzzword and a bit of an umbrella term, as the atmosphere vibrates with new research and discussion of how to understand and act in the human-influenced climate. While there is widespread agreement that humankind has critically impacted the Earth's functioning, deciding whether there is sufficient scientific evidence to formally replace the present epoch name, the Holocene, is another matter. Numerous researchers are addressing the issue, among other things discussing when the Anthropocene epoch can be said to begin. One common proposal is that the epoch was bombed into being in 1945 in Hiroshima and Nagasaki – and by the boom of consumption, industrial production and new technology after World War II.[23]

The atomic bomb is an important point of departure for Kudo's images of the chain reaction we ourselves have set in motion and of which we are part. His broadly analytical, metamorphic perspective[24] – destructively but constructively – points to the potential for thinking anew. The world is changing. That is how it is. But instead of panicking, Kudo urges us to see the potential for cultivating new habits in our new ecology.

Tine Colstrup is a curator at the Louisiana Museum of Modern Art. She has organized exhibitions of Hilma af Klint, Paula Modersohn-Becker, Louise Bourgeois, Marina Abramović and Pipilotti Rist.

Tetsumi Kudo, "Conversation with Kudo, Paris, 1974", questions and
nswers by Kudo. Originally published in *Kudo*, exhibition catalogue,
alerie Beaubourg, Galerie Vallois Paris, 1977. English translation by
ichael Gilson, 2008. Printed in this catalogue p. 36-37.

Nine works by Kudo were in the 1974 exhibition *Japan på Louisiana*
*apan at Louisiana*), including *"Pollution – Cultivation – New Ecology"*
*Portrait of Ionesco)*, 1970-71, which was acquired after the exhibition,
ollowed by the acquisition of *Cultivation by Radioactivity in the*
*ectronic Circuit*, 1968.

One positive consequence of this is that the works are generally in
ery good condition.

Kudo, op. cit., p. 36-37.

Retrospective introductions to Kudo's work can be found throughout
ne following two catalogues which are currently the most substantial
ublications on Kudo in English: Doryun Chong (ed.), *Tetsumi Kudo:*
*arden of Metamorphosis*, Walker Art Center, 2008 and Atsuhiko
nima et al. (ed.), *Your Portrait: A Tetsumi Kudo Retrospective*, National
useum of Art, Osaka, 2013. The latter is bilingual (Japanese/English)
nd includes a catalogue raisonné.

Political turbulence characterized Japan and influenced the Japanese
t scene at the time, for example in 1960 when the renewal of
merican-Japanese defence alliance and security act signed after World
ar II led to widespread protests. Alexandra Munroe, *Japanese Art After*
*945: Screaming Against the Sky*, Harry N. Abrams, 1994, p. 150-151.

I am referring here to the Japanese garden as a highly generic form.
ne analytical point occurred to me during a visit to the Zen garden at
e Tôfuku-ji temple, in Kyoto, which was laid out in the 1930s by the
ading garden designer Mirei Shigemori (1896-1975).

The cage has a rich art history, from Bosch, Bacon and Bourgeois to
ne present day. It would take a separate article to write Kudo's cages
to it.

We also meet "our own" portrait. Many of Kudo's works bear the
tle "Your Portrait", but at the most general level all the works can be
garded as such – as our portraits. "Your Portrait" was simply the title
the big retrospective exhibition of Kudo's work held in 2013-14 at the
nree main Japanese museums for his work: The National Museum of
rt, Osaka; The National Museum of Modern Art, Tokyo; and the Aomori
useum of Art.

**).** Atsuhiko Shima, "A Guide to Tetsumi Kudo", in Shima et al. (ed.), op.
t., p. 220 and Doryun Chong, "When the Body Changes into New Forms:
racing Tetsumi Kudo", in Chong (ed.), op. cit., p. 36.

**.** Shima, ibid.

**2.** Kudo, op. cit., p. 36. When the female sex appears in Kudo's works it
as a rule, embedded as folds in the middle of large and small hearts.

**3.** The same year, phallic forms became a main motif for Yayoi Kusama
. 1929), who in her so-called "accumulation sculptures" made in New
ork, clad furniture and objects in myriad phallic forms. Alexandra
unroe interprets this as a revolt against a patriarchal, moralistic and
ontrolling social model (Munroe, op. cit., p. 24 and p. 197). Kusama
erself has associated this type of work with a fear of sex, and in that
ght the works can be understood as reworking phallic anxiety by
cessively multiplying the form (*Yayoi Kusama: In Infinity*, exhibition
atalogue, Louisiana Museum of Modern Art, 2015, cf. the quote from
er autobiography, p. 46). Kusama's forms are far more abstract than
udo's, and while Kusama's bristle with potency, Kudo's variants of
npotent penises precisely do not.

**4.** Kudo's happening in Paris is included in Allan Kaprow's early book,
*ssemblages, Environments & Happenings*, 1966.

**5.** Chong, op. cit., p. 29-31.

**16.** *Monument of Metamorphosis*, 1969. Duration: 25 min. Produced by UNAC Tokyo, Masaomi Unagami. Camera: Yasuhiro Yoshioka. Music: Yasunao Tone.

**17.** In Japan, the butterfly is also a symbol of good fortune. Cf. the entry "Butterfly", in Jeremy Roberts, *Japanese Mythology A to Z*, 2nd ed., Chelsea House Publishers, 2010. The large monument was Kudo's gift to 1970. "For 1970," he signed it – hopefully, one must assume, among echoes of student revolt and a Vietnam War at its destructive peak. The penis cocoon is a symbol of change in power hierarchies over a broad front.

**18.** Whether Kudo himself ever called the text a "manifesto", I do not know, but as a rule it is designated as such in the literature on the artist.

**19.** Alexandra Munroe outlines this oppositional spirit in Munroe, op. cit., p. 19-25.

**20.** Ibid., p. 154-160.

**21.** Mike Kelley, "Cultivation by Radioactivity", in Chong (ed.), op. cit., p. 52.

**22.** The concept comes from the Dutch chemist Paul J. Crutzen.

**23.** An introduction to the theses and discussions of the Anthropocene can be found, e.g., in Heather Davis & Etienne Turpin's introductory article "Art & Death: Lives Between the Fifth Assessment & the Sixth Extinction", in Heather Davis and Etienne Turpin (eds.), *Art in the Anthropocene: Encounters Among Aesthetics, Politics, Environments and Epistemologies*, first edition by Open Humanities Press, 2015, http://openhumanitiespress.org/books/art-in-the-anthropocene, p. 3-29.

**24.** Kudo's metamorphic thinking interestingly points forward to thoughts in the sociologist Ulrich Beck's 2016 book *The Metamorphosis of the World*, in which Beck suggests that we should think of climate change in the perspective of metamorphosis, not just in the perspective of acute solutions, and that the metamorphosis perspective allows us to see more complex possibilities for creating brand new structural changes.

Pollution → CULTIVATION → Nouvelle écologie

Pollution de la nature!

Décomposition de l'humanité!

La fin du monde!

humanisme

Vous déclamez comme des acteurs tragiques au théatre. D'ailleurs, ces exclamations sont des mots à la mode aujourd'hui.

Mais cette situation n'est ni absolument catastrophique, ni à la mode (les mots à la mode).

Ceci est le processus inéluctable pour nous réformer nous mêmes, et qui entraine avec beaucoup de penitence.

Ceci veut dire que derrière cette situation il y a une grande Possibilité de révolution pour nous-mêmes.

Premièrement il y a la révolution de notre conception. C'est-à-dire, auto-effondrement de l'antagonisme primitif (conception de la confrontation) dans notre conception.

L'antagonisme primitif ⇒ L'humanité contre la nature
⇒ L'humanité contre les animaux ⇒ L'humanité contre-
la machine (instrument), etc. → ······
······ → (privilège de l'humanite). ?

Probablement, cette conception fondamental (antagonisme-primitif) est née du christianisme.

Dans notre histoire, cet antagonisme a fait un "FILET" —(NET)— compligné et intéressant.

Par example, l'esclavage, le colonialisme, les relations entre la bourgeoisie et prolétariat, le nationalisme (racisme), le capitalisme les entreprises monopolisatrices, etc., etc. ······ et la guerre, Mais maintenant, ce "FILET" est cassé, et est en train de se métamorphoser (en mue).

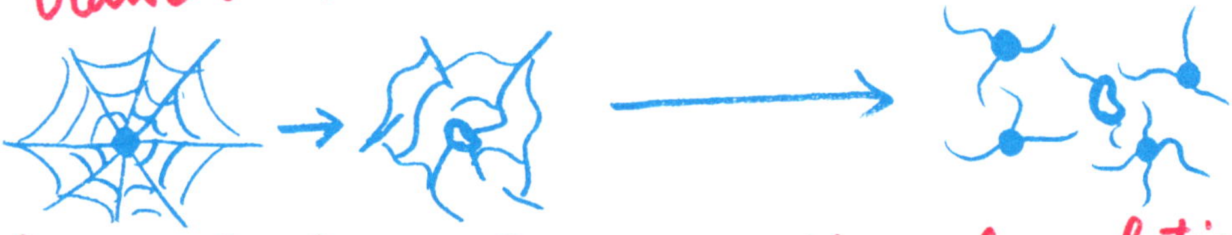

La relation fondamentale, c'est-à-dire, la relation de l'humanité contre la nature et de l'humanite contre l'instrument est en train de se métamorphoser
Par example, dans l'histoire, comme l'esclavage à été aboli, comme la relation entre la bourgeoisie et le prolétariat doit être changée, notre conception d'aujourd'hui est aussi en train de subir une metamorphose.

"La nature conquise" commence à se venger de l'humanité, en se servant de la pollution et de l'instrument (machine) qui ont été fabriqués par l'humanité pour l'égoisme des humains, et qui, bien au contraire, commencent maintenant à décomposer l'humanité.

Cette situation bouleverse les gens.

Mais je trouve un espoir et une possibilité pour notre RÉVOLUTION dans cette situation.

Est-ce un paradoxe ?

Ou une hypothèse énoncée par un Alcoolique ?

N'importe comment, il est important de penser sur le rapport de la nature polluée avec l'électronique proliférée (mécanisme), la décomposition de l'humanité (humanisme) et la vieille et traditionnelle hiérarchie des valeurs.

Elles se décomposent et se pénètrent les unes contre les autres (l'humanité contre la nature, l'humanité contre le mecanisme – électronique. etc.) et iront former une écologie complètement ——

— nouvelle dans notre société et dans le cosmos.
Ceci veut dire que la conception de DOMINATION — (antagonisme primitif)
— sera détruite par la décomposition et l'infiltration des unes contre les autres et elles commencent à inaugurer une époque de "contrôle mutuel" et de "culture mutuelle".

L'humanité est contrôlée par la nature,
la nature est cultivée par l'humanité,
l'électronique contrôle et cultive l'humanité,
l'humanité contrôle et fait proliférer l'électronique.
Et la nature contient l'électronique.

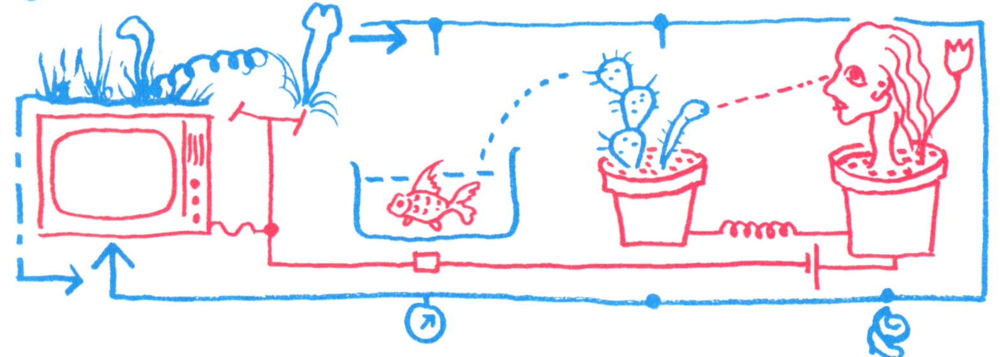

Dans ce nouveau système écologique, il n'est pas possible que seule la dignité humaine reste hautaine comme un roi.

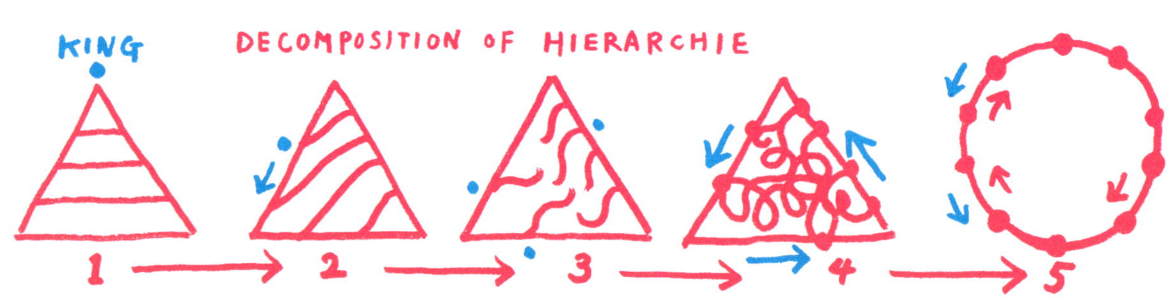


No. 4.
KUDO.

Mais il est très difficile d'enlever le sentiment de privilège (dignité humaine) et le sentiment de colonialisme de la tête de l'humanité, qui s'appelle elle même "HUMANISTE".

Pour ce faire, une révolution humaine réelle et fondamentale sera necessaire !
Peut-être, elle doit réformer l'instinct —
La cellule du gène et du cerveau,
en irradiant de la radioactivité sur leurs corps, pour réformer leurs têtes conservatrices et égoistes.

Radioactivity

Ceci peut vous rappeler le "fascisme", – l'image d'irradier de la radioactivité contre le corps humain
Mais il sera plutôt utile de châtrer "le sentiment de privilège" et "le fascisme" dans la nouvelle écologie.
Qu'est-ce qui est nécessaire maintenant ?
Pour notre coopération dans le nouveau système écologique, ——————

pour la révolution de nos conceptions,
et pour la réelle connaissance de
nous-mêmes dans la nouvelle écologie?

Je pense qu'il sera nécessaire d'adopter
l'hypothèse intuitive de la jeune génération —
jeunes artistes, Étudiants, etc.

Je prophétise maintenant la croissance
de la nouvelle écologie dans le marécage
de la "nature polluée" et de
"l'humanité en décomposition".

Aujourd'hui, je vous offre —
le petit modèle de notre
Nouvelle Écologie.

1971. paris
tetsumi KUDO

Pollution of nature! Decomposition of humanity! (humanism)!
The end of the world!

You declaim like tragic actors in the theatre. Besides, these exclamations are fashionable words nowadays.
But this situation is neither absolutely catastrophic nor fashionable (fashionable words).
This is the ineluctable process for reforming ourselves, and which seduces with much repentance.
This is to say that behind this situation there is a great possibility of revolution for us personally.
Firstly, there is the revolution in our conception. That is to say, collapse under its own weight of the primitive antagonism (conception of confrontation) in our conception.

The primitive antagonism → humanity against nature → humanity against animals → humanity against the machine (instrument), etc. → "Human privilege."
This fundamental conception (primitive antagonism) was probably born out of Christianity.
In our history this antagonism has made a complicated and interesting NET.
For example, slavery, colonialism, relations between the bourgeoisie and the proletariat, nationalism (racism), monopolistic enterprises, capitalism and war, etc., etc.
But now, this "NET" is broken, and is being metamorphosed (moulting).

The fundamental relationship, in other words the relationship of humanity against nature and humanity against the instrument, is in the process of metamorphosing itself.
For example, historically speaking, as slavery was abolished, as the relationship between the bourgeoisie and the proletariat must be changed, our present-day conception is also in the process of undergoing a metamorphosis.
"Conquered nature" is starting to take its revenge on humanity, making use of pollution and of the instrument (machine) which have been made by humanity for the egoism of humans, and which, quite to the contrary, are now starting to decompose humanity.
This situation is throwing people into confusion.
But I find hope and a possibility for our revolution in this situation. Is this a paradox? Or a hypothesis expressed by an alcoholic?
No matter how, it is important to think about the relationship of polluted nature to the proliferation of electronics (mechanism), the decomposition of humanity (humanism) and the old and traditional hierarchy of values

First published, in French, as part of the artist's contribution to *Tetsumi Kudo: Pollution Cultivation New Ecology Your Portrait*, exh. cat. (Amsterdam: Stedelijk Museum, 1972). The translated text comes from Colin Naylor and Genesis P-Orridge, eds., Contemporary Artists (London: St. James Press, 1977)

hey are decomposing and interpenetrating, each against he others (humanity against nature, humanity against nechanism — electronics, etc.) and will come to form a ompletely new ecology in our society and in the cosmos. his means that the conception of "domination" (primitive ntagonism) will be destroyed by the decomposition and nfiltration of the ones by the others and they will begin o inaugurate an age of "mutual control" and of "mutual ulture."

lumanity is controlled by nature, nature is cultivated by umanity, electronics controls and cultivates humanity, umanity controls and causes to proliferate electronics. nd nature contains electronics.

n this new ecological system, it is not possible that human ignity alone should retain the hauteur of a king. But it is ery difficult to remove the sentiment of privilege (human ignity) and the sentiment of colonialism from the head of umanity, which calls itself "humanist."

o do that, a real and fundamental human revolution will e necessary!
erhaps it must irradiate the instinct — the cells of the enes and of the brain — by irradiating their bodies vith radioactivity, to reform their conservative and goistical heads.

his may remind you of "fascism" — the idea of irradiating he human body with radioactivity.

ut it will rather be useful to castrate the "sentiment of rivilege" and "fascism" in the new ecology.
Vhat is now necessary?
or our cooperation in the new ecological system, for the evolution of our conceptions, and for the real knowledge f ourselves in the new ecology?

think that it will be necessary to adopt the intuitive ypothesis of the young generation — young artists, tudents, etc.

now prophesy the growth of the new ecology in the wamp of "polluted nature" and "decomposing humanity."

oday, I offer you the small-scale model of our new cology.

1971, Paris
Tetsumi Kudo

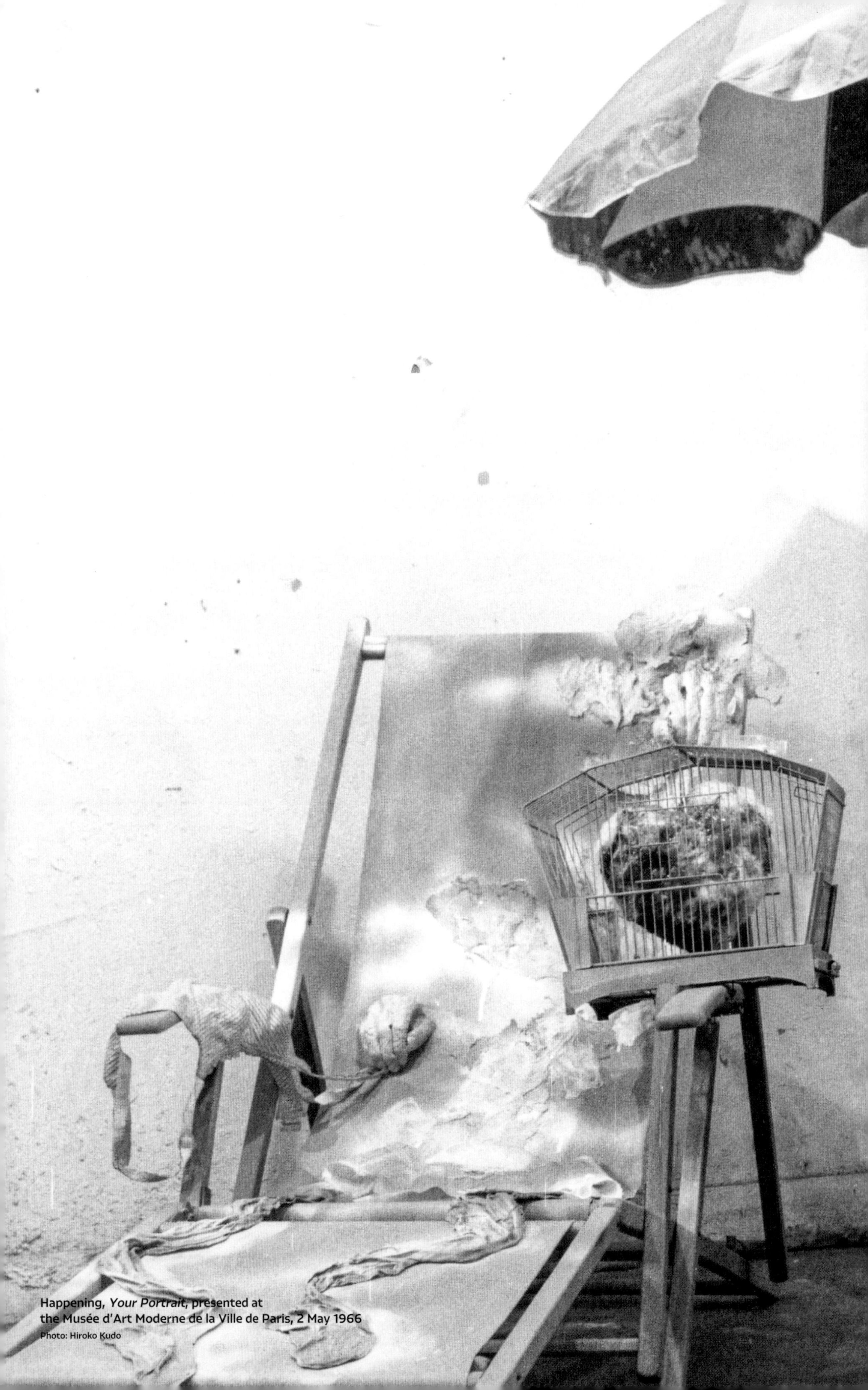

Happening, *Your Portrait*, presented at
the Musée d'Art Moderne de la Ville de Paris, 2 May 1966
Photo: Hiroko Kudo

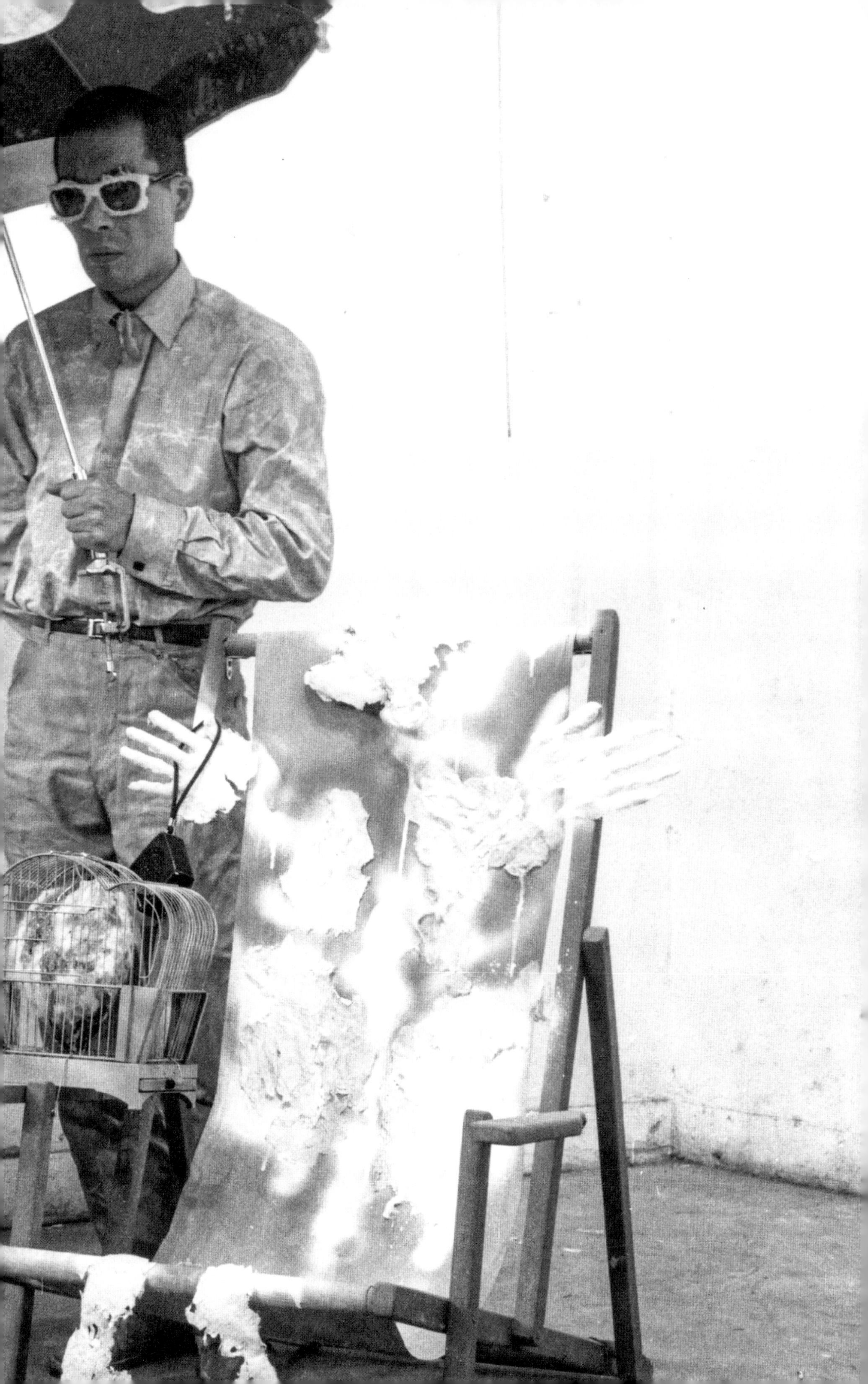

***I had a shock when I visited Kudo's recent exhibition in Paris. One of the works represents men cultivated with goldfish in an aquarium, and the work entitled Grafted Garden shows fragmented bodies of men connected to plants and insects by electrical wires. A heated Nichrome coil wraps around the phallus. Worms and the brain agglutinate, and on the polluted plants, tiny transistors proliferate like mold. Are works like these expressions of sadism as a driving force in Kudo's dream world?***
It's not a dream world, it's your current situation. It's your portrait decomposing amid polluted nature and the tide of technology. This decomposition of humanity does not signal its death; in reality, we are being decomposed, we are being metamorphosed, and we are being kept alive. My work consists in making you cognizant of this situation in the form of a visual maquette.

***Does that mean we are being kept like worms in the septic pit of polluted nature and technology? In that case, what has happened to the dignity of humanity?***
You're forgetting that we dug the pit ourselves. History shows us that humanity has conquered, parceled out, and exploited nature as it pleased, and in so doing tortured it. Now humanity is reaping pollution as nature's vengeance. Technology, in its primitive state, was meant to be an instrument for conquering nature, so we had to train it, like a slave, so as to protect human dignity. But with the expansion of our egocentricity — which seeks only human dignity — technology flooded in, and we are now witnesses, in this giant pit, to this spectacle of decomposing dignity and collapsing egocentricity.

***Could you give us some explanations of "pollution — cultivation — new ecology"?***
You and I are slow (idiotically so) to acknowledge pollution, and a certain process is necessary to achieve that. First of all, to have seen little birds stuck fast in oil slicks, fish with twisted vertebrae, and to have been moved by that. Then to have let mercury and cadmium into our bodies and been paralyzed as a result, or to have lost consciousness after breathing in a toxic gas. SO, after having experimented with this comic process, we notice that we have lost our lover, nature. It is impossible for man "as he must be" and human dignity to exist by themselves. To be able to confront polluted, parceled-out nature, we have to achieve a conception of human dignity as decomposed, polluted. From this perspective, I am reflecting on the relationship between nature, humanity, and technology. I could schematize this as follows: humanity viewed as susceptible to being transformed by polluted nature; technology transformed and multiplied by humanity's complex; nature protected and cultivated by that technology. These three elements — nature, humanity, technology — control and cultivate one another in a closed loop. I call this relationship pollution — cultivation — new ecology.

***But, given the bloody state in which the hands, feet, and head are shown, after having been cut off, violently connected to these iron tubes and electronic components, we perceive nothing but a kind of despai which is its own end. In that case, we can't conceive of new ecology.***
One of the reasons we are allergic to the new ecology is that it is still in an infantile, violent stage. Another reason is that our illusion of human dignity is being brutally deconstructed by technology. When we realize that the attitude man has adopted toward nature has been characterized by violence and ignorance, we can grasp this situation. If a rejection reaction occurs between nature and man, in the form of pollution, it is normal that there should also be a rejection reaction (in a cruel form) between man and technology. We can consider the tormented scenes in my works — in which human body parts are sadistically grafted onto electronic components, while bleeding and emitting pus — as a visual expression of our rejection reaction towar technology.

***So does that mean we should be content to observe this violence inherent in technology, as it torments people like cattle in a slaughterhouse, ripping blood an pus from them?***
That's not it. In his rotting state, man opposes the violent intervention of technology, allowing his blood and pus to flow. This rotten state is allowing the decomposition of humanity to progress, and at the sar time oxidizing and transforming technology. So now we have a new situation, one of reciprocal transformation and decomposition. In the bog of transformation and decomposition, a new communication between technology and humanity is produced. To translate this new relationship into visual language, I am showing two maquettes, entitled Graft and Symbiosis. The first depicts a process of reciprocal decomposition and transformation, a process born of the rejection reaction between humanity and technology. The seconc presents the possibility of a biological community between polluted nature, decomposed humanity, and transformed technology.

***You use the symbol of the sexual organ very often in your works. Why do you use only the male sex as a symbol?***
I have a lot of respect for the female sex and I use it in my works, but I think there is nothing like the symbol of the male organ detached from the body to symbolize the decomposition of human dignity. The female sex is so natural. Conversely, the phallus seems artificial and quite comical, in both form and function. For example, a phallus kept with goldfish in an aquarium symbolizes your portrait as well as the dignity of the coelacanth raised by technology. The phallus grafted onto a cactus in a greenhouse ensures its existence thanks to worms and snails. The phallus playing the role of a regulator in the television's electronic circuit can be a member of the new ecology only through its connection to the transistor and the capacitor. In this situation the phallus as a symbol for human dignity, gives up its privileges

- in other words, its existence is assured solely by the bandonment of its right. So here you learn of a new elationship between humanity and nature by means f this comic but adorable phallus.

***'our explanation reminds us of biology, botany, urgical transplantation. What does art signify to you?***
n today's society, in which economics, politics, and echnology are bound up in a very complex manner, rt cannot be a decorative element serving a state or n ideology. Art must be one of the media that serve o provoke doubt and defiance in us: it is a provocative ommunication between you and me, who are living n a septic pit of technology. In this sense, art is a naquette through which we reflect, and question verything. Doubt everything. What is our place in the niverse? What is human freedom in the universe? Vhat is human freedom in the universe? What is ndividual freedom in society?

***Vhy have you lived for so long in Paris, far rom Japan?***
t's an advantage for me, being away from japan, yet vithout being assimilated into French society, because hat way I can position myself between Japan and urope I can also biologically study and compare the wo societies.

***Vhat do you think of Japan?***
apan is a bunch of narrow islands, occupied by 10 million people. That society is a model of the nformation society connected by evolved mass nedia. To realize this, all you have to do is think of a igh-speed blender. In the whirlwind of information, verything is spinning at dizzying pace. Man himself is lso an informational element. If you stay there, you an no longer see or observe either yourself or the vorld. In that whirlwind, there is no freedom to doubt r to provoke. In that whirlwind, driven by relentless peed, individuals tend to spin faster and faster but, onversely, each individual's freedom vector tends owards zero in the extreme. Japanese society can be ompared to a kind of cyclotron.

***Vhat is Japan like, away from that whirlwind?***
ince the atom bomb at Hiroshima, Japan has been a ab rat for direct experimentation — with radioactivity, t the time of the explosion itself; then, after the war, t has been an experimental model for economical rowth as an economical animal; then, an experimental ield for the worst pollution in the world; finally, as a ample of a human group in which the mass media are he most highly developed. So Japan, as a laboratory, nd the Japanese, as loyal lab rats, offer you the esults of all that experimentation. To put it ironically, ne could say that Japan serves other people — that is, ou — as a martyr.

Originally published in *KUDO*, exh. cat.
(Paris: Galerie Beaubourg, Galerie Vallois, 1977).
English translation by Michael Gilson, 2008

# TETSUMI KUDO

# BIOGRAPHY

By Joshua Mack

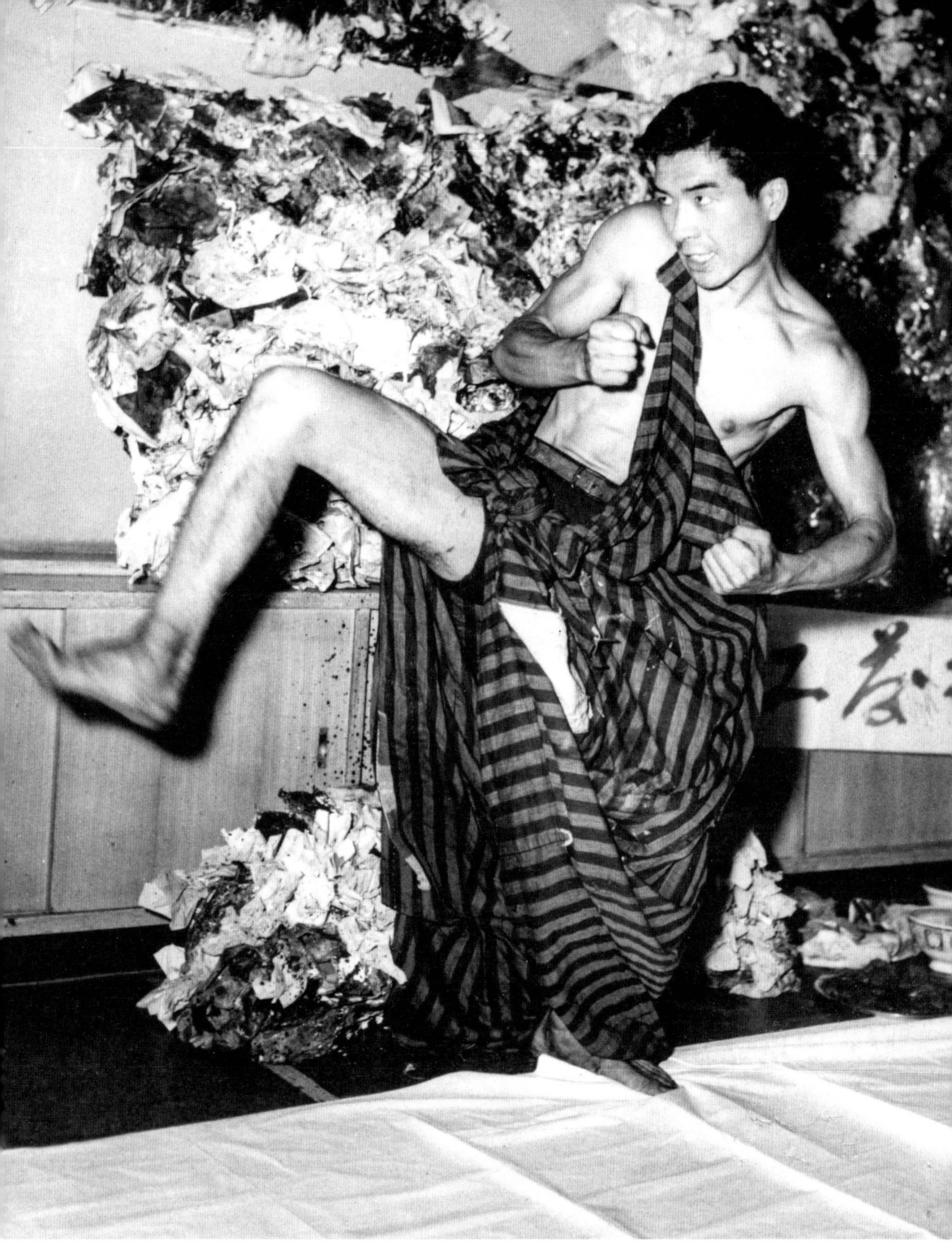

do at Mimatsu Shobō Gallery in Shimbashi, Tokyo, summer 1958

otographer unknown

**1935:** Kudo is born on 23 February in Osaka. His father, Masayoshi Kudo, is a painter in the "Western" modernist style. His mother, Yoshioko Kudo, teaches at a girls' high school.

**1942:** To escape wartime privation, the family evacuates to the father's hometown in Northern Japan.

**1945:** Kudo's father dies of tuberculosis at age 39.

**1949:** Kudo, his mother, and two siblings resettle in Okayama, Mrs. Kudo's hometown, in Western Japan.

**1954-58:** Kudo attends Tokyo National University of Fine Art. He maintains a contrary attitude towards traditional pedagogy and supplements his education by reading pamphlets on astrophysics, set theory, and quantum mechanics.

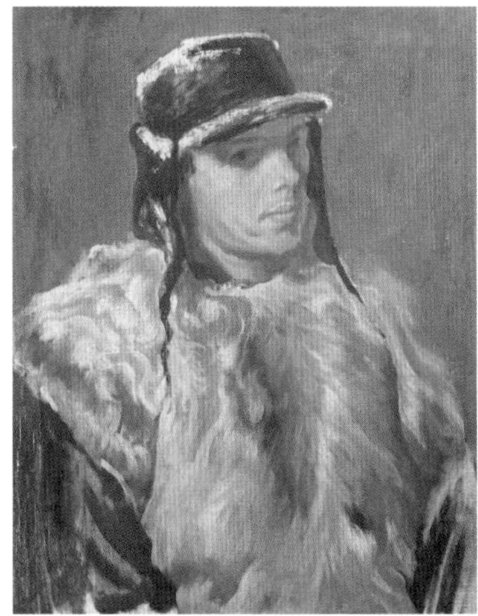

**Masayoshi Kudo:**
***Self Portrait in Furs*, c. 1943**
Hirosaki City Museum

**1958-62:** Kudo graduates university in March 1958. Between 1957 and 1961 he organizes seven one-person exhibitions often accompanied by happening-like events, a precedent noted by the American artist Allan Kaprow in his seminal book, *Assemblages, Environments and Happenings* (1966).

He also exhibits regularly in the annual Yomiuri Independant, the most significant venue for contemporary art in Japan. In a review of the 1960 exhibition, the critic Yoshiaki Tono dubs his work, "Proliferating Chain Reaction (B)", which incorporates store bought brushes, "Anti-art junk". The term becomes the byword for art in Japan critiquing consumerism and political conformity. Kudo, however, remains leery of joining artistic groups and objects to the moniker. Rather he believes his work, whose titles often include "chain reaction", represents a model of the complex interactions and influences among individuals in a society — or chain reactions.

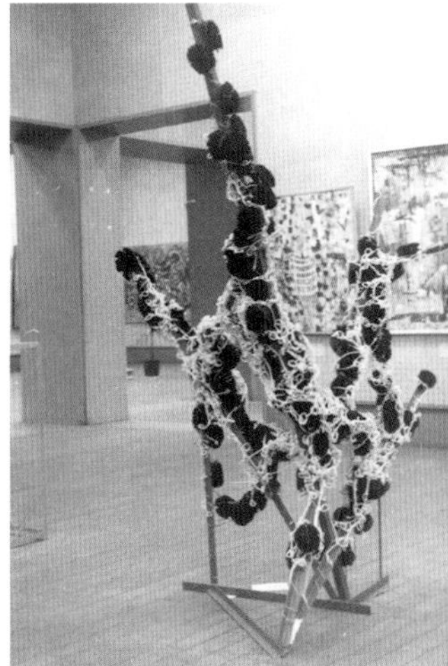

***Proliferating Chain Reaction (B)*, whereabouts unknown**
Photo: Hiroko Kudo

**1962:** Kudo wins the grand prize in the *Second International Young Artists Pan-Pacific Exhibition* which includes a grant of $1,500 to study in Paris. He and wife, Hiroko, move to Paris. In June they visit Venice just prior to the opening of the Biennale where they meet the Austrian artist Friedensreich Hundertwasser whom they had encountered previously in Tokyo. He provides entrée to the French art scene.

**1963-69:** Kudo comes to believe that the hierarchical structure of European Humanism, which emphasizes the individual and places man above nature, is false. He considers our failure to understand our world holistically as the root cause of colonialism, racism, and environmental degradation. In response he develops a series of works in which store-bought items like dolls and kitchenware are placed inside boxes painted like dice. He also uses small pet cages creating vignettes in which body parts fuse with transistors and circuit boards. Their titles often include the words "your portrait". He intends them as models of the human condition meant to inspire viewers to reconsider their position in society and nature.

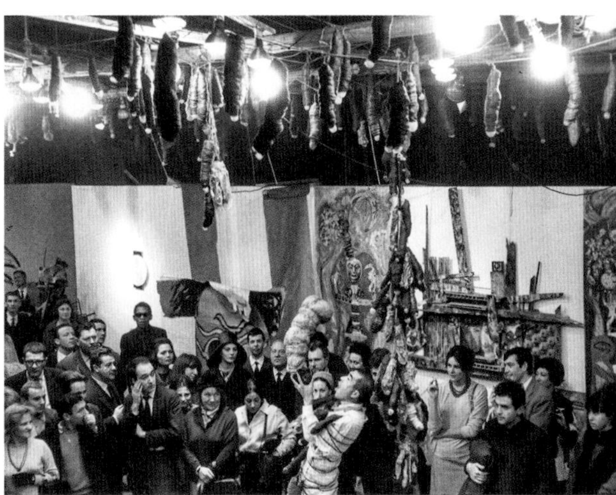

**Happening, *Philosophy of Impotence*, presented at Cinéma-Studio de Boulogne, Paris, February 1963**
Photo: Hiroko Kudo

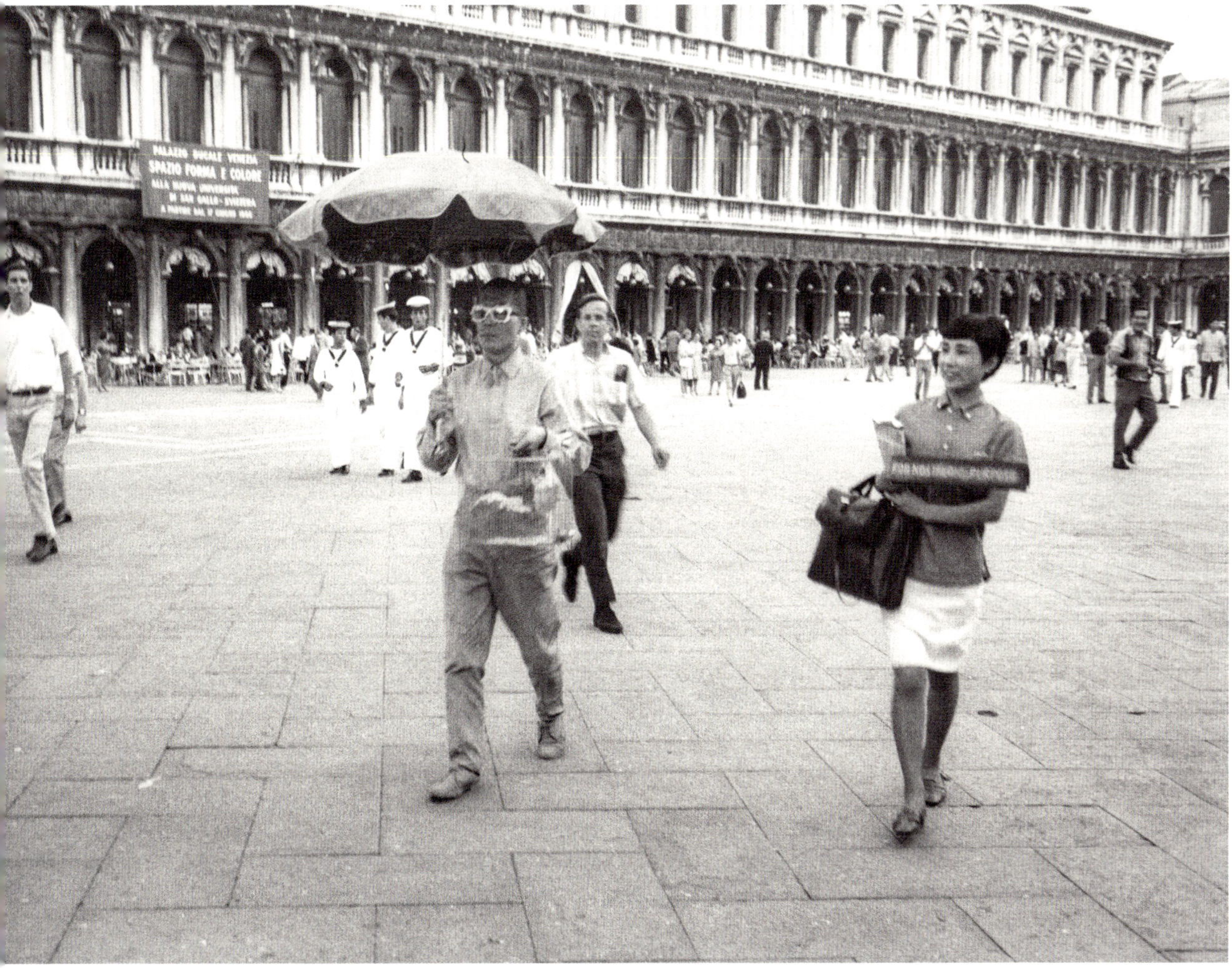

ppening, *Quiet Event, Your Portrait*, presented at Piazza San Marco in Venice, June 1966
to: Shunk Kender

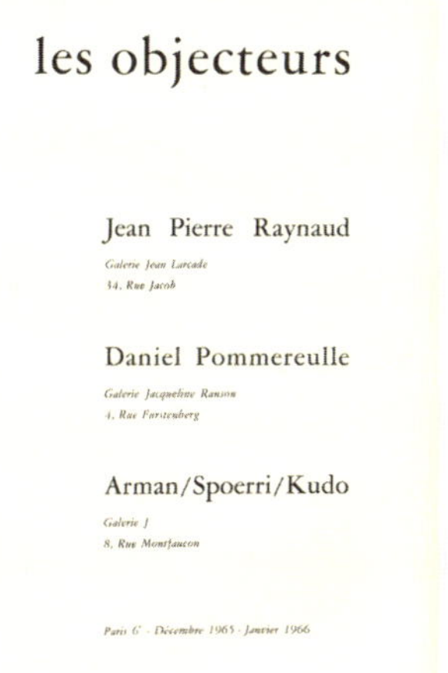
les objecteurs

Jean Pierre Raynaud

*Galerie Jean Larcade*
*34, Rue Jacob*

Daniel Pommereulle

*Galerie Jacqueline Ranson*
*4, Rue Furstenberg*

Arman/Spoerri/Kudo

*Galerie J*
*8, Rue Montfaucon*

*Paris 6e - Décembre 1965 - Janvier 1966*

*s Objecteurs*, Galerie J, Paris, 1965-66

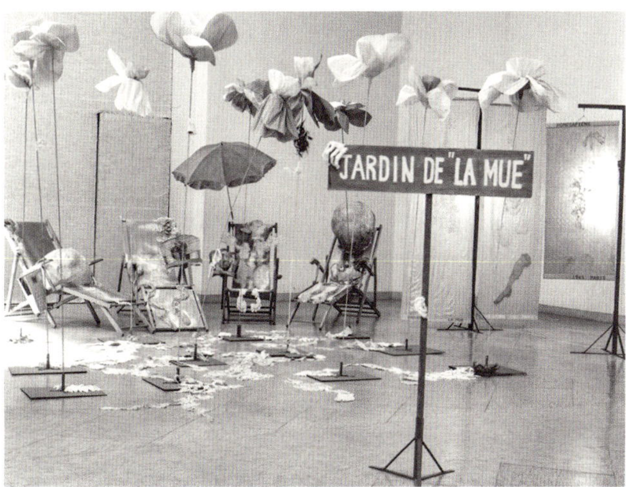


Installation *Garden of Molt (Jardin de "La Mue")* in group exhibition *Le monde en question ou vingt-six peintres de contéstation* at Musée d'Art Moderne de la Ville de Paris, 1967
Photo: Hiroko Kudo

In Paris he quickly becomes associated with French artists such as Arman, Erró, and Jean-Jacques Lebel. Lebel invites him to participate in an exhibition at the Galerie Raymond Cordier.

**In 1964** the Dutch curator Wim Beeren includes Kudo in *Nieuwe Realisten* (New Realists), a global survey of contemporary figuration and realism at the Gemeente Museum in The Hague. The show travels to Vienna and Berlin. He exhibits regularly in France and Holland, often inaugurating his shows with happenings attended, by among others, French-American artist Marcel Duchamp and the venerable gallerist Ileana Sonnabend, who had recently opened her Parisian venue. He develops a strong collector base, particularly in the Netherlands and France.

**1969:** In June, Kudo returns to Japan for nine months during which he creates *Monument of Metamorphosis*, a massive carving on the shear face of Mt. Nokogiri south of Tokyo. Resembling a giant phallus and a cocoon the work expresses his belief that people must shed their tenacious belief in individuality and adopt a more holistic understanding of society and nature.

**1970:** Kudo returns to Europe. He inaugurates his first one-person museum show at the Kunstverein für die Rheinlande und Westfalen, Düsseldorf. It includes 61 works. Here he meets the Romanian-French author and playwright Eugène Ionesco. He accepts the commission to design the sets of a television film of Ionesco's story *La vase* (Mud). Ultimately, Kudo concludes Ionesco is no longer a radical figure but an embodiment of European egoism and creates work incorporating distorted images of his face.

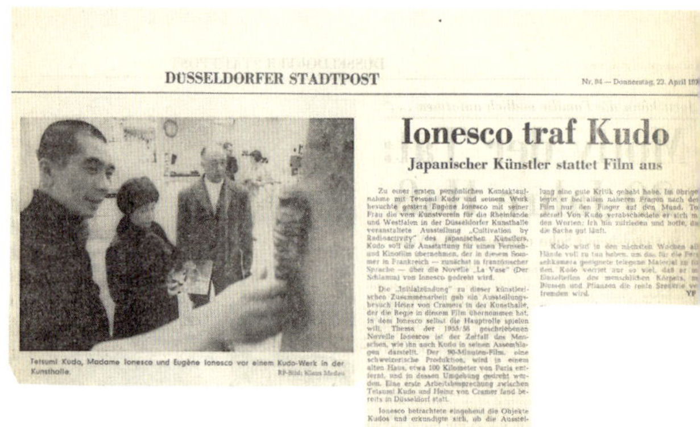

DÜSSELDORFER STADTPOST — Nr. 94 — Donnerstag, 23. April 19[illegible]

**Ionesco traf Kudo**

**Japanischer Künstler stattet Film aus**

Zu einer ersten persönlichen Kontaktaufnahme mit Tetsumi Kudo und seinem Werk besuchte gestern Eugène Ionesco mit seiner Frau die vom Kunstverein für die Rheinlande und Westfalen in der Düsseldorfer Kunsthalle veranstaltete Ausstellung „Cultivation by Radioactivity" des japanischen Künstlers. Kudo soll die Ausstattung für einen Fernseh- und Kinofilm übernehmen, der in diesem Sommer in Frankreich — zunächst in französischer Sprache — über die Novelle „La Vase" (Der Schlamm) von Ionesco gedreht wird.

Die „Initialzündung" zu dieser künstlerischen Zusammenarbeit gab ein Ausstellungsbesuch Heinz von Cramers in der Kunsthalle, der die Regie in diesem Film übernommen hat, in dem Ionesco selbst die Hauptrolle spielen will. Thema der 1955/56 geschriebenen Novelle Ionescos ist der Zerfall des Menschen, wie ihn auch Kudo in seinen Assemblagen darstellt. Der 90-Minuten-Film, eine schweizerische Produktion, wird in einem alten Haus, etwa 100 Kilometer von Paris entfernt, und in dessen Umgebung gedreht werden. Eine erste Arbeitsbesprechung zwischen Tetsumi Kudo und Heinz von Cramer fand bereits in Düsseldorf statt.

Ionesco betrachtete eingehend die Objekte Kudos und erkundigte sich, ob die Ausstellung eine gute Kritik gehabt habe. Im übrigen [illegible]

Kudo wird in den nächsten Wochen [illegible] YP

Tetsumi Kudo, Madame Ionesco und Eugène Ionesco vor einem Kudo-Werk in der Kunsthalle.

Article with photograph of Eugène Ionesco and his wife visiting Kudo' solo exhibition in *Düsseldorfer Stadtpost*, 23 April, 1970

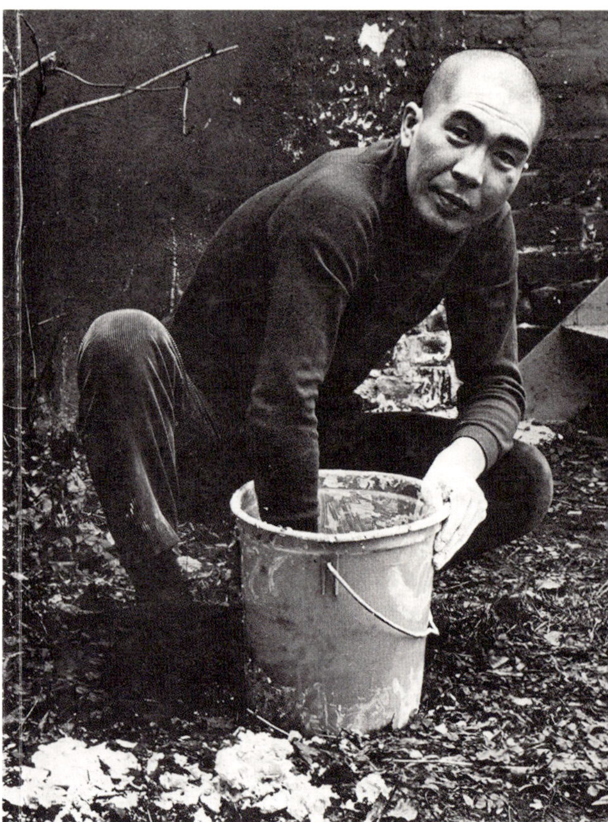

Cover of catalogue for the exhibition at Kunstverein für die Rheinlanc und Westfalen, Düsseldorf, 1970

Photo: Brigitte Hellgoth

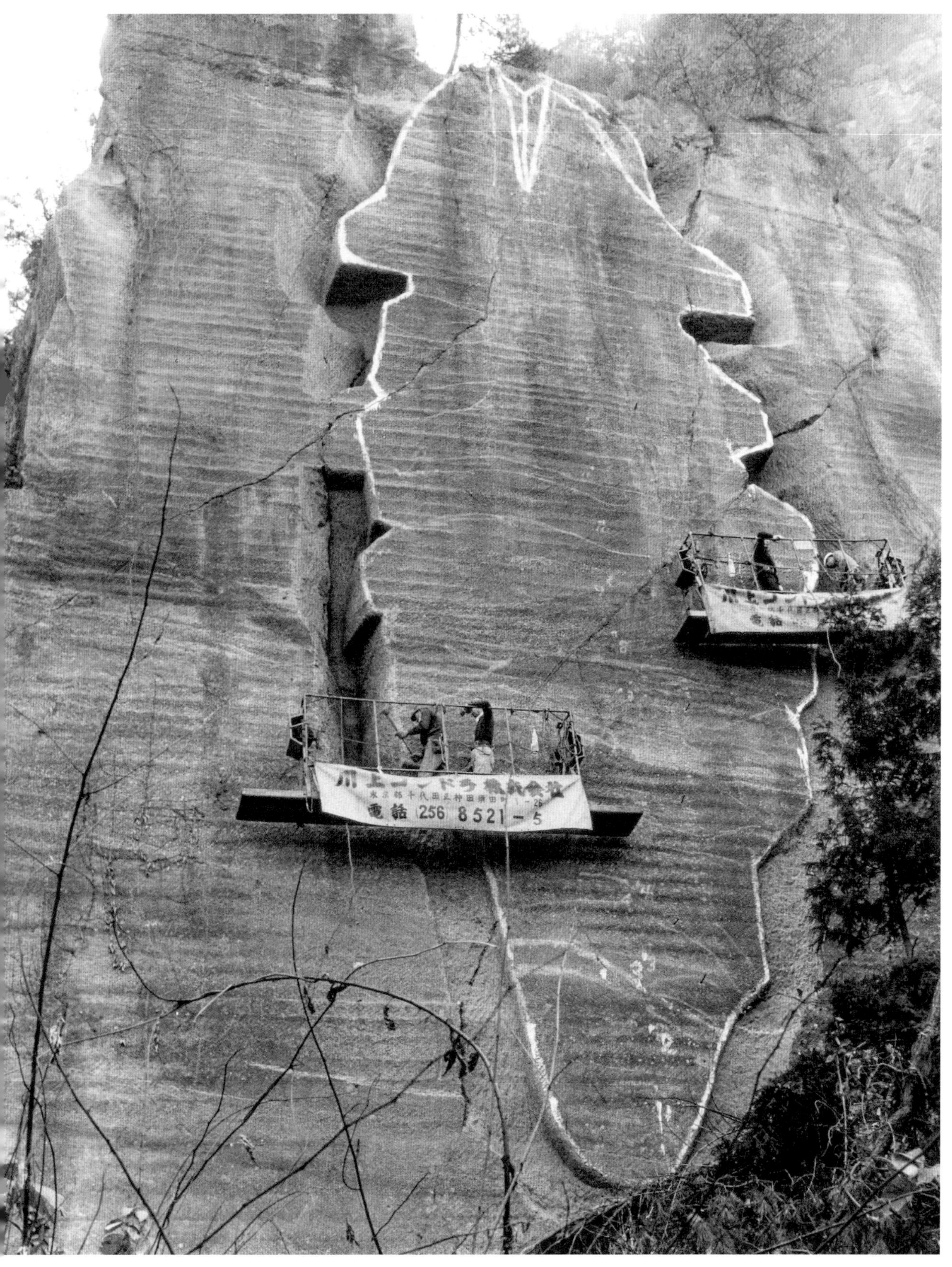


*onument of Metamorphosis*, 1970
otographer unknown

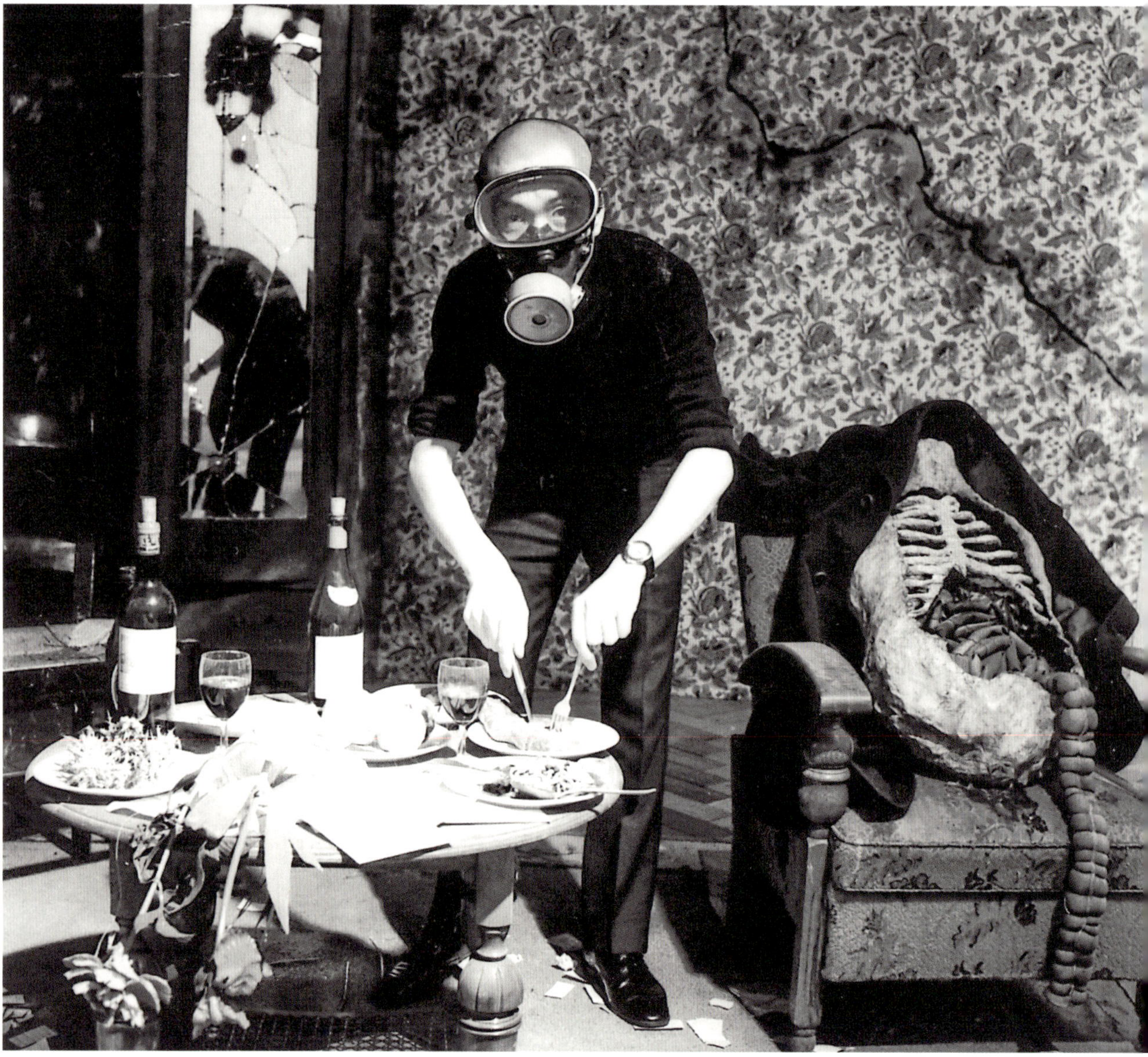

Exhibition view of the solo show *Tetsumi Kudo: Pollution – Cultivation – New Ecology – Your Portrait* at Stedelijk Museum Amsterdam, 1972
Photo: Hiroko Kudo

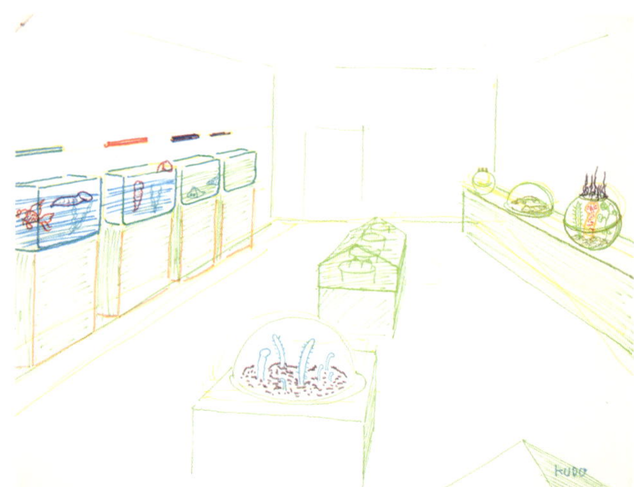


Plan drawing for installations in the exhibition *Tetsumi Kudo: Pollution Cultivation New Ecology You Portrait*, Stedelijk Museum Amsterdam, 1972, felt-tip on ink paper, 28 x 39 cm
Courtesy the Estate of Tetsumi Kudo, Tokyo

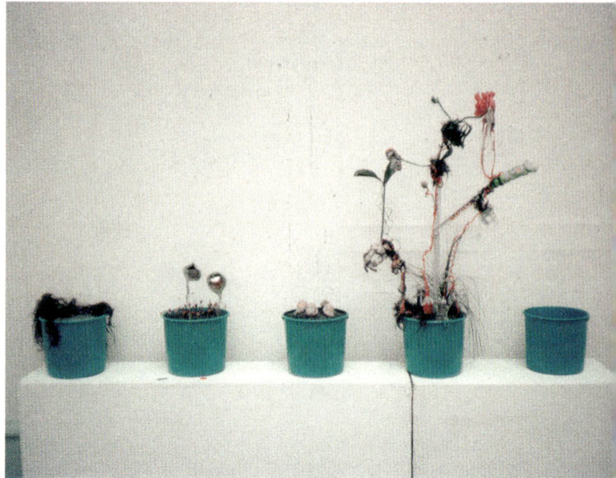

Exhibition view of the group exhibition *Dødsspringet på Charlottenborg*, 1976
Photo: Hiroko Kudo
Opposite page, left: exhibition catalogue

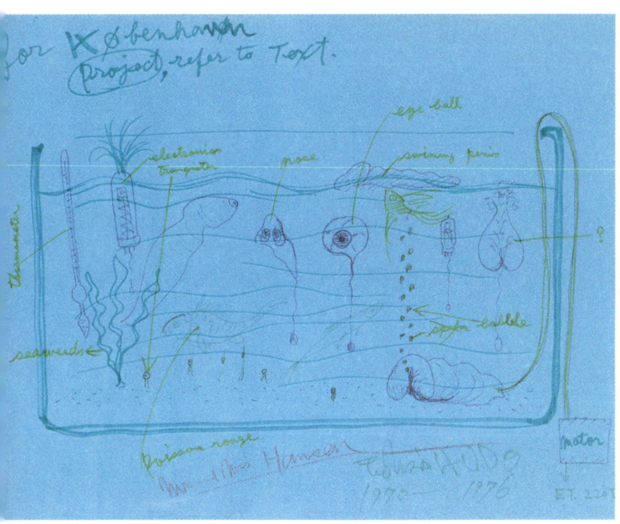


roject for Copenhagen, 1970-76
ixed technique on paper, 50 x 65 cm
urtesy Galerie Christophe Gaillard and Galerie 1900-2000

**1972:** The Stedilijk Museum, Amsterdam, hosts a major solo exhibition *Pollution – Cultivation – New Ecology – Your Portrait*. Many of the works are housed in aquarium, models of greenhouses, or clear plastic balls. They resemble sci-fi landscapes in which body parts and electronic components glow in phosphorescent colors. Following the "New Ecology" of the show's title, the works present Kudo's idea that technology, nature and humanity influence and nurture each other in a closed circuit.

**1974:** His work is included in *Japan på Louisiana* at the Louisiana in Humlebæk. The show travels to Göteborg Konstmuseum and Henie Onstad Kunstsenter in Oslo. He exhibits again in Denmark in 1976 in *Dødsspringet på Charlottenborg*. He visits Copenhagen on both occasions and several of his works enter Danish collections.

Kudo's mother dies on 7 May, 1974. The loss and increasing financial pressure due to global recession and a cooling of the art market precipitates a psychological impasse. His work becomes more introspective and spiritual exploring themes of memory, heredity, and artistic crisis.

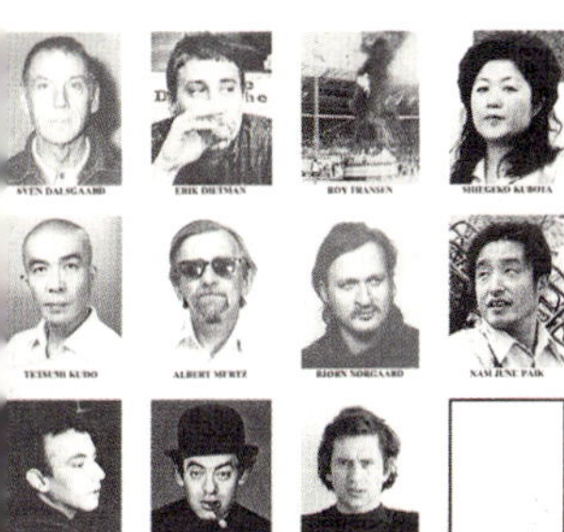


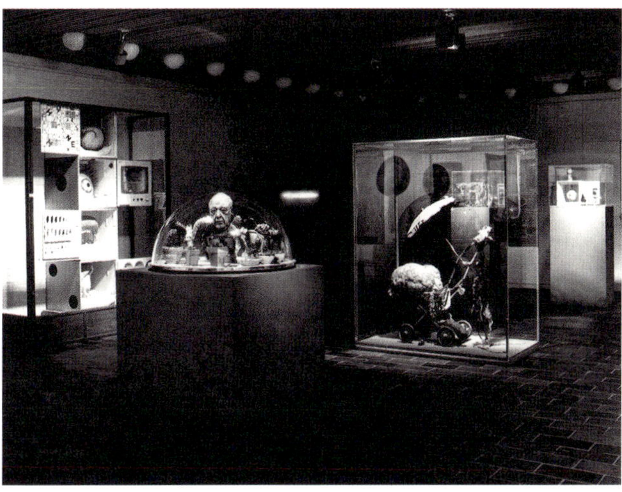

Exhibition view of the group exhibition *Japan at Louisiana* at Louisiana Museum of Modern Art, 1974

**1980:** In April, he performs at the Centre Pompidou which had acquired six of his works. He is hospitalized for alcoholism in June, 1980.

**1981:** He begins a series using string and thread exploring cosmologies of time, memory, cultural continuity, and the mystical structure of Japanese society. These are completely abstract and appear to break with his past work, but they all share a fundamental interest in the structures of nature and society.

**1983-90:** In 1983 he begins splitting his time between Paris and Japan, where he has several gallery and museum exhibitions. His work is also included in major surveys of Japanese Art in Oxford and at the Centre Pompidou in Paris.

He is diagnosed with throat cancer in 1987. He creates his last works in 1988 but continues to exhibit.

Kudo dies of colon cancer on 12 November, 1990 in Tokyo.

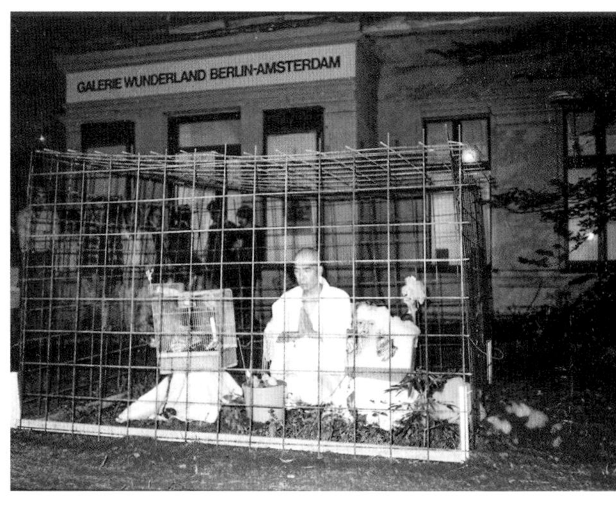


Kudo presenting his ceremony *Meditation – Buddha in Berlin* in the garden of Galerie Wunderland in Berlin, 19 August 1978
Photo: Hiroko Kudo

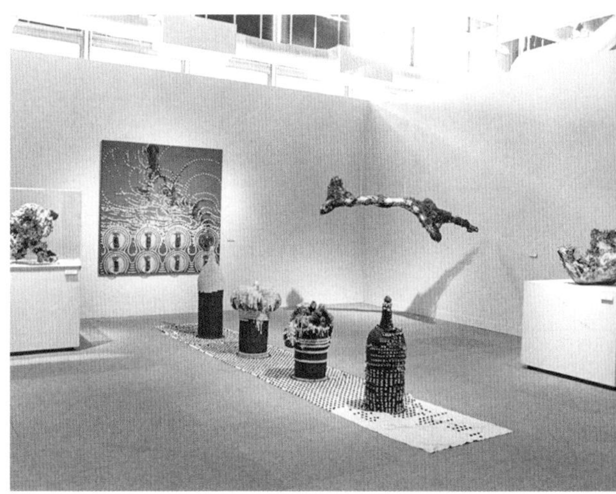

Kudo's section, with works from 1957 to 1961, in the exhibition *Japon des avant-gardes, 1910-1970* at Musée National d'Art Moderne, Centre Georges Pompidou, Paris, 1986-87
Photo: Manabu Matsunaga

**1990 to the present:** Since his death, Kudo has been the subject of major retrospectives at the National Museum of Modern Art Osaka (1995 and 2013-14) both of which toured in Japan; at La Maison Rouge, Paris, 2007; at the Walker Art Center, Minneapolis, USA, 2008; and the Fridericianum, Kassel, Germany, 2016. Both Paul McCarthy and Mike Kelley have cited him as influences. His work is currently included in the opening installation at the recently expanded Museum of Modern Art in New York.

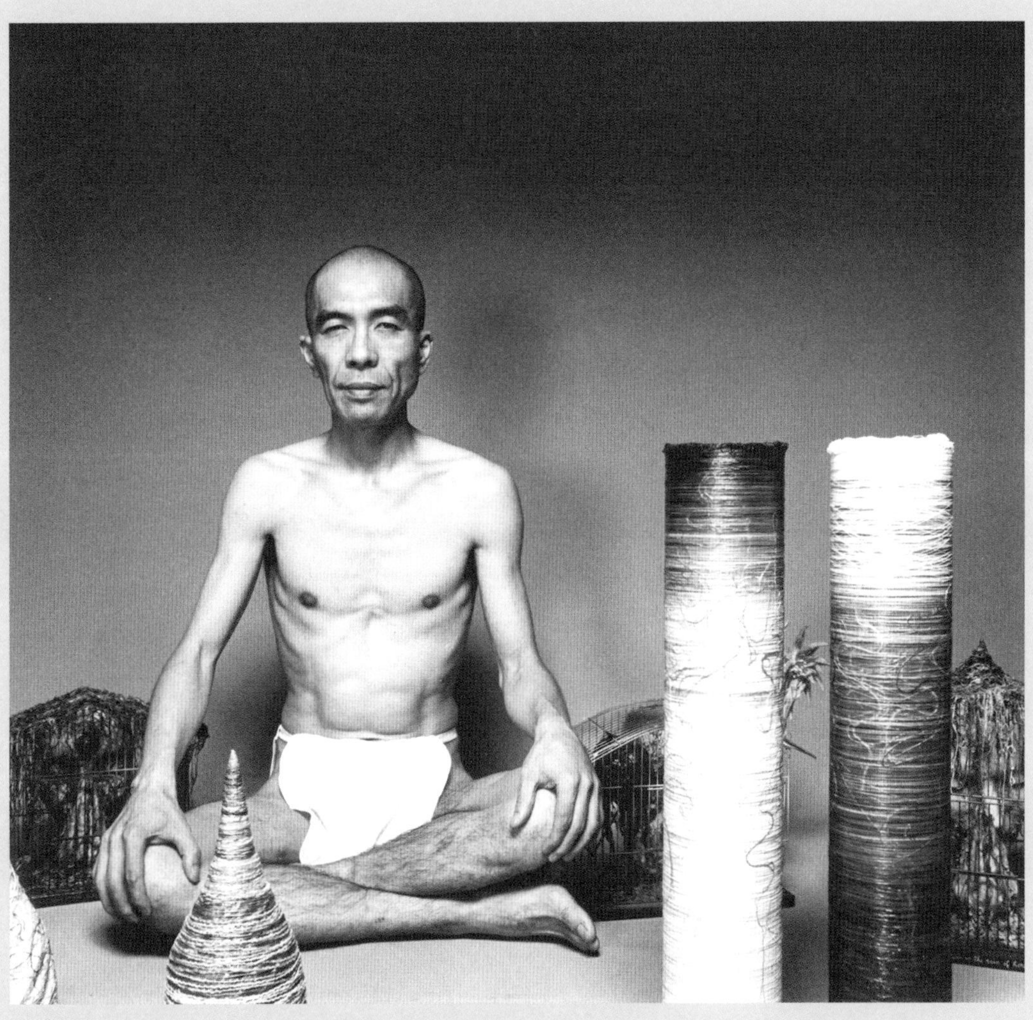

Kudo with works from the *Black Hole* series in the exhibition *Kudo 1981* at Sōgetsu Museum, Tokyo, 1981
Costume: Hiroko Kudo, portrait of Kudo: Anzaï

***Your Portrait B,*** 1962
Wooden cube with various objects and materials
30 × 30 × 30 cm
mumok – Museum moderner Kunst Stiftung Ludwig Wien,
Former Hahn Collection, Cologne
Acquired in 1978

***Souvenir la Mue – 1965 Homo sapiens,*** 1965
Souvenir of Molt – 1965 Homo Sapiens
Moulded paper, glue
26,5 × 11 × 1 cm
Kunsten Museum of Modern Art Aalborg

***Project for "Becht Garden",*** 1965
Felt-tip pen, paint on paper
50 × 65 cm
Agnes & Frits Becht Collection,
The Netherlands

***For Your Living Room – For Nostalgic Purpose,*** 1966
Cage, cotton, plastic, polyester, resin, paint, pills
43,5 × 51 × 30,5 cm
Private Collection,
Courtesy Hauser & Wirth and Andrea Rosen Gallery

***Souvenir "La Mue",*** 1967
Souvenir of Molt
Cage, artificial roses and various found objects and materials
61 × 38 × 24 cm
Private Collection

***Souvenir – La Mue (Memory-Pupal Skin),*** 1967
Souvenir of Molt (Memory-Pupal Skin)
Cage, acrylic on plastic flowers and mixed media
35,5 × 39,5 × 25,5 cm
Private Collection,
Courtesy Hauser & Wirth and Andrea Rosen Gallery

***CULTIVATION,*** 1967
UV tube, papier maché, paint, wire
175 × 63 × 50 cm
Collection Fabre

***Flowers,*** 1967-68
From: Garden of the Metamorphosis in the Space Capsule, 1968
10 artificial flowers, paper, iron
H: 250 cm
Private Collection,
Courtesy Hauser & Wirth and Andrea Rosen Gallery

***Cultivation by Radioactivity in the Electronic Circuit (Pink Flower),*** 1968
Plastic, plexi glass, polyester
65,5 × 25,5 × 25,5 cm
Courtesy of Andrea Rosen Gallery

***Cultivation by Radioactivity in the Electronic Circuit,*** 1968
Perspex (pmma), resin, paper, metal, neon tube
Object: 42 × 120 × 110 cm
Base: 142 × 131 × 122 cm
Collection Stedelijk Museum Amsterdam

***Cultivation by Radioactivity in the Electronic Circuit,*** 1968
Mixed media
2 parts with individual dimensions
Total dimension: 148 × 100,5 × 133,5 cm
Louisiana Museum of Modern Art, Humlebæk, Denmark

***Portrait of Ionesco and/or the End of Some Generation,*** 1970
Cage, iron, plastic and paper
112 (incl. book) × 41 × 40 cm
Collection Stedelijk Museum Amsterdam

***Portrait d'artiste,*** 1968-75
Portrait of the Artist
Cage, plastic, resin, metal, wool, paper, masonite, plywood, paint
29 × 45 × 32 cm
FNAC 1638
Centre national des arts plastiques (France)

***Cultivation of Nature & People Who Are Looking at It,*** 1970
Plastic bucket, artificial soil, cotton, plastic, resin, adhesive, paint, screws
24 × 23,5 × 23,5 cm
Courtesy of Andrea Rosen Gallery

***Cultivation of Nature & People Who Are Looking at It,*** 1970
Plastic bucket, mirror, snail shells, adhesive, paint, hair, screws
19 × 23 × 23 cm
Courtesy of Andrea Rosen Gallery

***Cultivation of Nature & People Who Are Looking at It,*** 1970
Plastic bucket, polyester, adhesive, resistors, hair
35 × 30 × 30 cm
Private Collection

***Cultivation of Nature & People Who Are Looking at It,*** 1970-71
Plastic bucket, plastic, mirrored glass, papier maché, cotton, artificial soil, resin, adhesive, paint, artificial hair
36 × 23 × 23 cm
Private Collection

***Cultivation of Nature & People Who Are Looking at It,*** c. 1970
Plastic bucket, soil, resin, glue, cellulose, hair, paint and electronic diagrams
35 × 30 × 30 cm
Courtesy Galerie Christophe Gaillard and Galerie 1900-2000

***Cultivation of Nature & People Who Are Looking at It,*** 1970-71
Painted resin, snail shells, soil, vacuum tube, hair, adhesive, plexi glass
28 × 26 × 26 cm
Console 42,5 × 36 × 32,5 cm
Gothenburg Museum of Art

***Cultivation by Nature & People Who Are Looking at It,*** 1970-71
Plastic, artificial soil, glass, cotton, vacuum tubes, hair, resin
33 × 26 × 26 cm
Private Collection,
Courtesy Hauser & Wirth and Andrea Rosen Gallery

***"Pollution – Cultivation – New Ecology" (Portrait of Ionesco),*** 1970-71
Mixed media
50 × 100 cm
Louisiana Museum of Modern Art, Humlebæk, Denmark

***Votre Portrait,*** 1970-79
Your Portrait
Mixed media
50 × 46 × 25 cm
Private Collection,
Courtesy Hauser & Wirth and Andrea Rosen Gallery

***Untitled,*** 1971
Plastic, resin and electronic devices under plexi dome
25 × 53,5 cm
Collection Antoine de Galbert, Paris

***Translation Painting by Computer A,*** 1971
Computer painting on canvas
293 × 214 cm
FNAC 89787
Centre national des arts plastiques (France)

***Translation Painting by Computer B,*** 1971
Computer painting on canvas
300 × 223 cm
FNAC 89788
Centre national des arts plastiques (France)

***Untitled,*** 1971
Mixed media
17,5 × 38 × 20,5 cm
Private Collection,
Courtesy Hauser & Wirth and Andrea Rosen Gallery

***Pollution – cultivation – nouvelle écologie (B),*** 1971
Pollution – Cultivation – New Ecology (B)
Wood, artificial flowers, artificial soil, cotton, plastic, polyester, resin, snail shell, transistors, adhesive, paint
58 × 12 × 24 cm
Agnes & Frits Becht Collection, The Netherlands

***Pollution,*** 1971-73
Wood, artificial grass, resin, artificial flower, cotton, plastic, polyester, artificial snail shell, toy earthworm, adhesive, paint
61 × 30 × 8 cm
Private Collection

***Esclavage de Conservation de l'espèce humaine,*** 1972
Slavery of Conservation of the Human Race
Cage with various objects and materials
33 × 42 × 27 cm
mumok – Museum moderner Kunst Stiftung Ludwig Wien,
Former Hahn Collection, Cologne
Acquired in 1978

***Cultivation,*** 1972
Cage, wood, plastic, cotto[n], paint, snail shells, spray paint, artificial soil, hair, resin, thermometer
28 × 33 × 23,5 cm
Private Collection,
Courtesy Hauser & Wirth and Andrea Rosen Gallery

***Sans titre,*** 1972
Untitled
Plastic bucket, plastic, resin, cellulose, paint, soil, electronic resistors, TSF tube on wooden base
63,5 × 46 × 37 cm
Courtesy Galerie Christophe Gaillard and Galerie 1900-2000

***Origine de la pollution,*** 1972-73
The Origin of Pollution
Mixed media
63 × 24,5 × 5 cm
Private Collection,
Courtesy Hauser & Wirth and Andrea Rosen Gallery

***La Liberté de l'étalon,*** 1972-77
The Stud's Freedom
Cage, paint, artificial soil, cotton, plastic, polyester, resin, string
45,5 × 33,5 × 20,5 cm
Private Collection,
Courtesy Hauser & Wirth and Andrea Rosen Gallery

***Pollution Cultivation New Ecology,*** 1974
Spray paint, watercolour, pencil and pen and ink on serigraph
50 × 64,5 cm
Private Collection

***Votre Portrait,*** 1974
Your Portrait
Screenprint on paper
56,5 × 90 cm
Private Collection,
Courtesy Hauser & Wirth

***Bonheur,*** 1974
Happiness
Cage, paint, artificial soil, plastic flowers, cotton, plastic, resin, string, cigarettes, thermometer, Aspro tablets, circuit boar[d]
28,5 × 48,5 × 22 cm
Courtesy of Andrea Rose[n] Gallery

*uddha in Paris. 1éditation entre utur programmé t mémoire nregistrée,* 1976
uddha in Paris. editation between rogrammed Future and ecorded Memory
age, metal, plastic, yarn, ood
5 × 27 × 18 cm
rivate Collection

*ossil in Hiroshima,* 976
pray paint on paper with mbossings
pcs, each 54,5 × 50 cm
rivate Collection, courtesy oevenbruck, Paris

*ortrait of the rtist in the Crisis,* 978
age, woolen yarn, emperature gauge, nitting needles, wood
0 × 45,5 × 22 cm
rivate Collection, ourtesy Hauser & Wirth

*luman Bonsai - Freedom of eformity — eformity of reedom,* 1979
rtificial soil, resin, plastic, ood, paint, cotton, wire, etal chain, glass beads
3,5 × 74,5 × 21,5
rivate Collection, ourtesy Hauser & Wirth nd Andrea Rosen Gallery

*eteindre l'hérédité hromosomique ar le pétrole et la adioactivité,* 1979
edyeing Chromosomal eredity with Petroleum nd Radioactivity
age, paint, artificial soil, astic flower, plastic, olyester, resin and string
9,5 × 38 × 26 cm
ourtesy of Andrea Rosen allery

*aradise,* 1980
age, paint, plastic flower, astic, metal coins, resin
3 × 36 × 20,5 cm
rivate Collection, ourtesy Hauser & Wirth

# TETSUMI KUDO WORKS

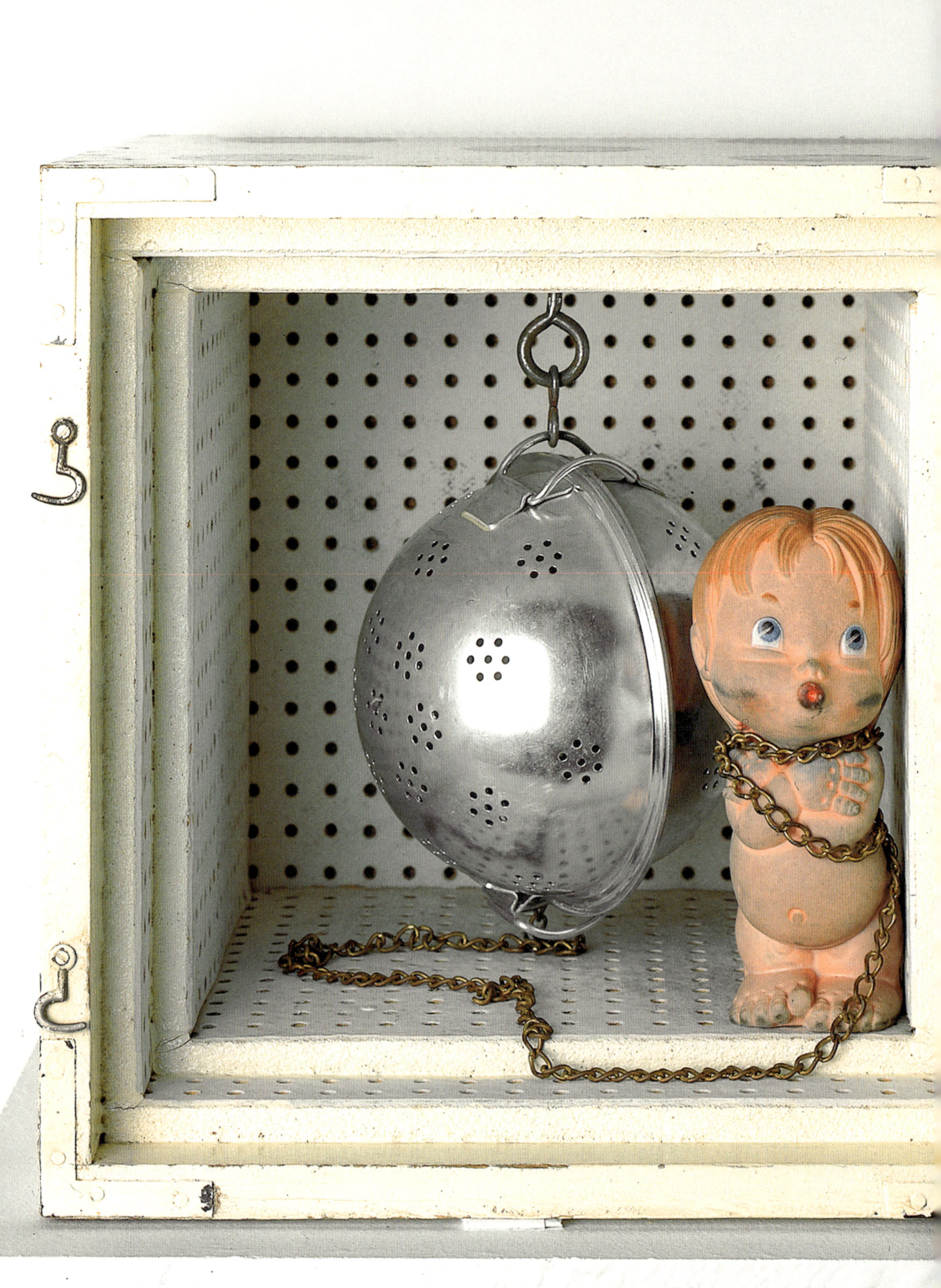

*Your Portrait B*, 1962

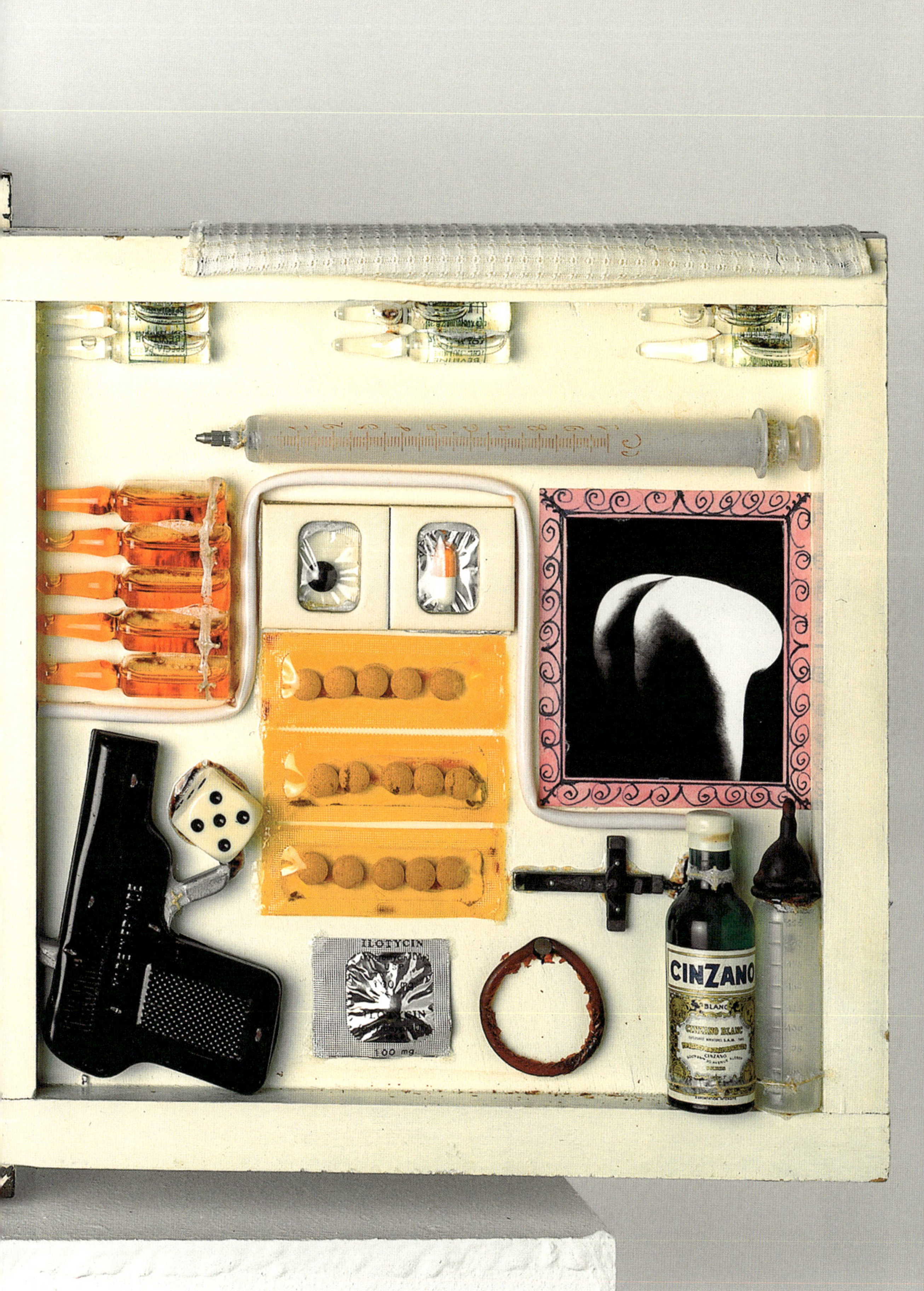
ILOTYCIN
100 mg.
CINZANO
BLANC

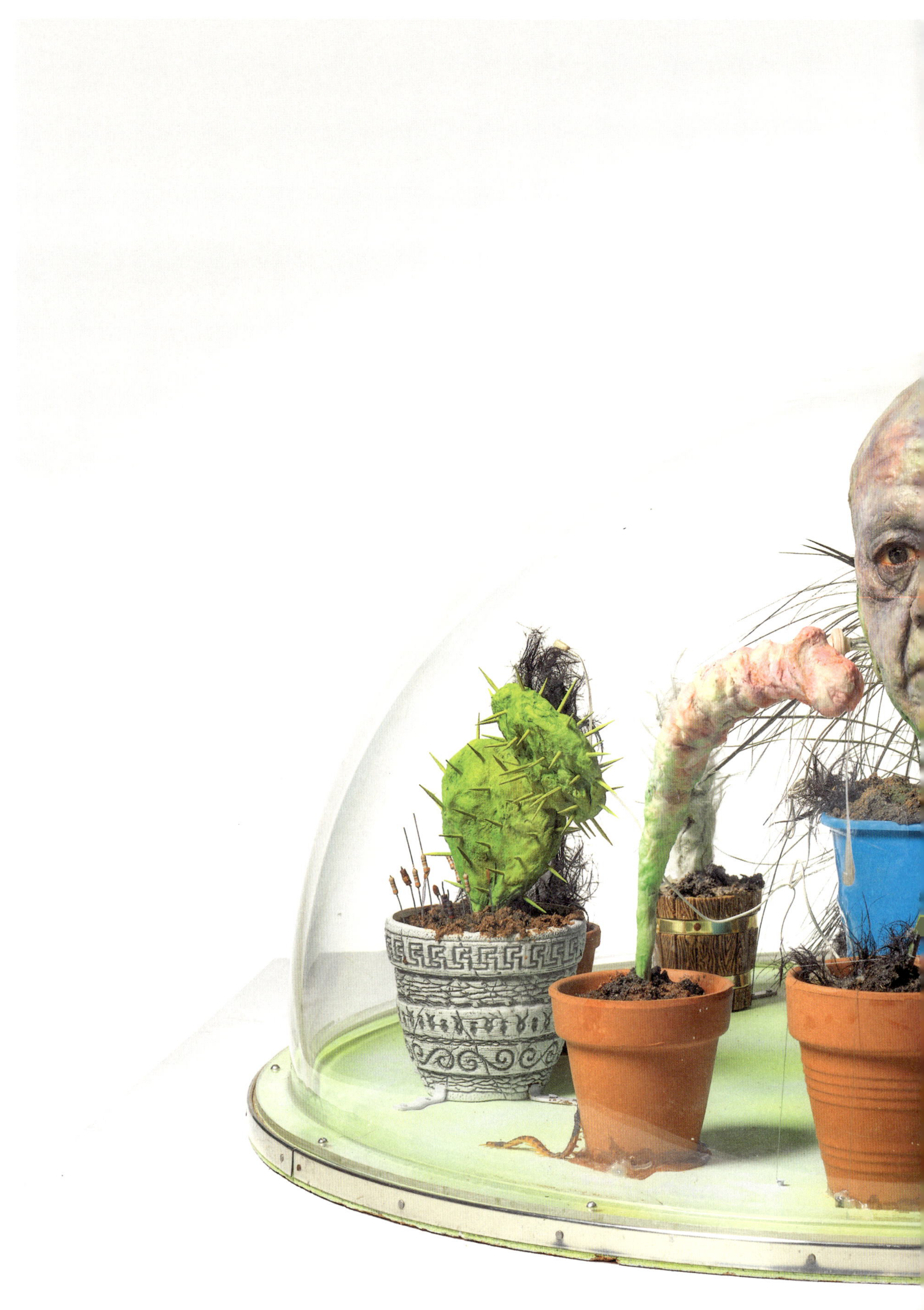

*"Pollution – Cultivation – New Ecology" (Portrait of Ionesco)*, 1970-71

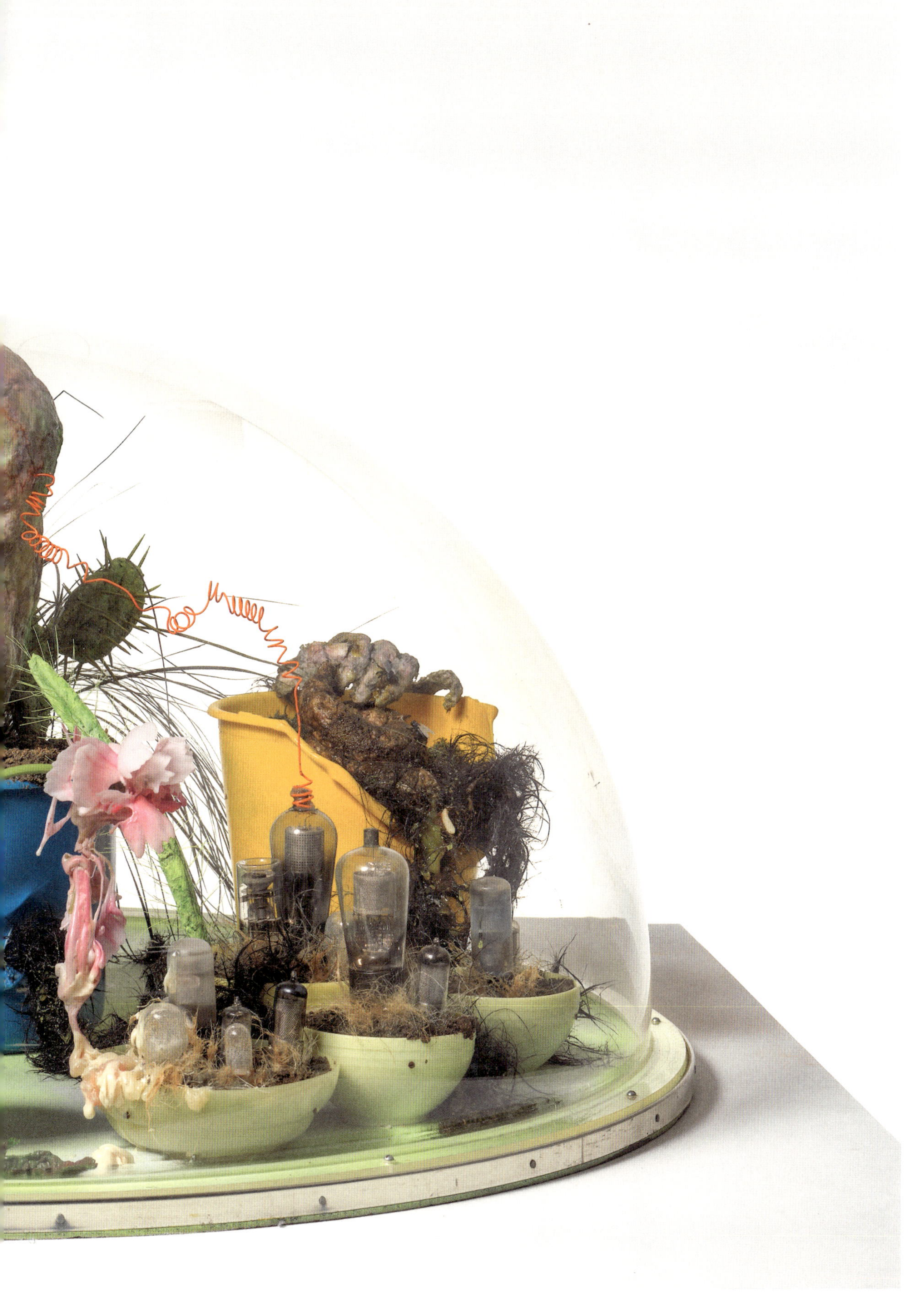

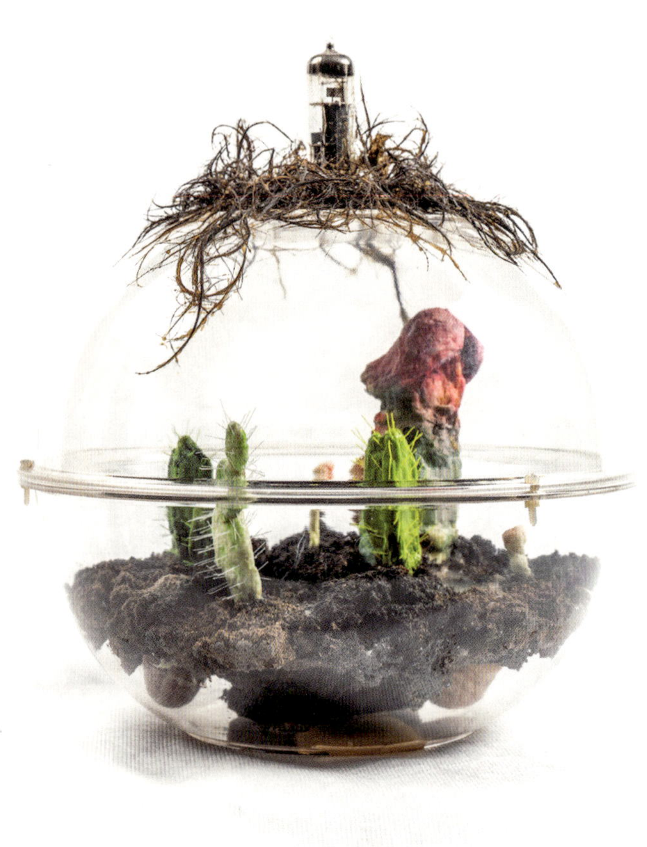

*Cultivation of Nature & People Who Are Looking At It* , 1970-71

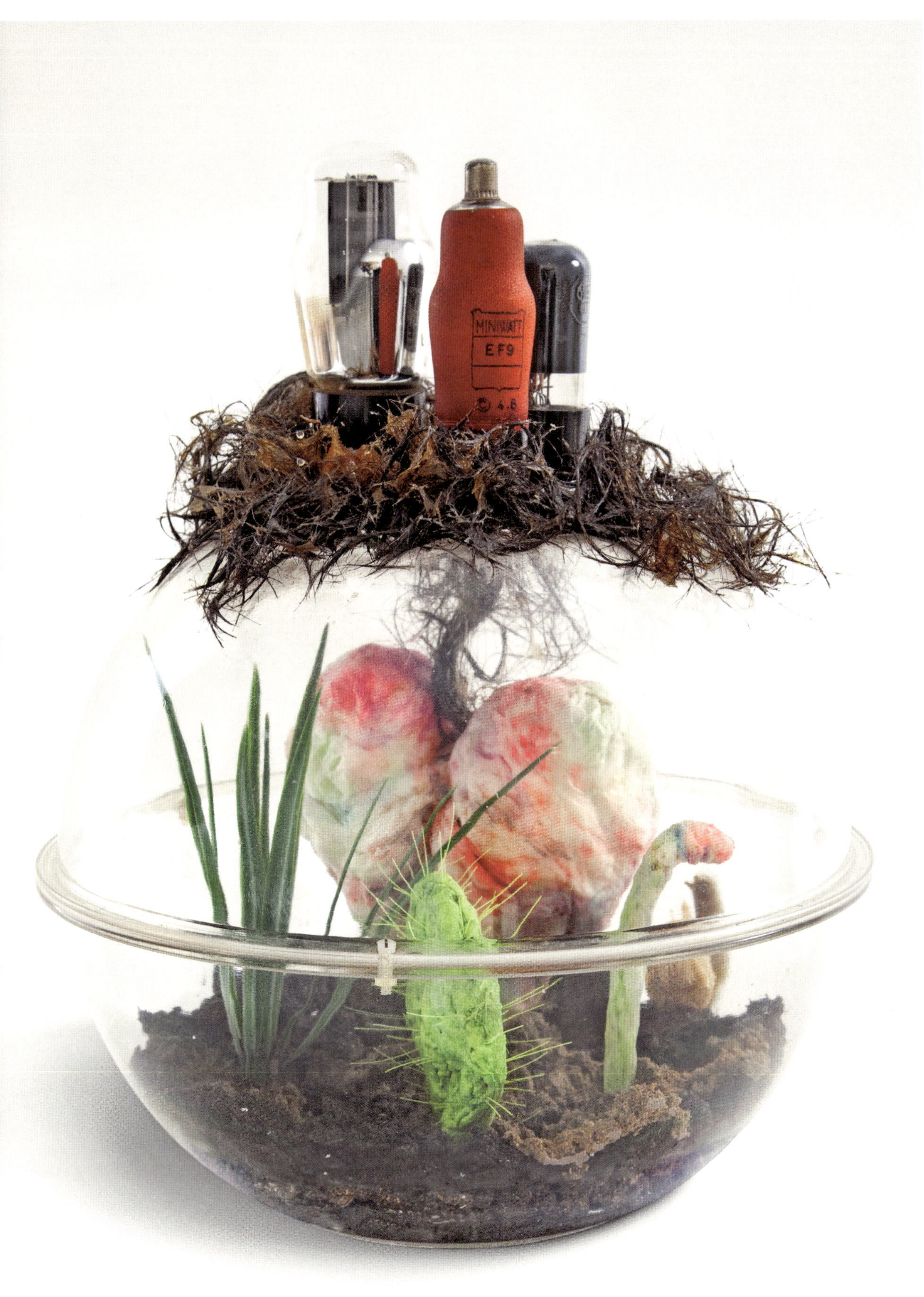


*ultivation by Nature & People Who Are Looking at It*, 1970-71

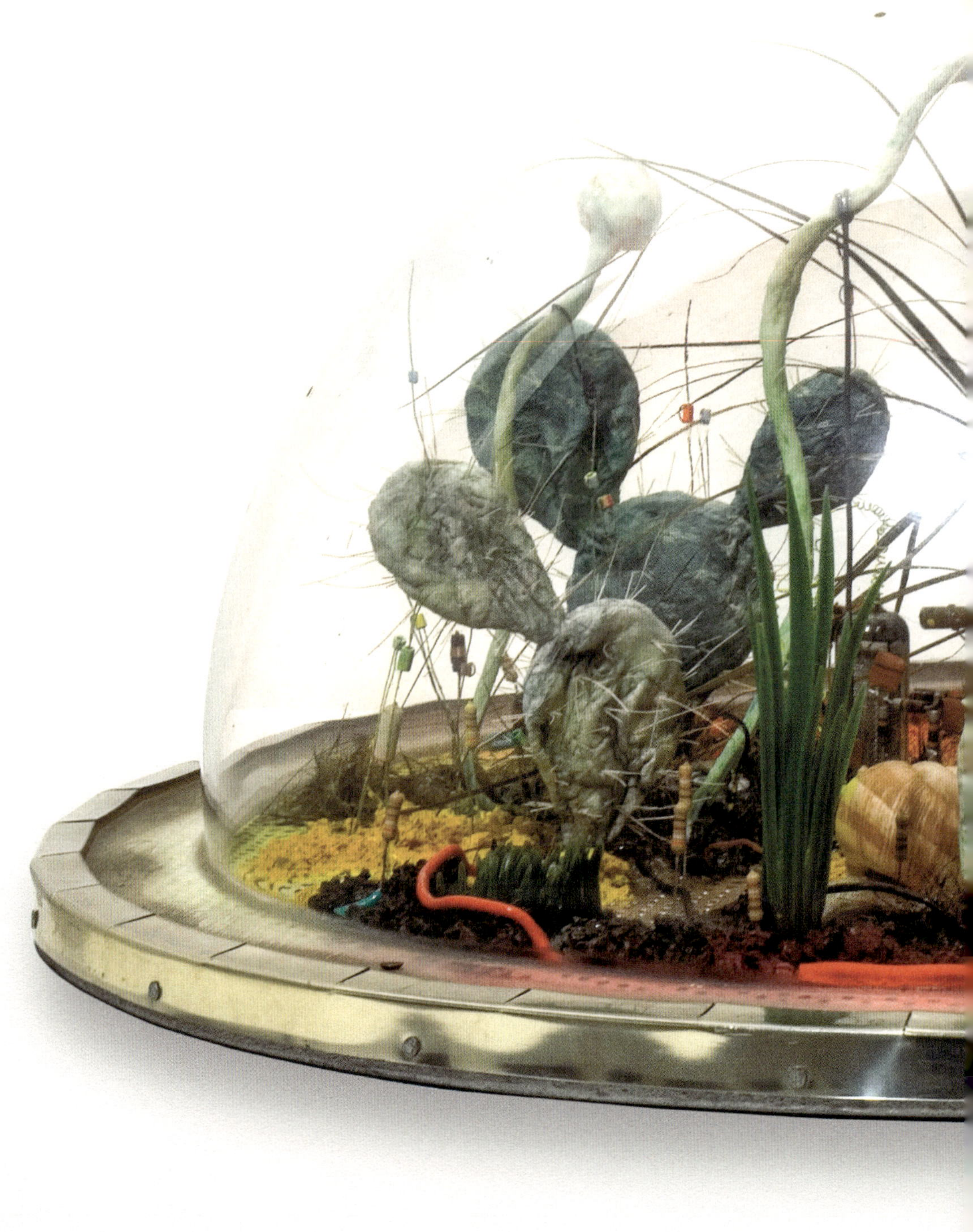

*Untitled*, 1971

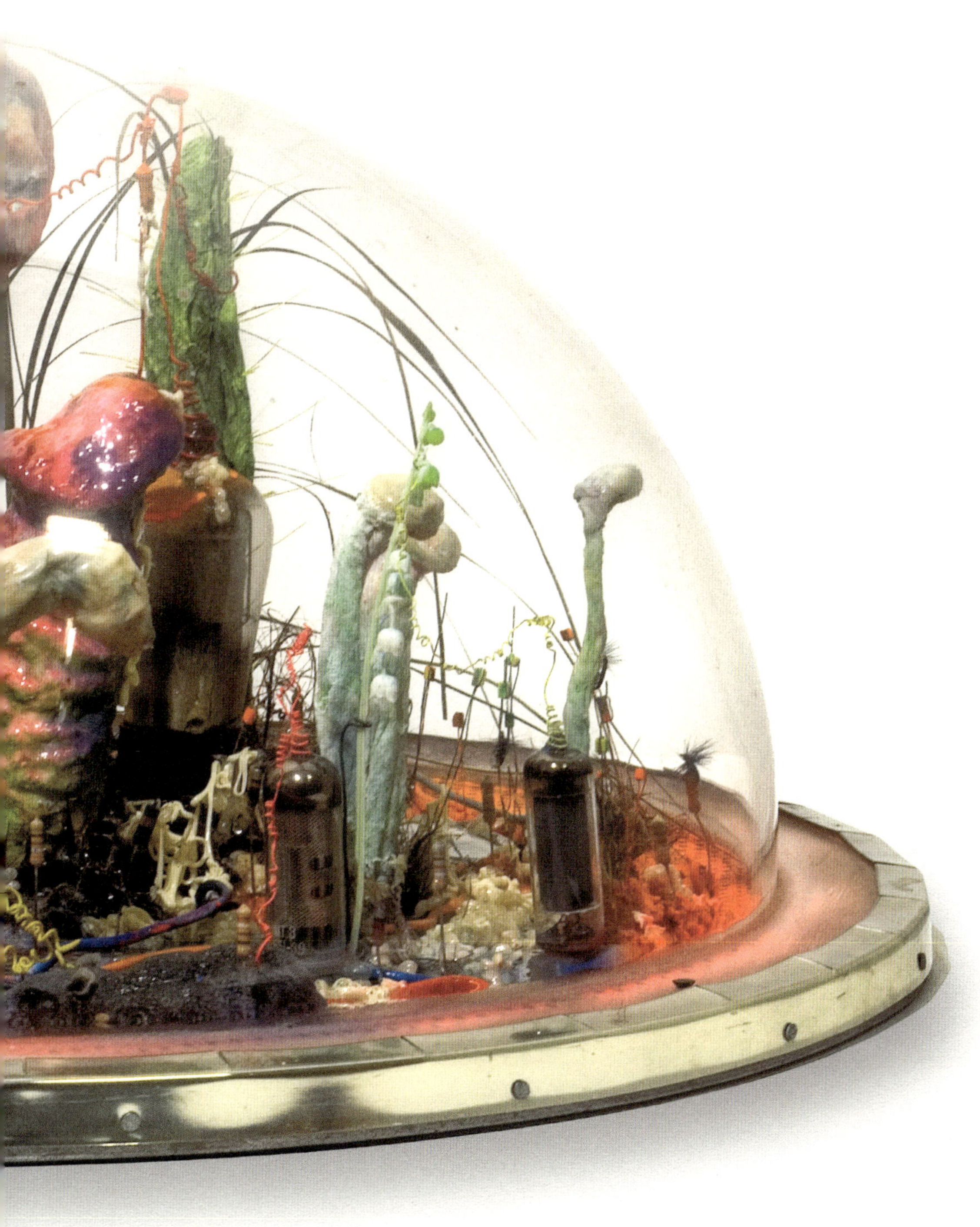

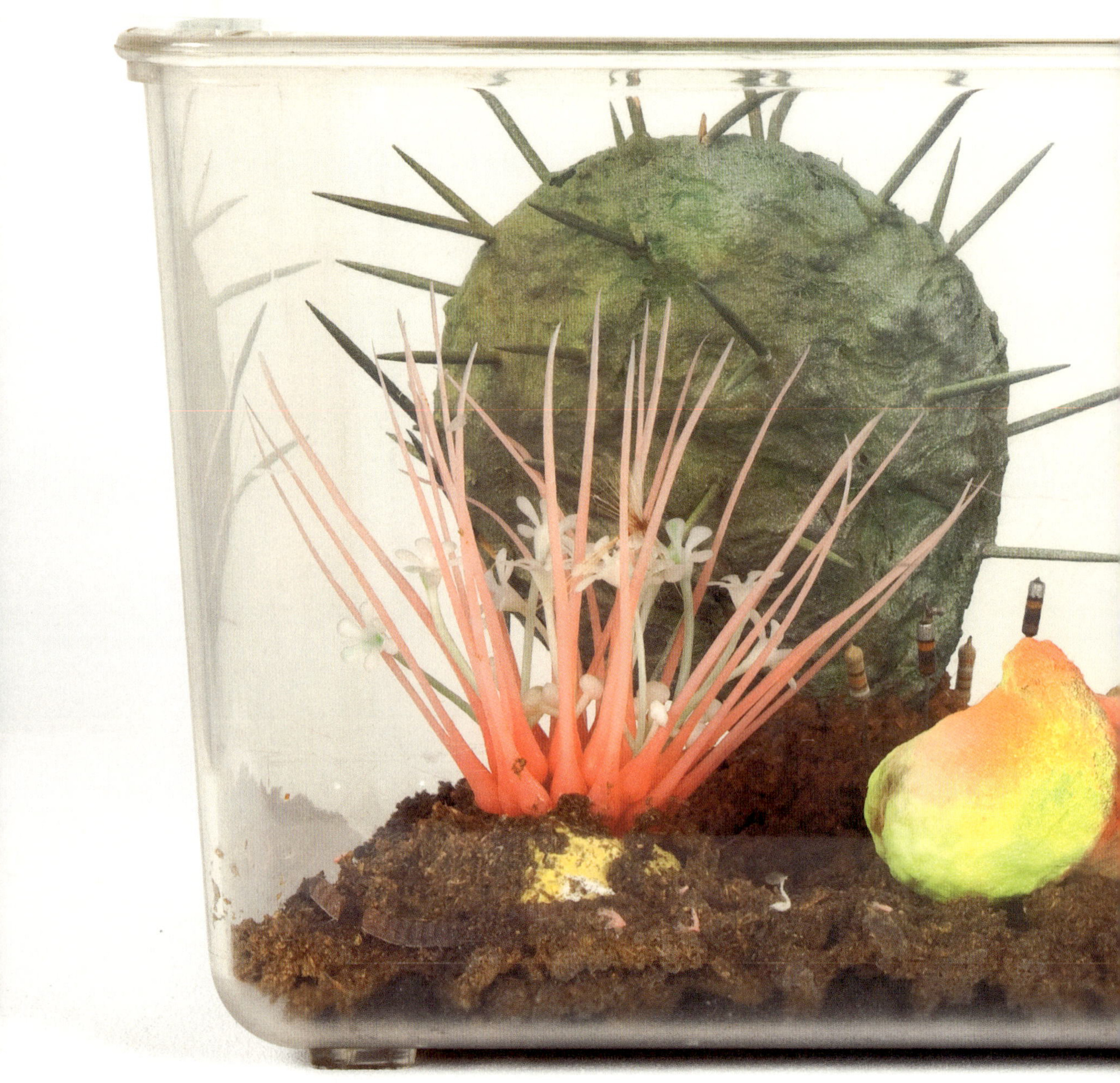

*Untitled*, 1971

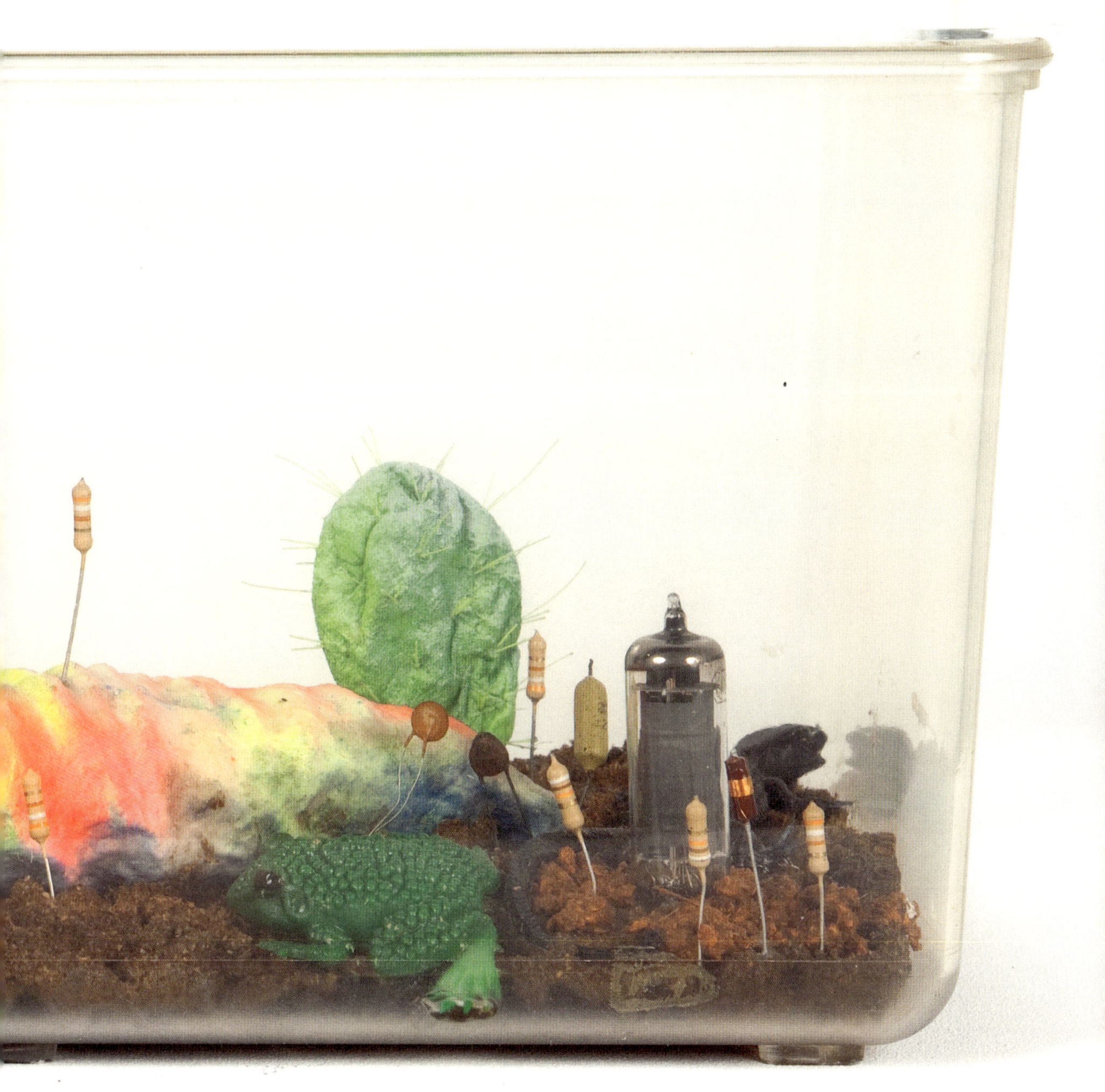

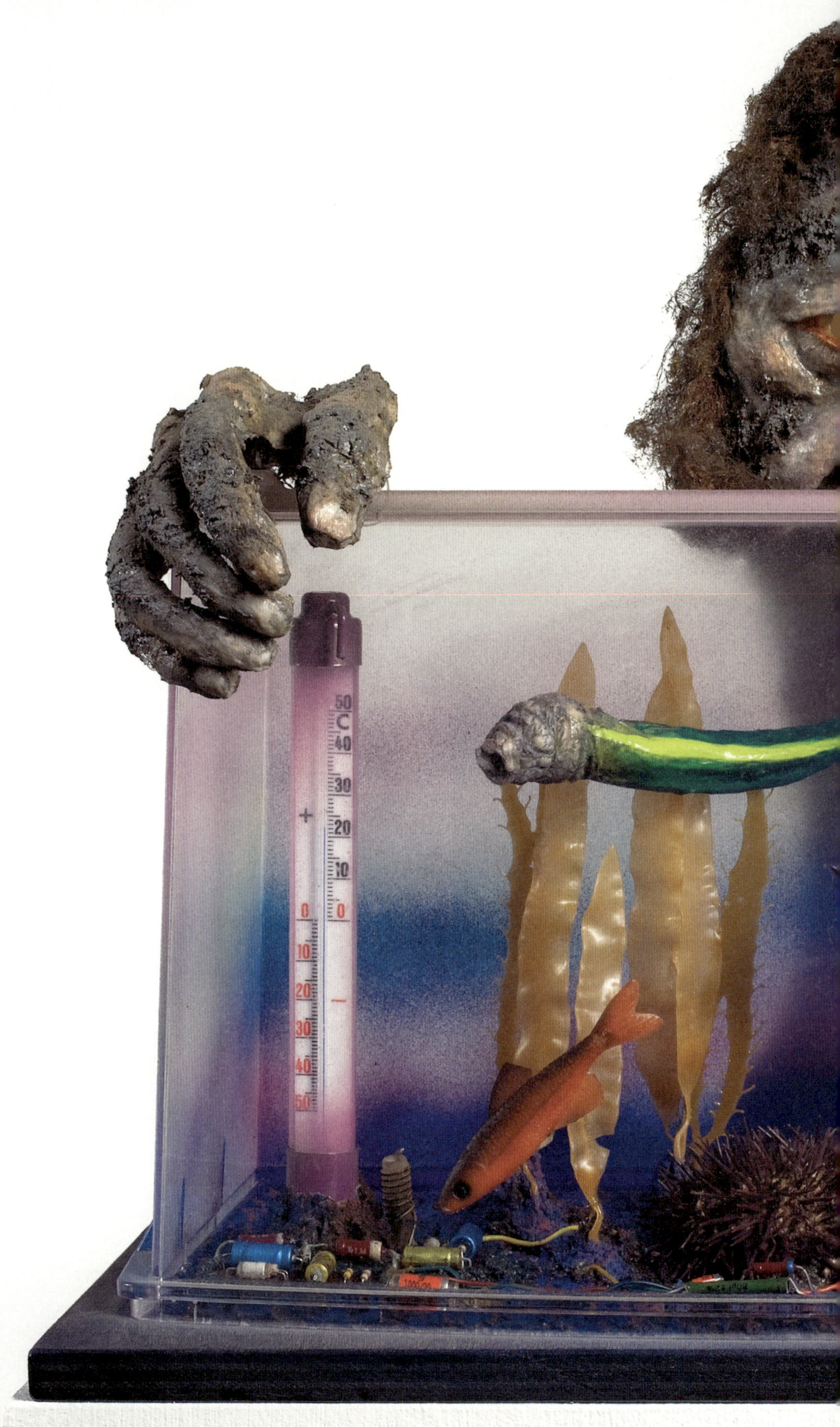

*Votre Portrait*, 1970-79

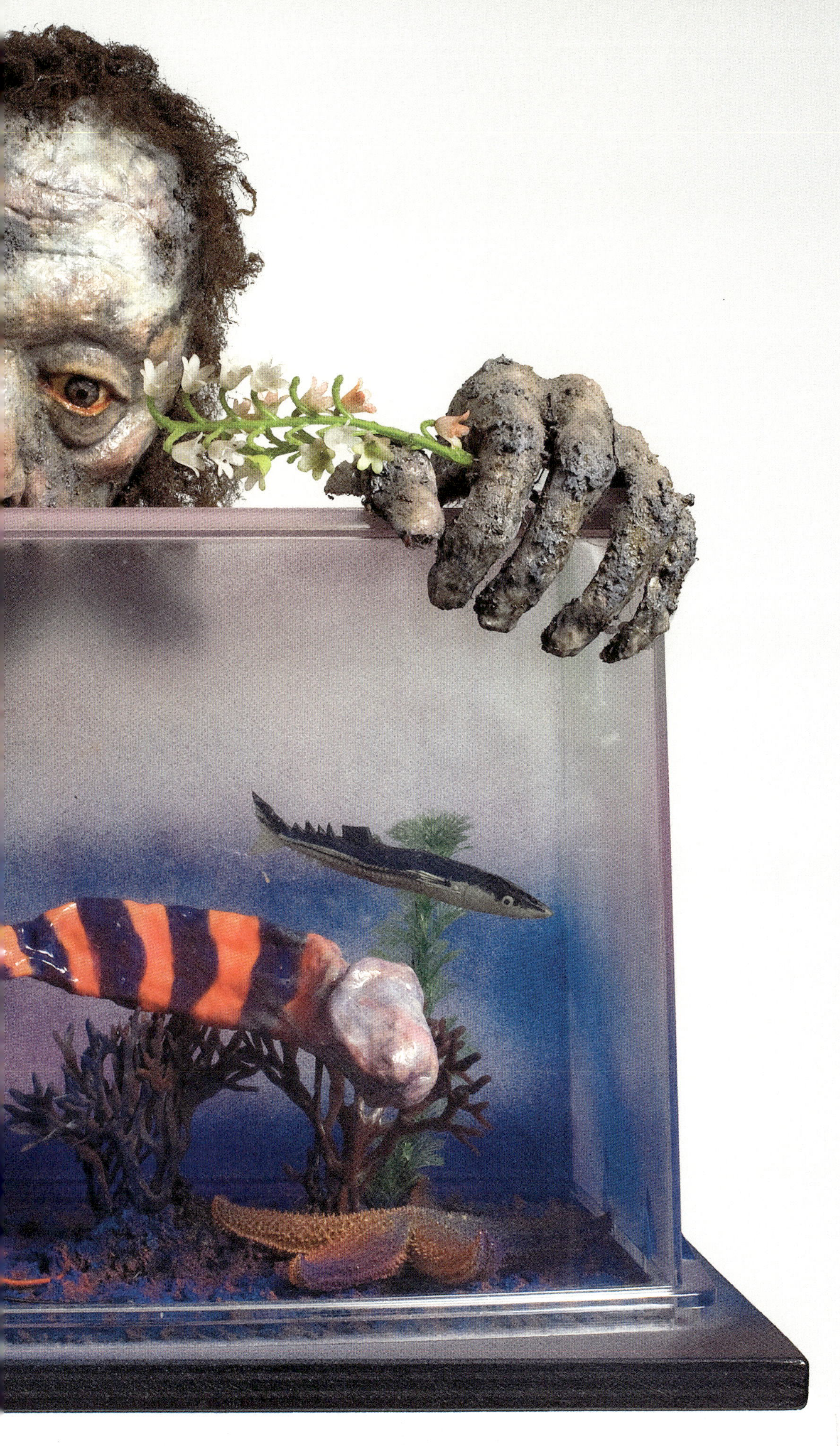

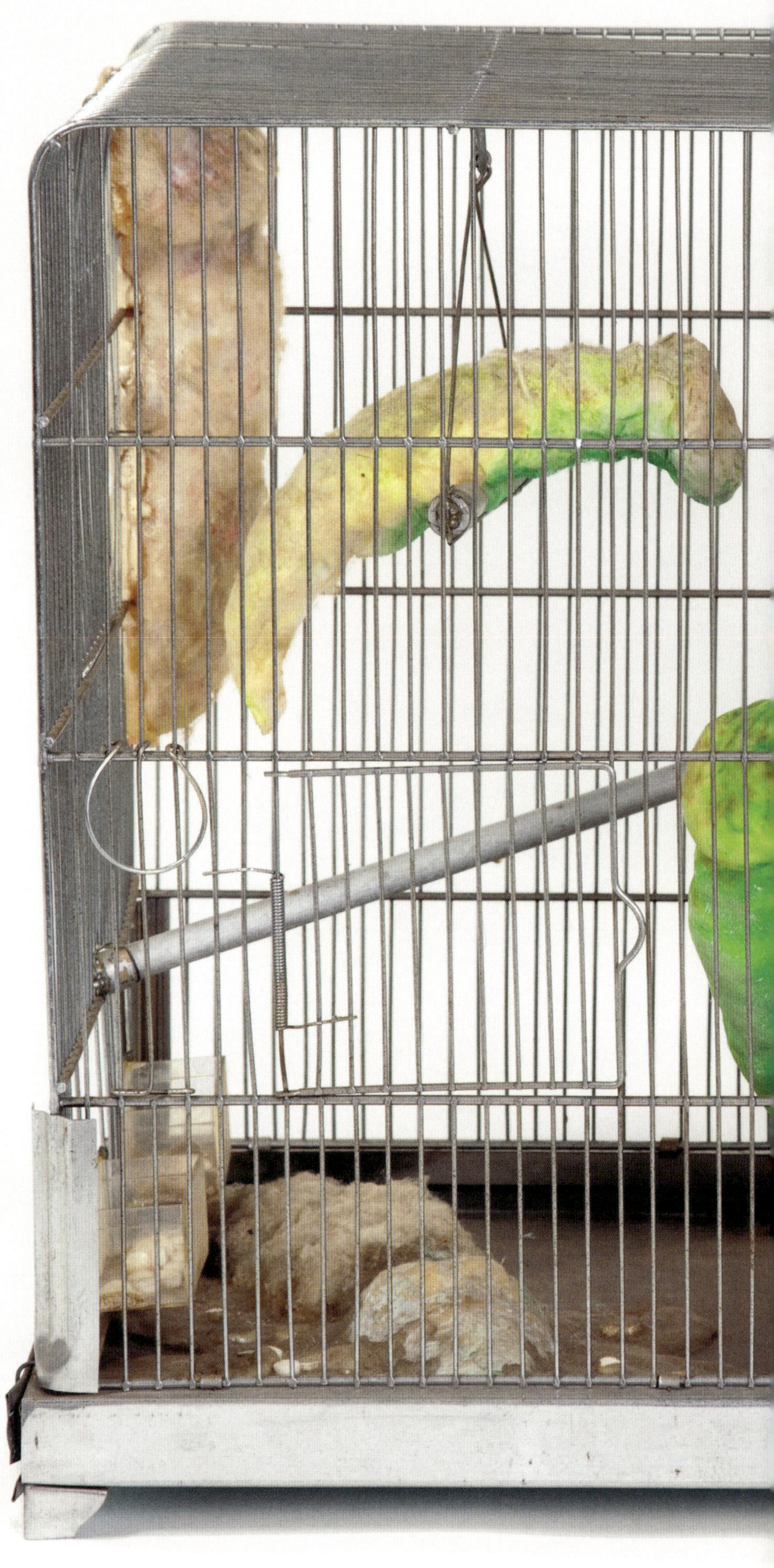

*For Your Living Room – For Nostalgic Purpose*, 1966

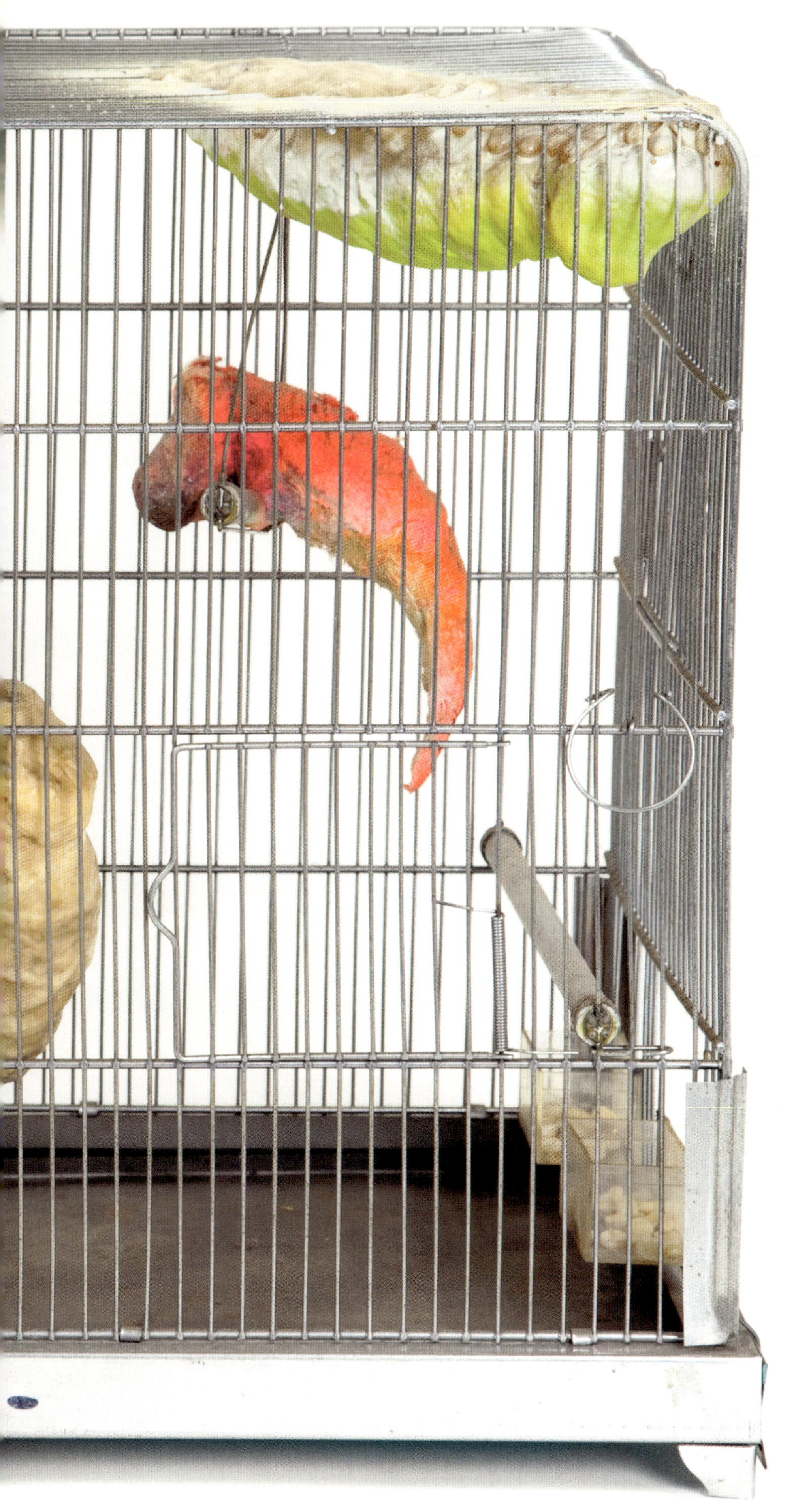

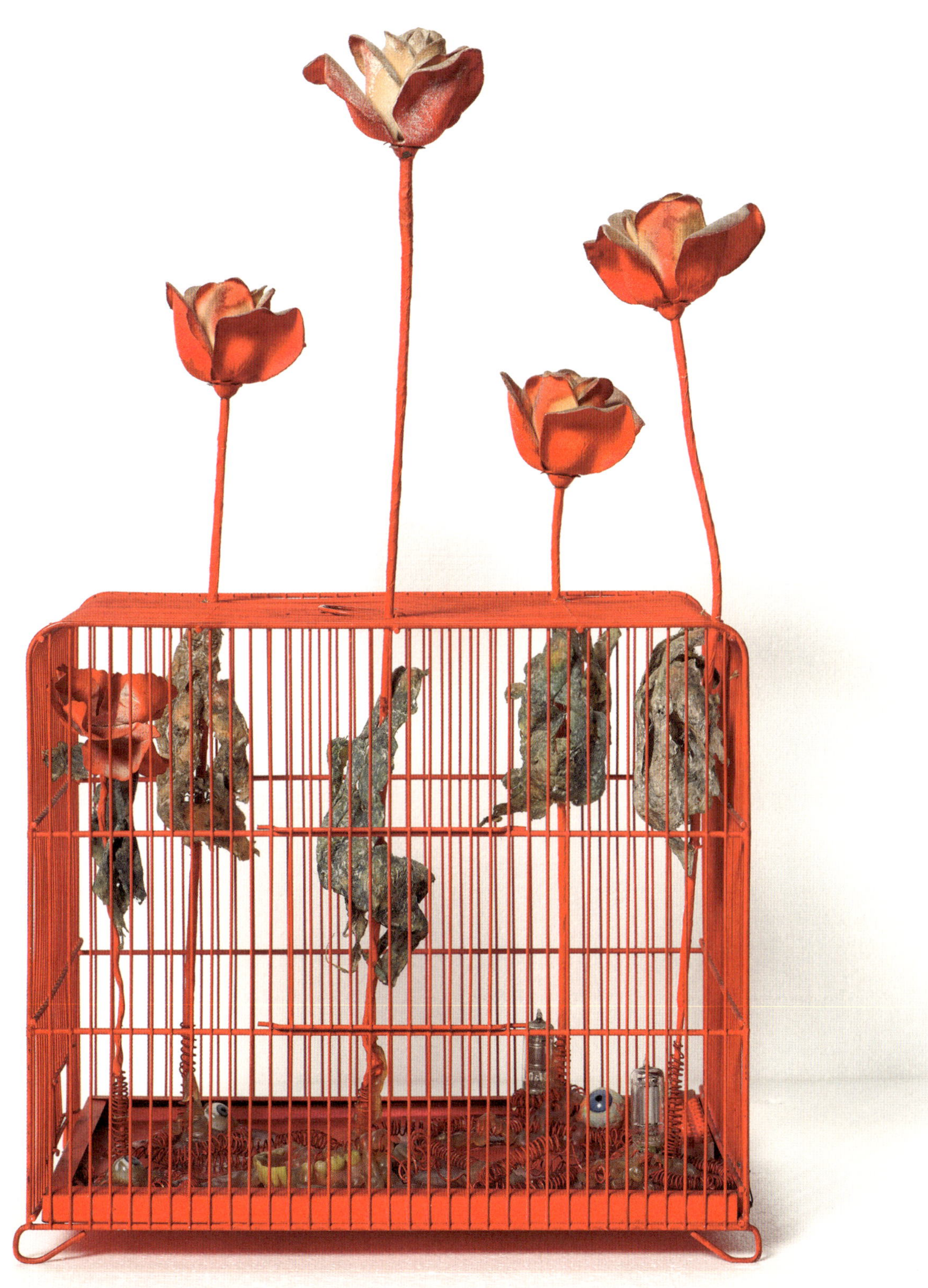

*ouvenir "La Mue"*, 1967

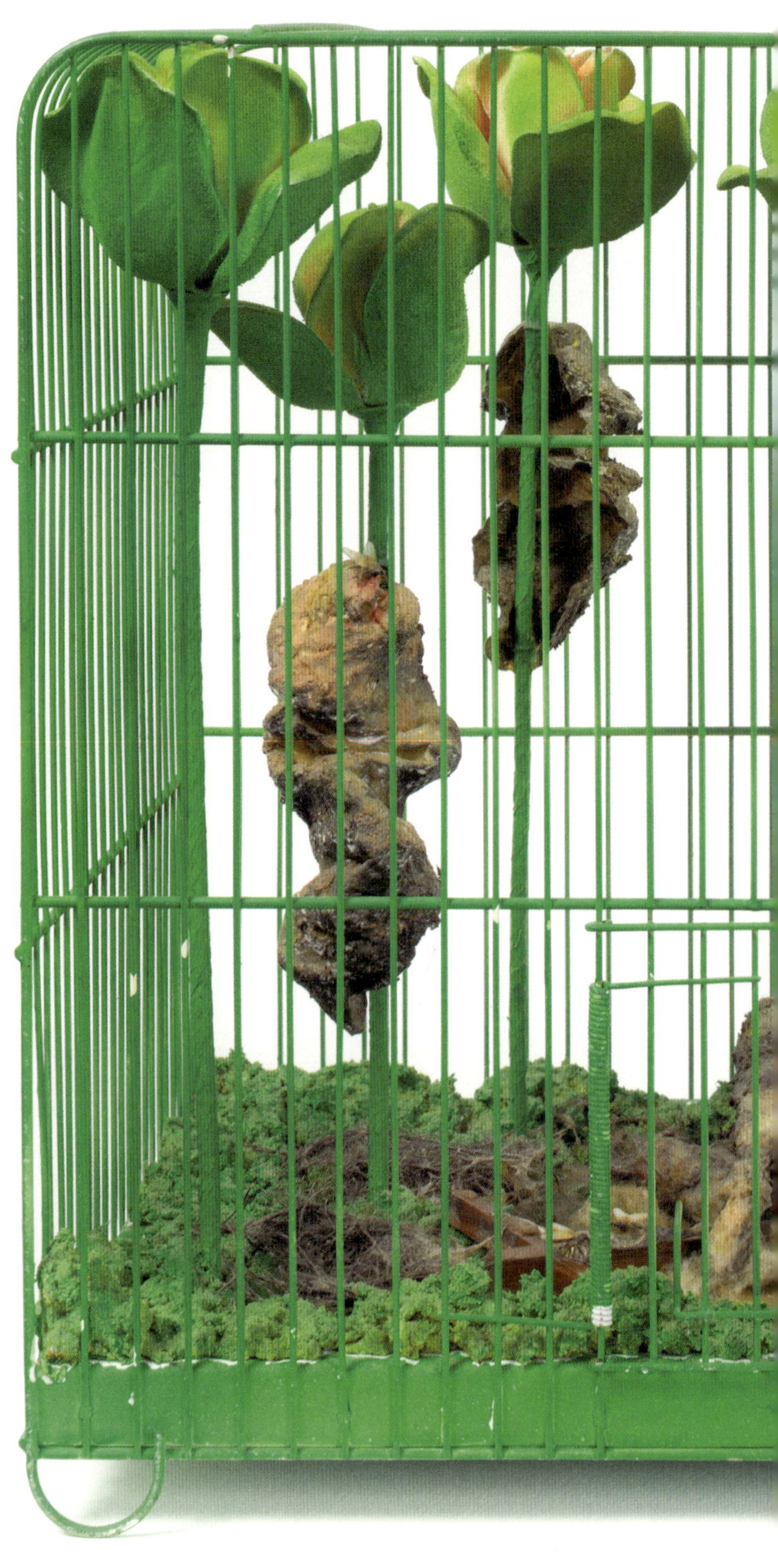

*Souvenir – La Mue (Memory-Pupal Skin)*, 1967

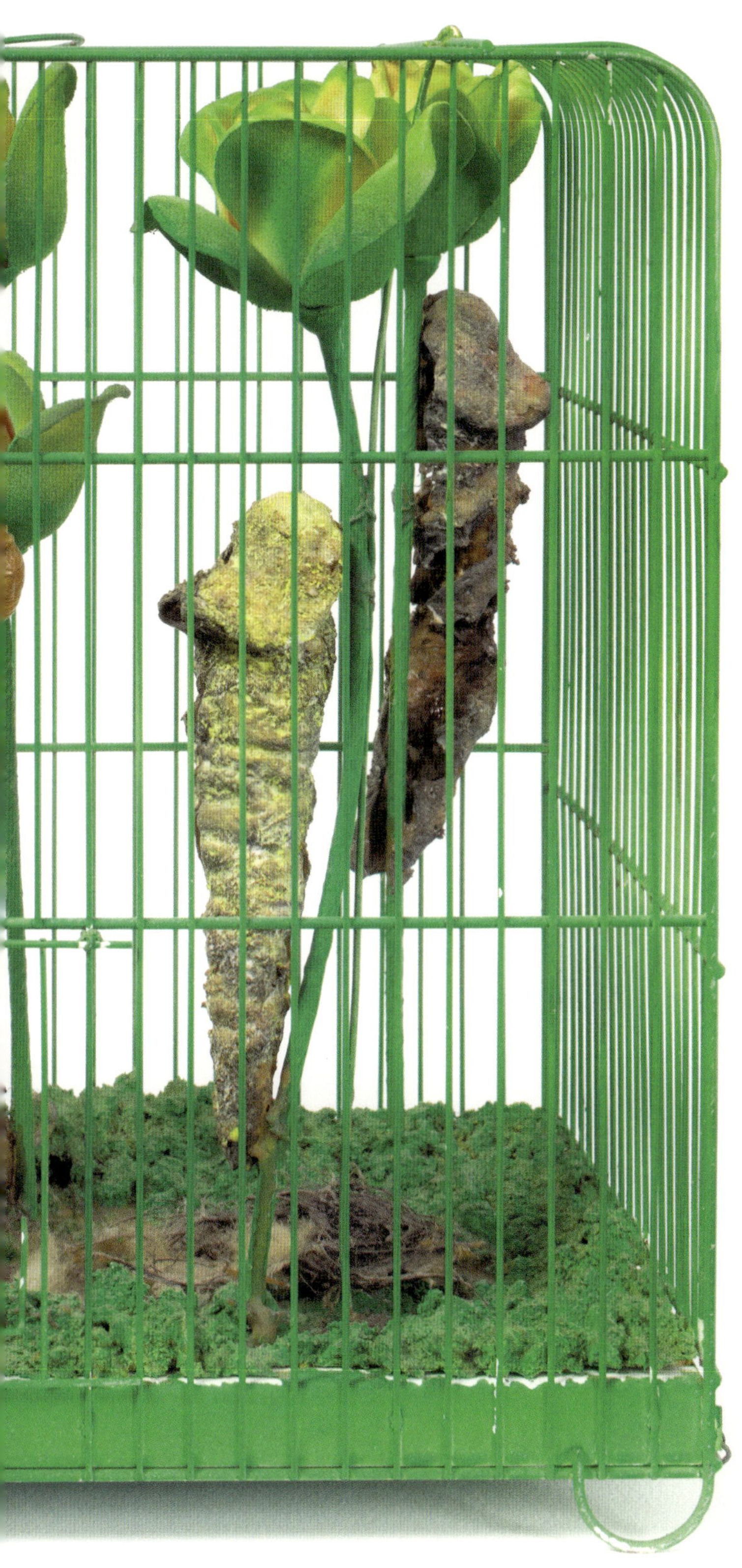

*Portrait of Ionesco and/or the End of Some Generation*, 197

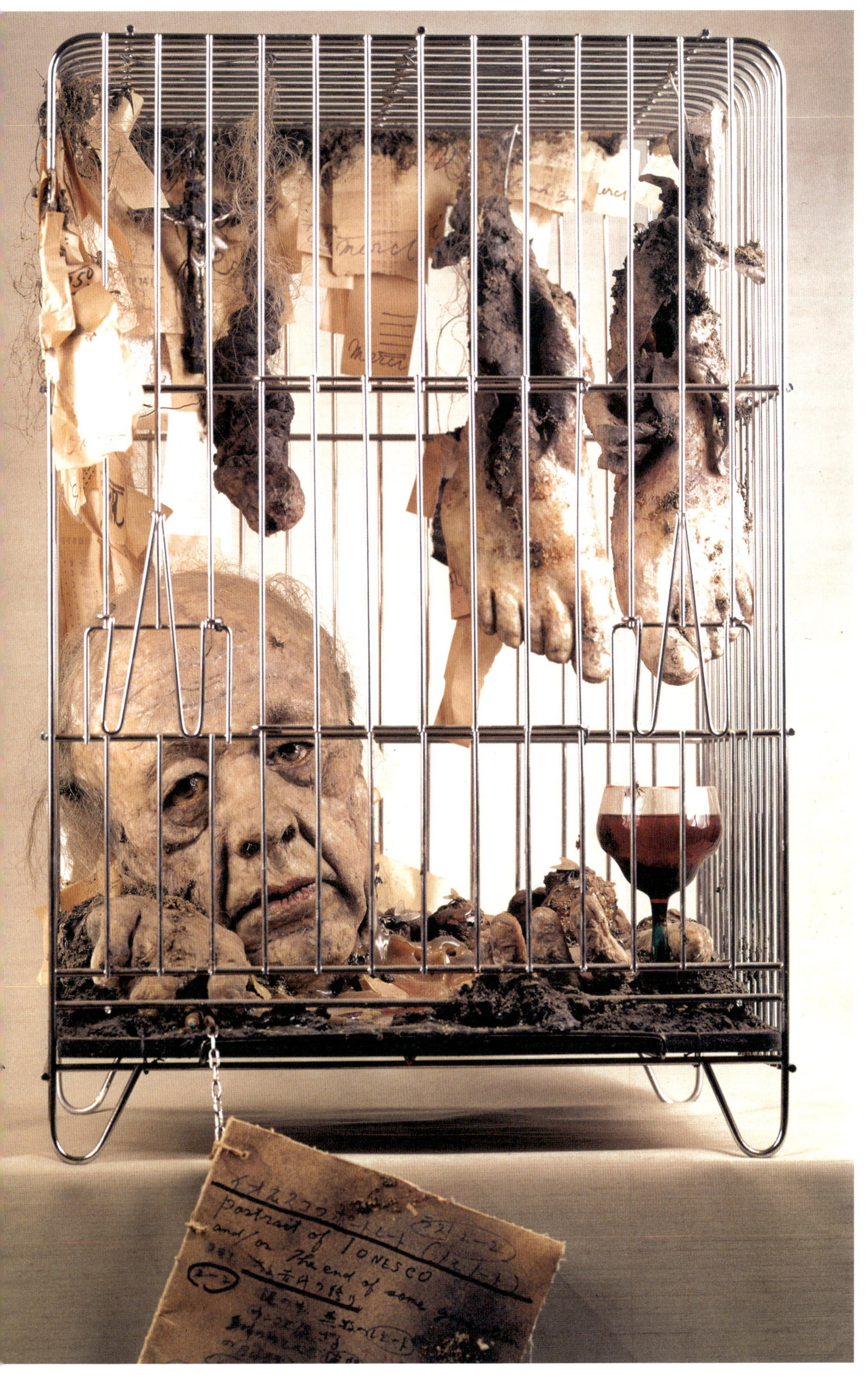
Portrait of IONESCO
and/or The end of some

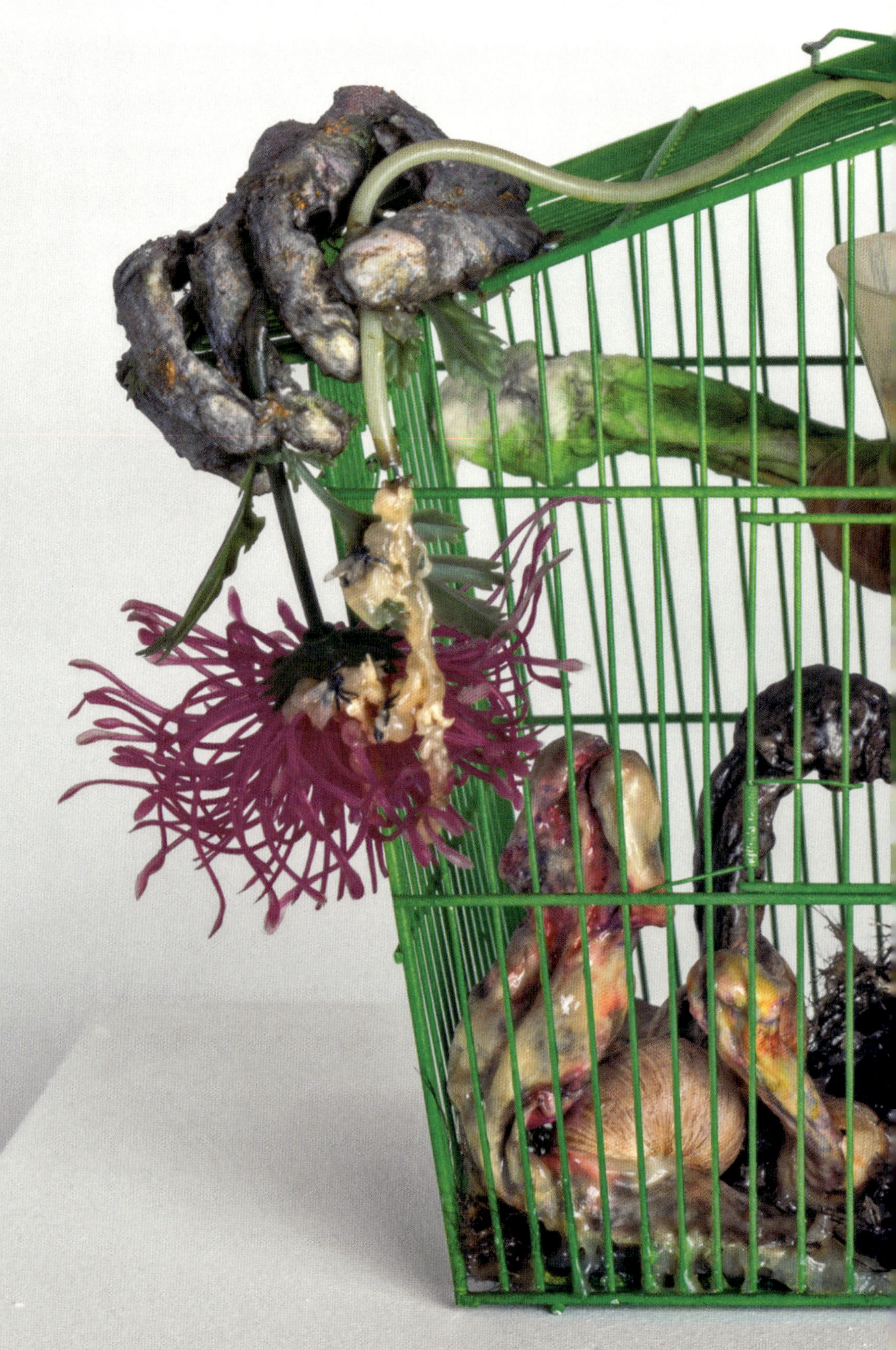

*Esclavage de Conservation de l'espèce humaine*, 1972

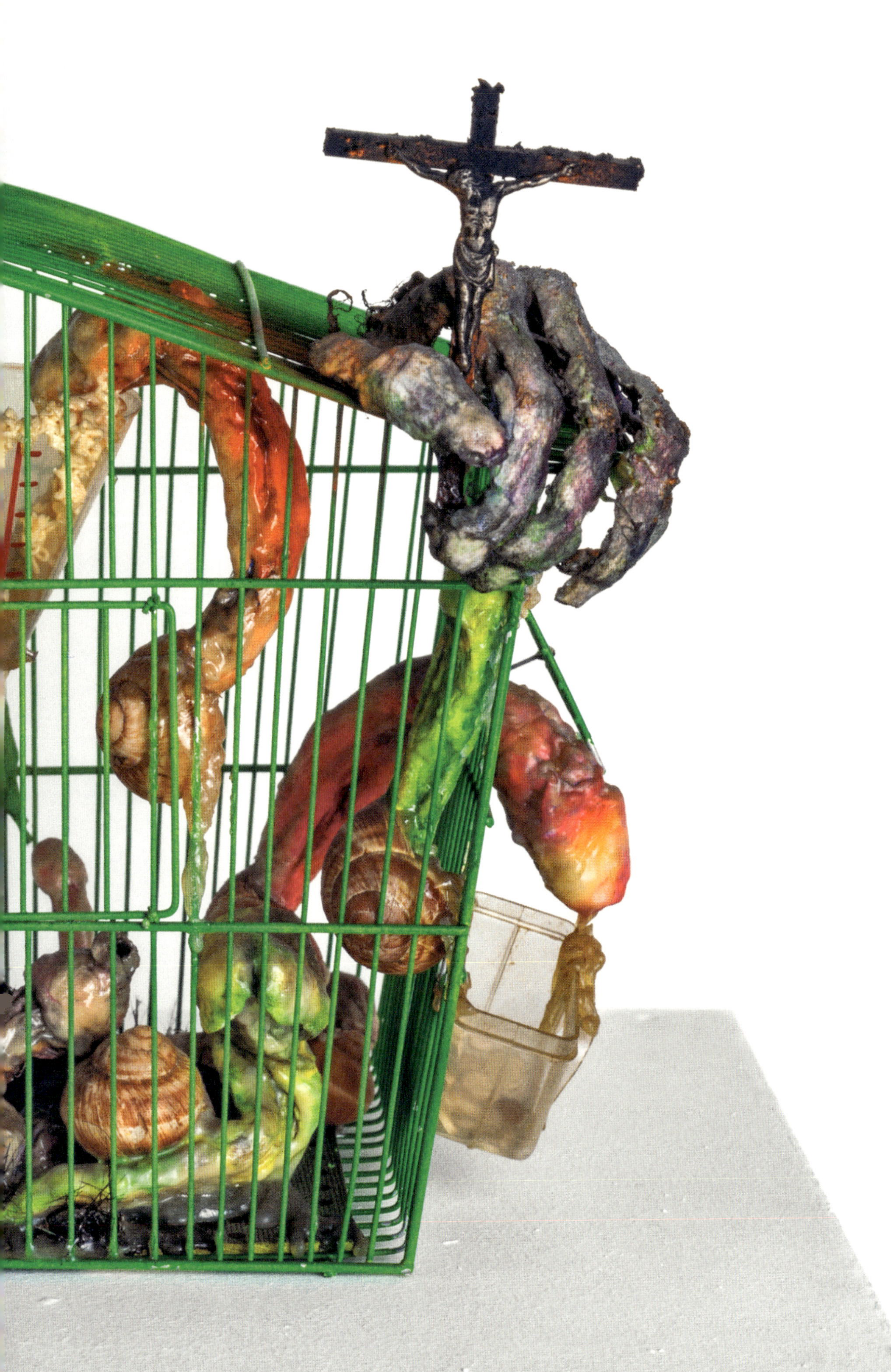

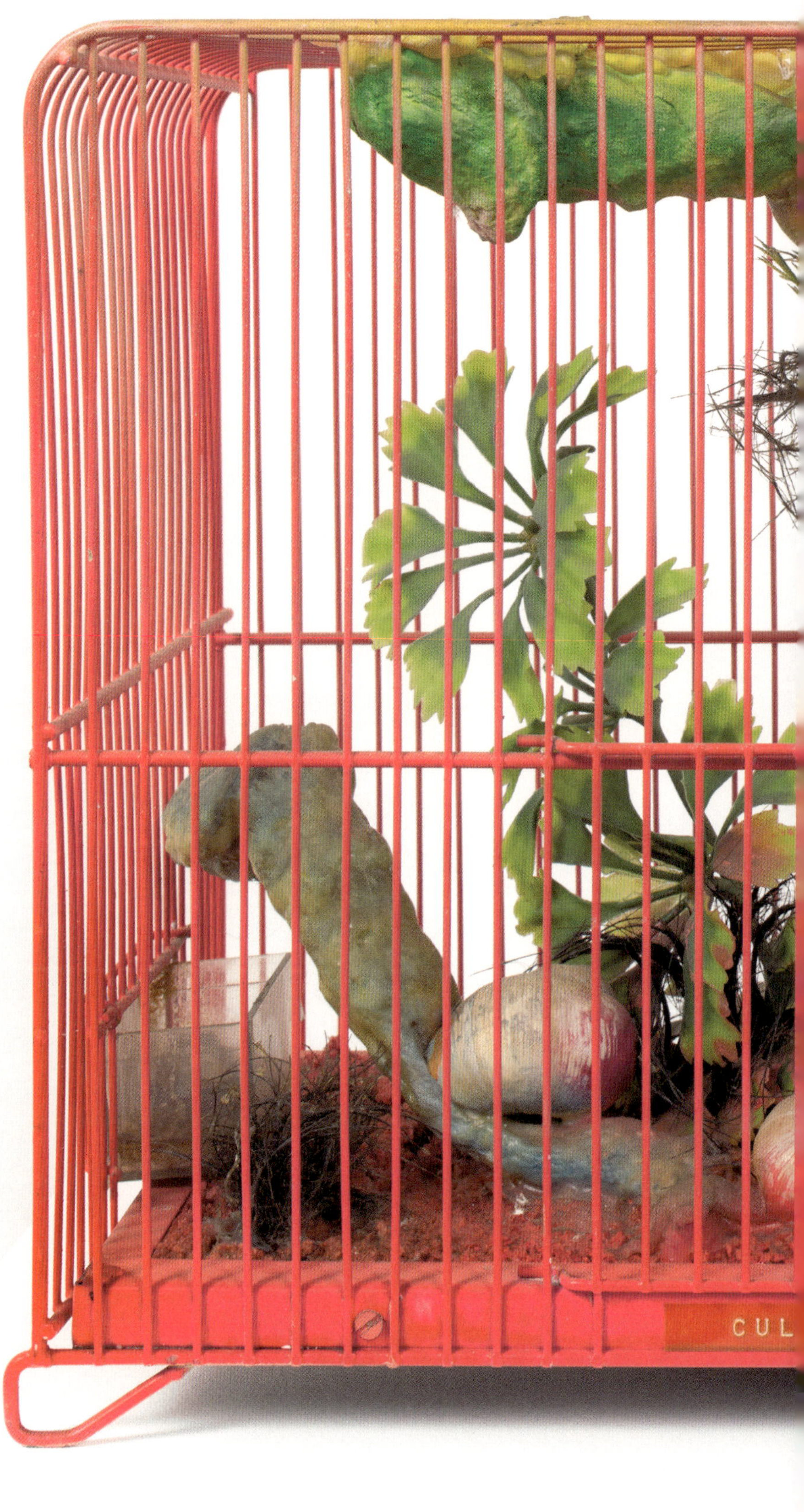


*Cultivation*, 1972

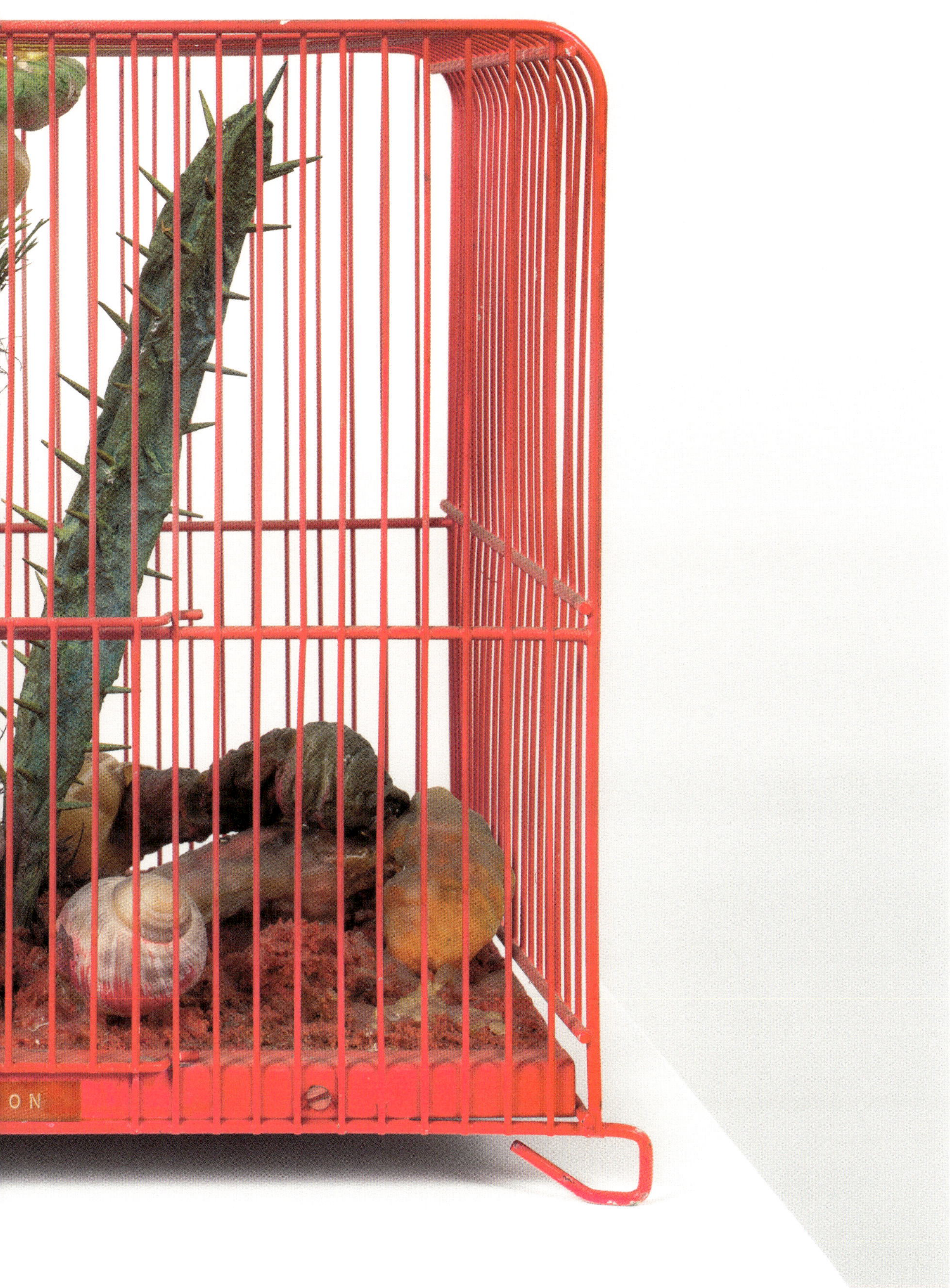

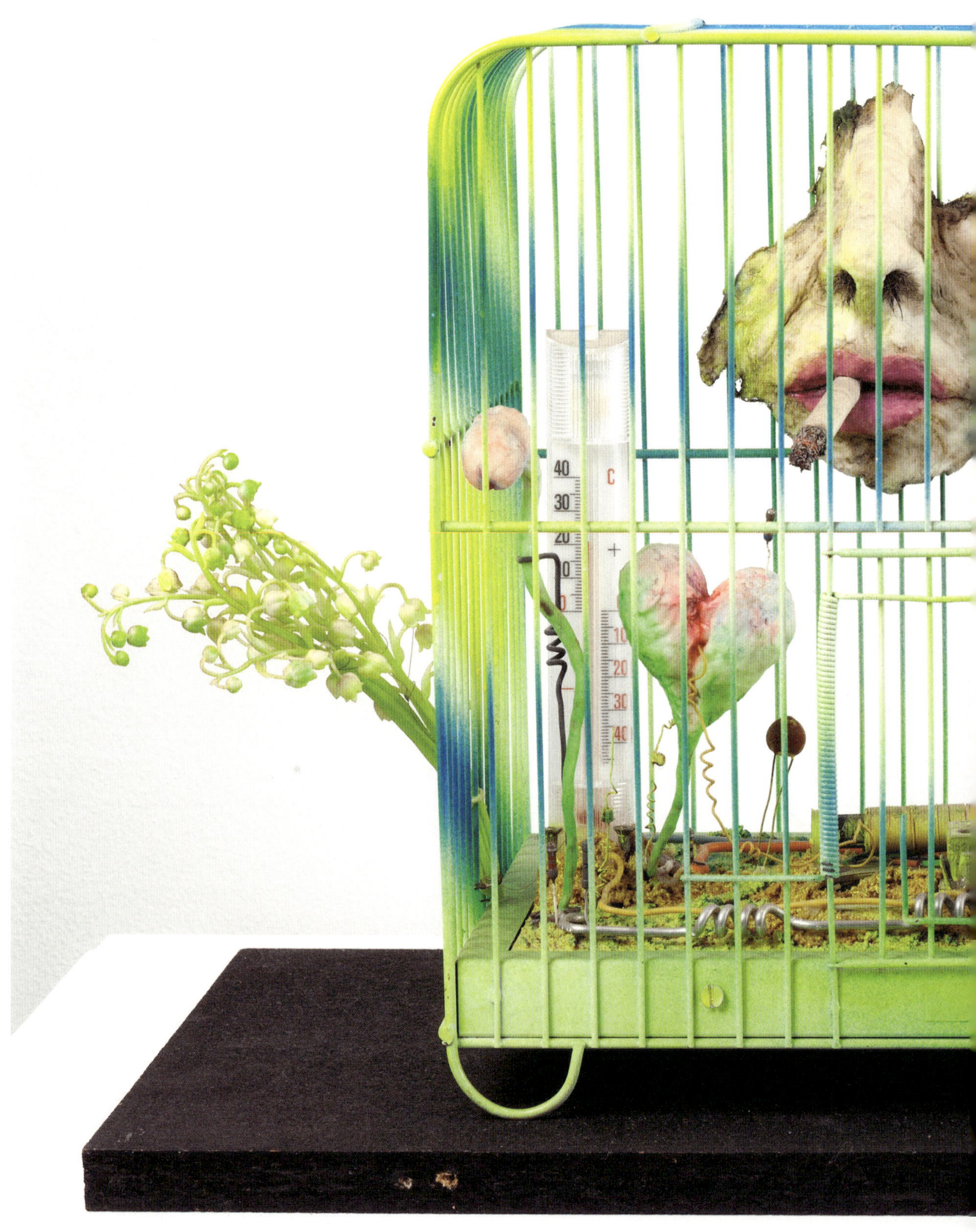

*Bonheur*, 1974

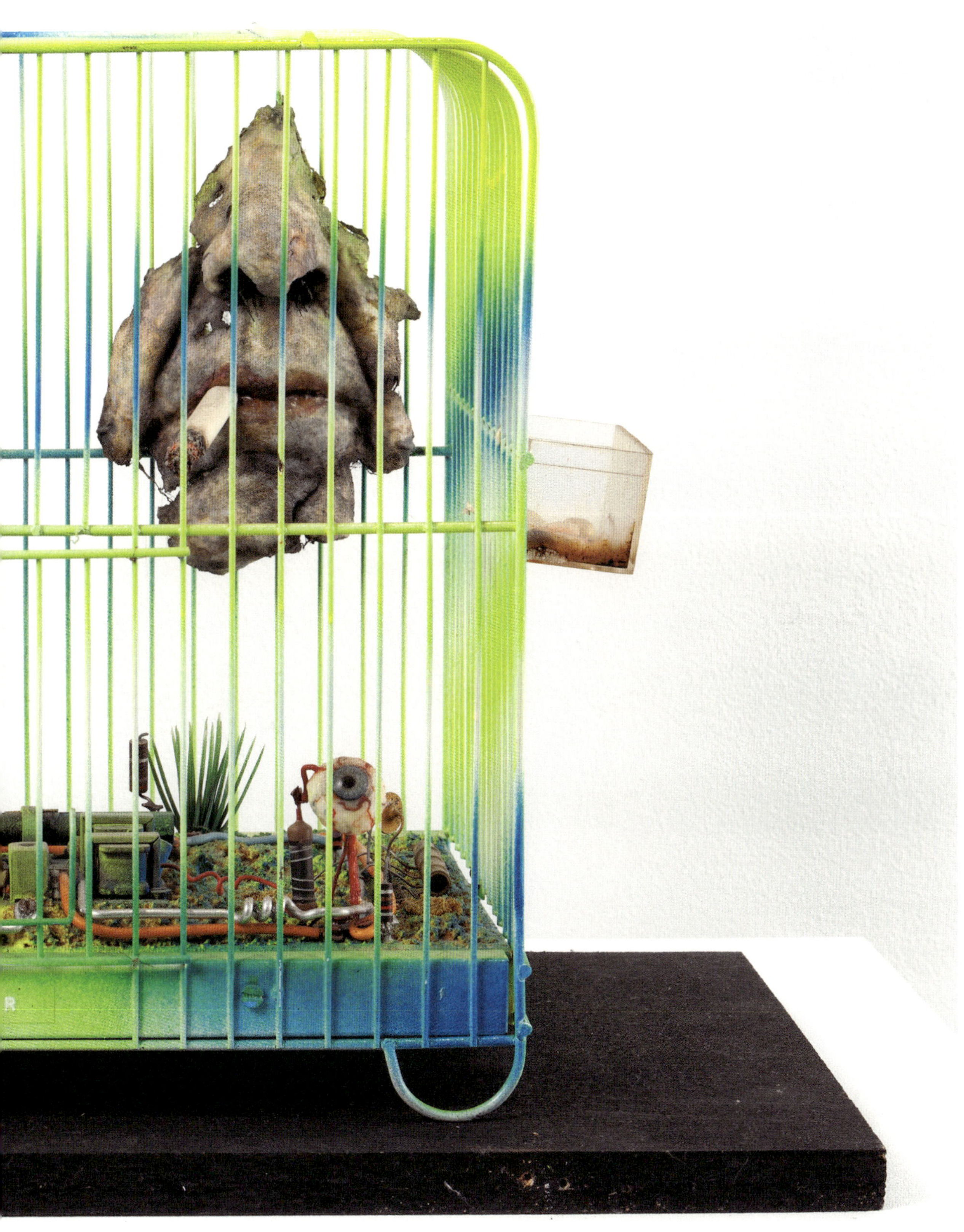

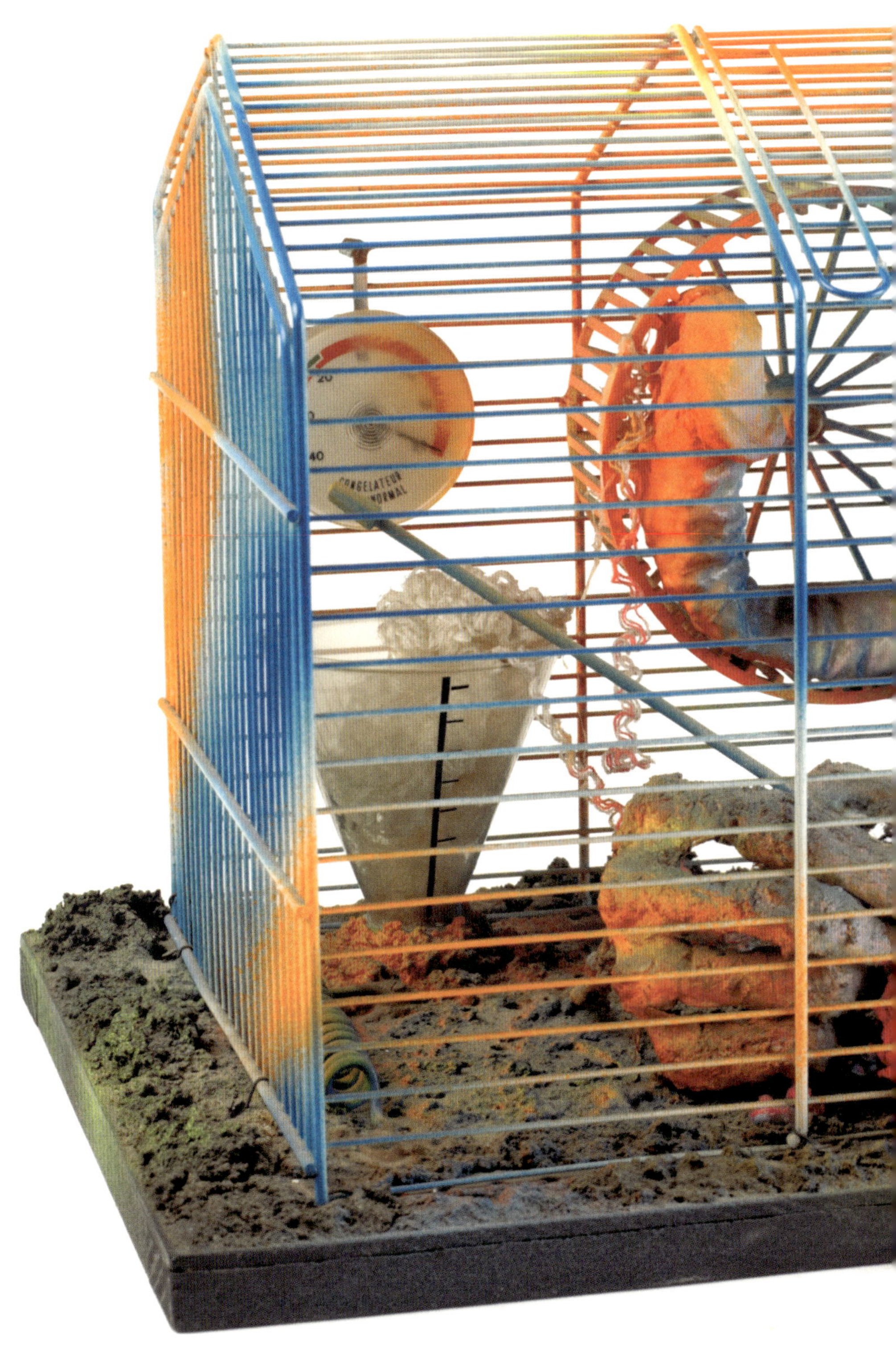


*Portrait d'artiste*, 1968-75

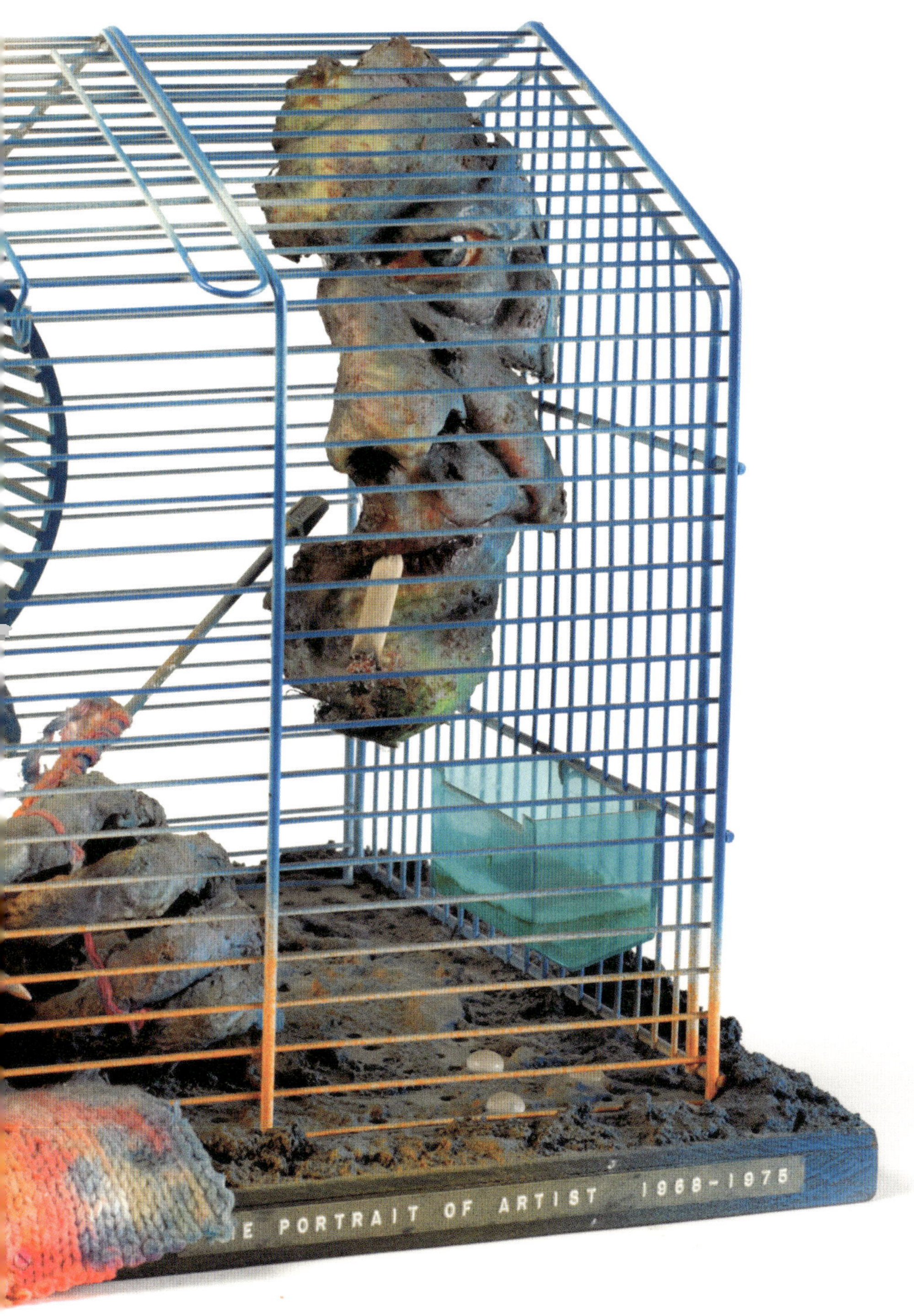
E PORTRAIT OF ARTIST 1968-1975

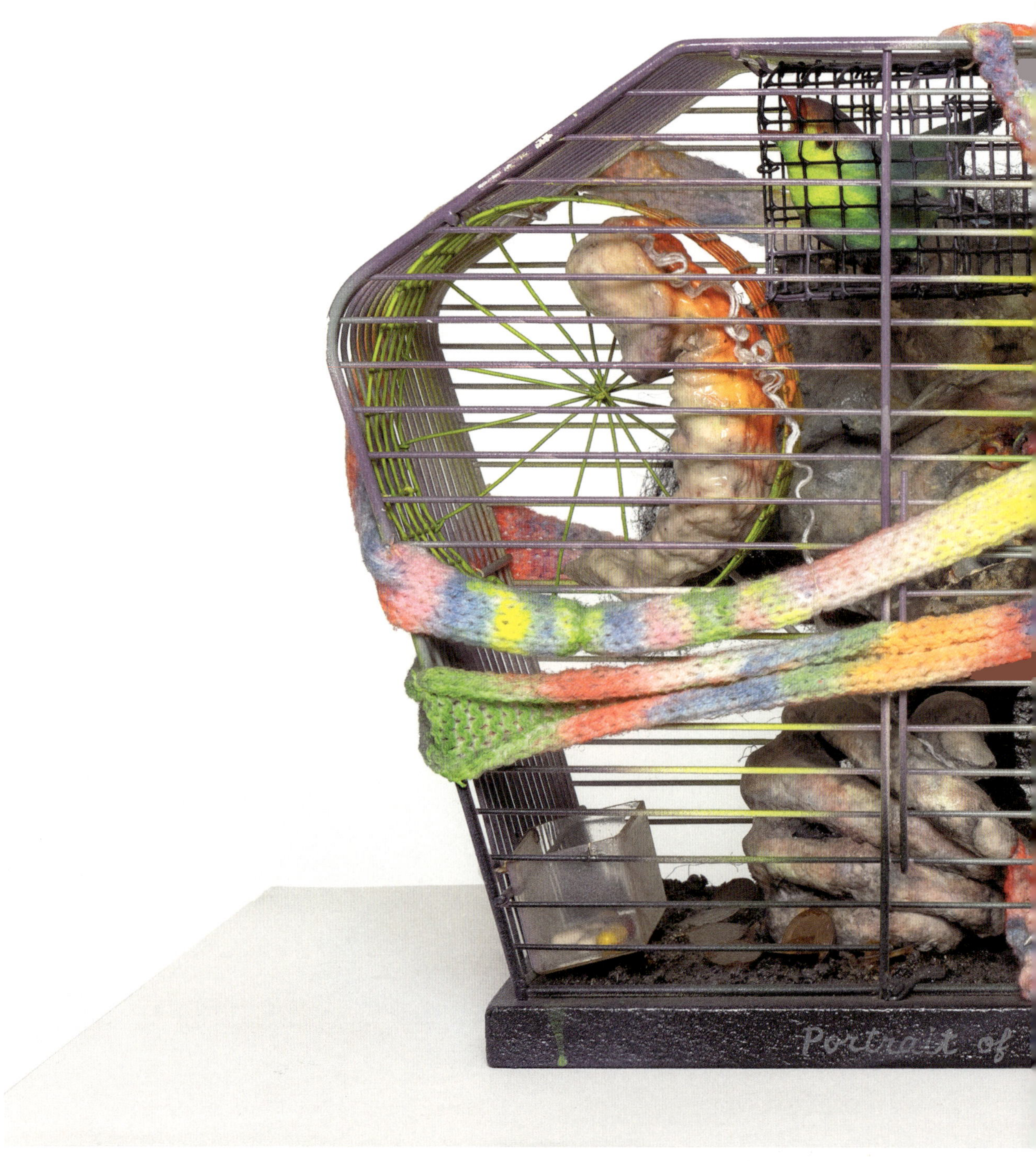


*Portrait of the Artist in the Crisis*, 1978

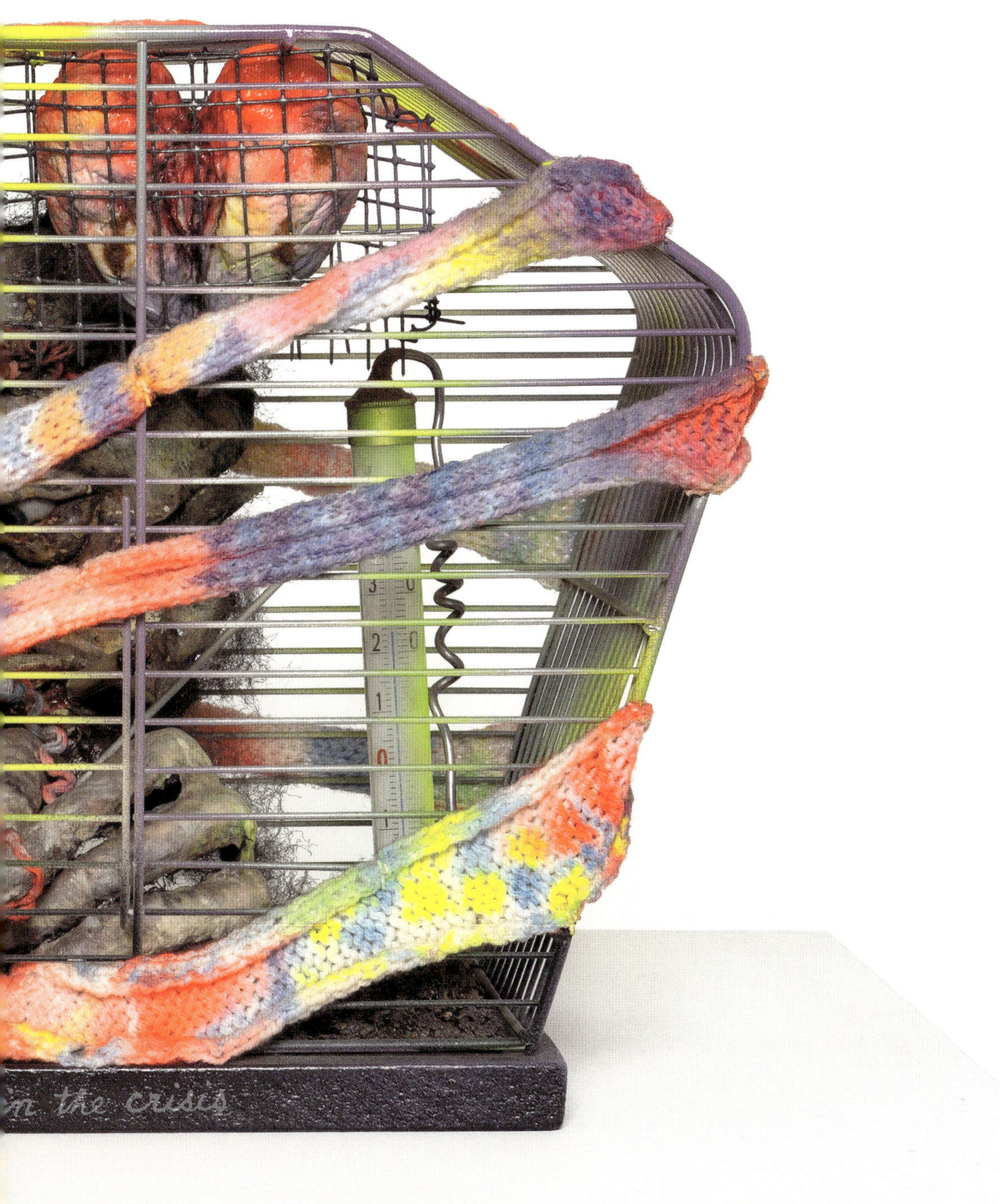
n the crisis

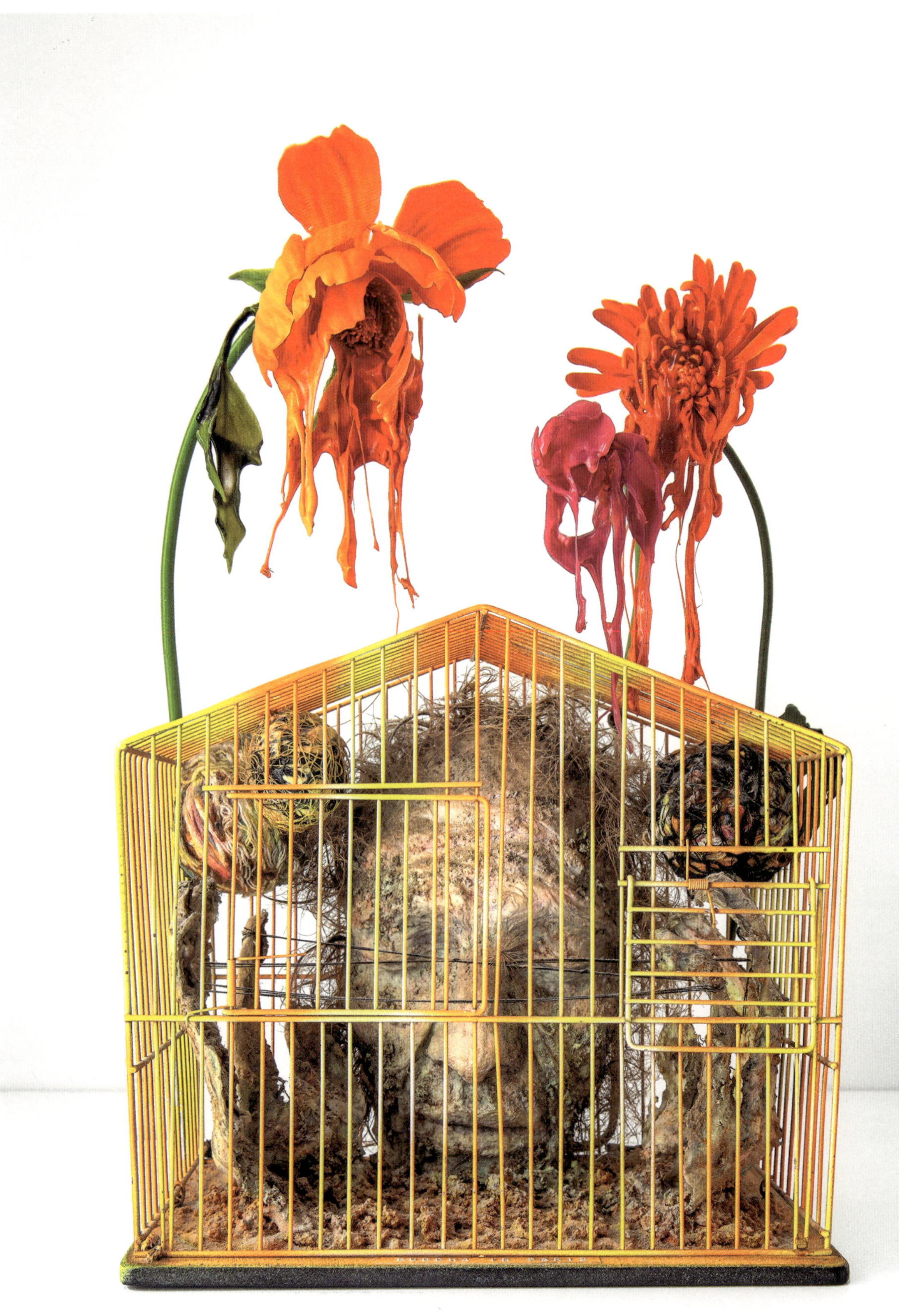

*Buddha in Paris. Méditation entre futur programmé et mémoire enregistrée*, 1976

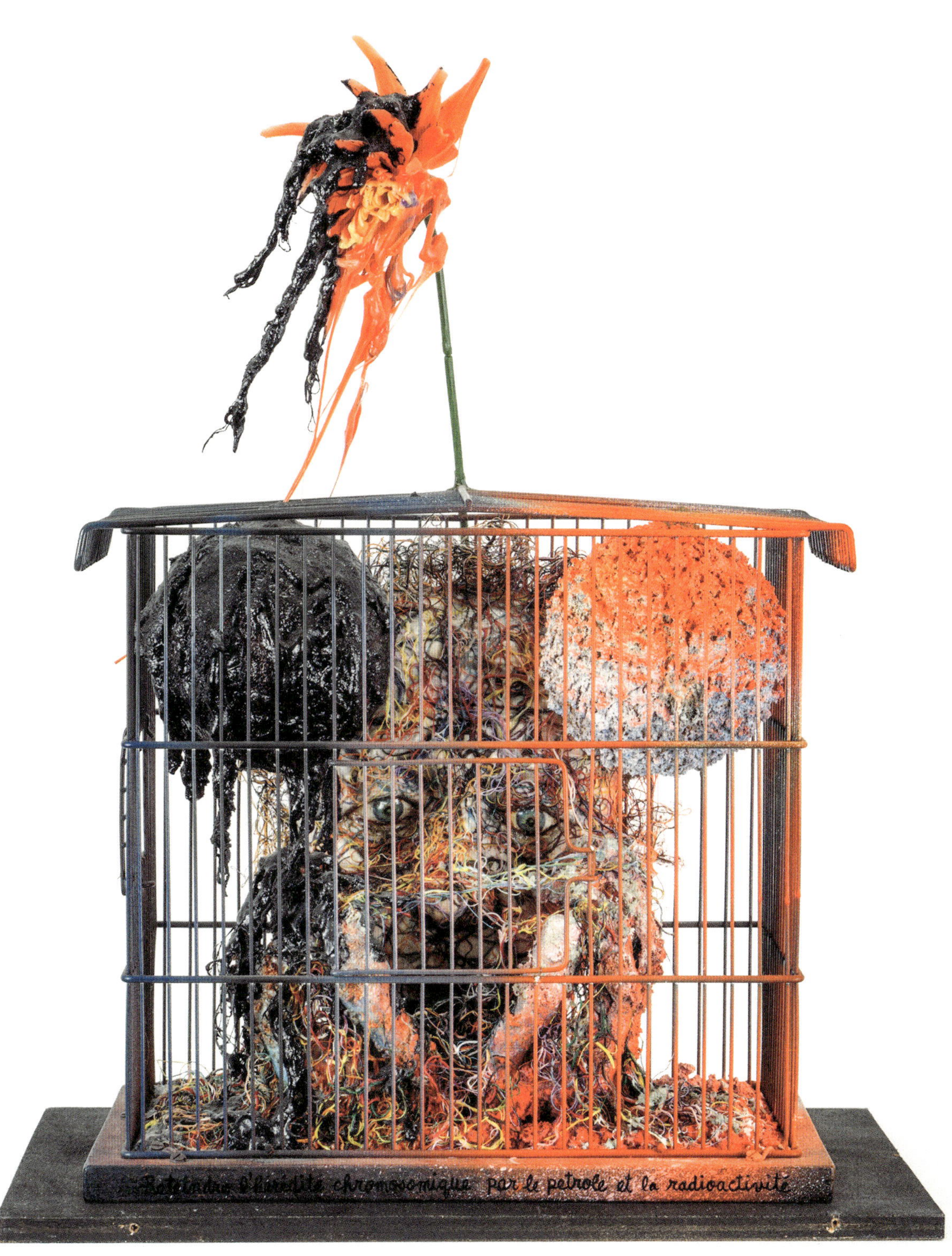


*Reteindre l'hérédité chromosomique par le pétrole et la radioactivité*, 1979

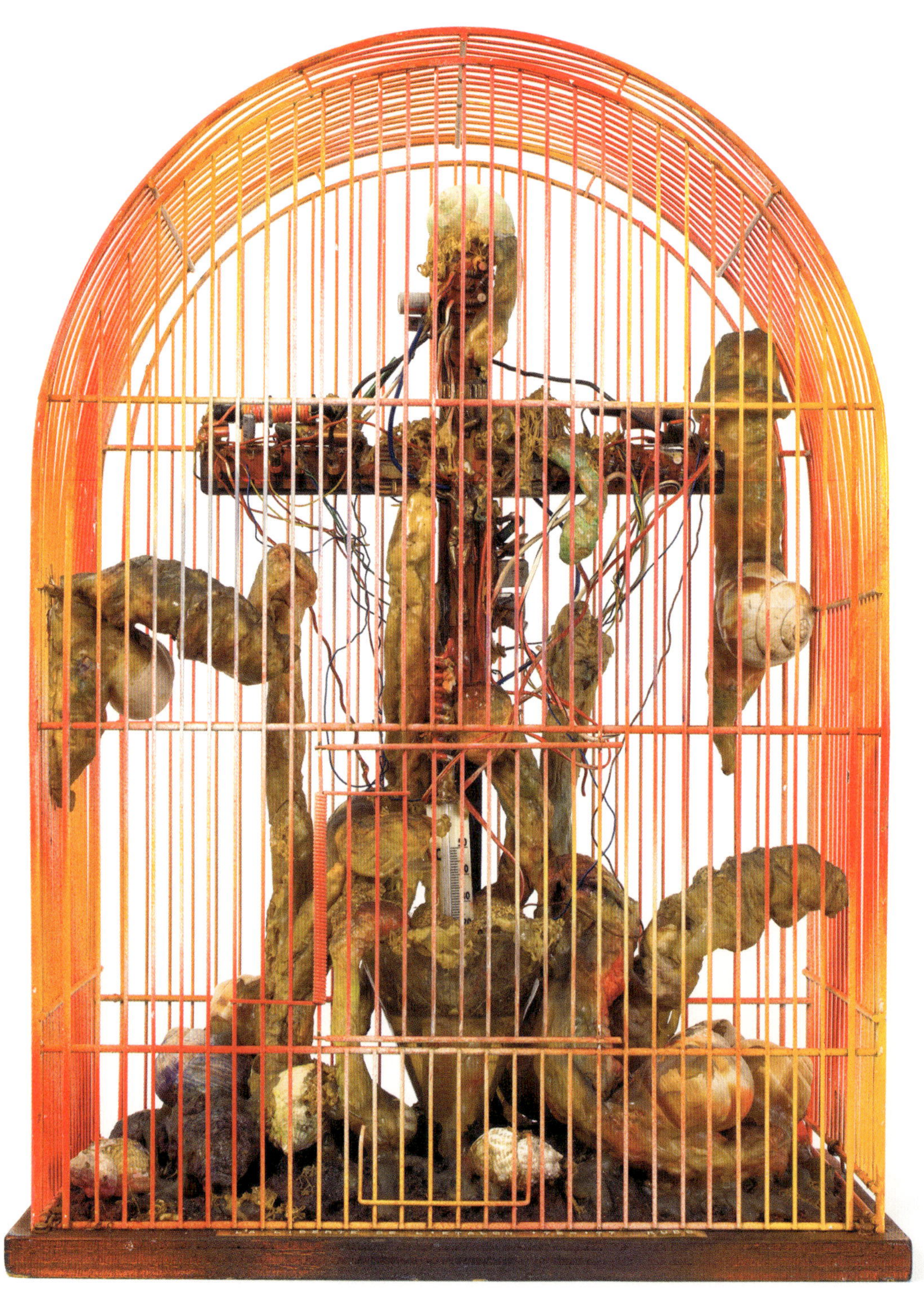

*La liberté de l'étalon*, 1972-1977

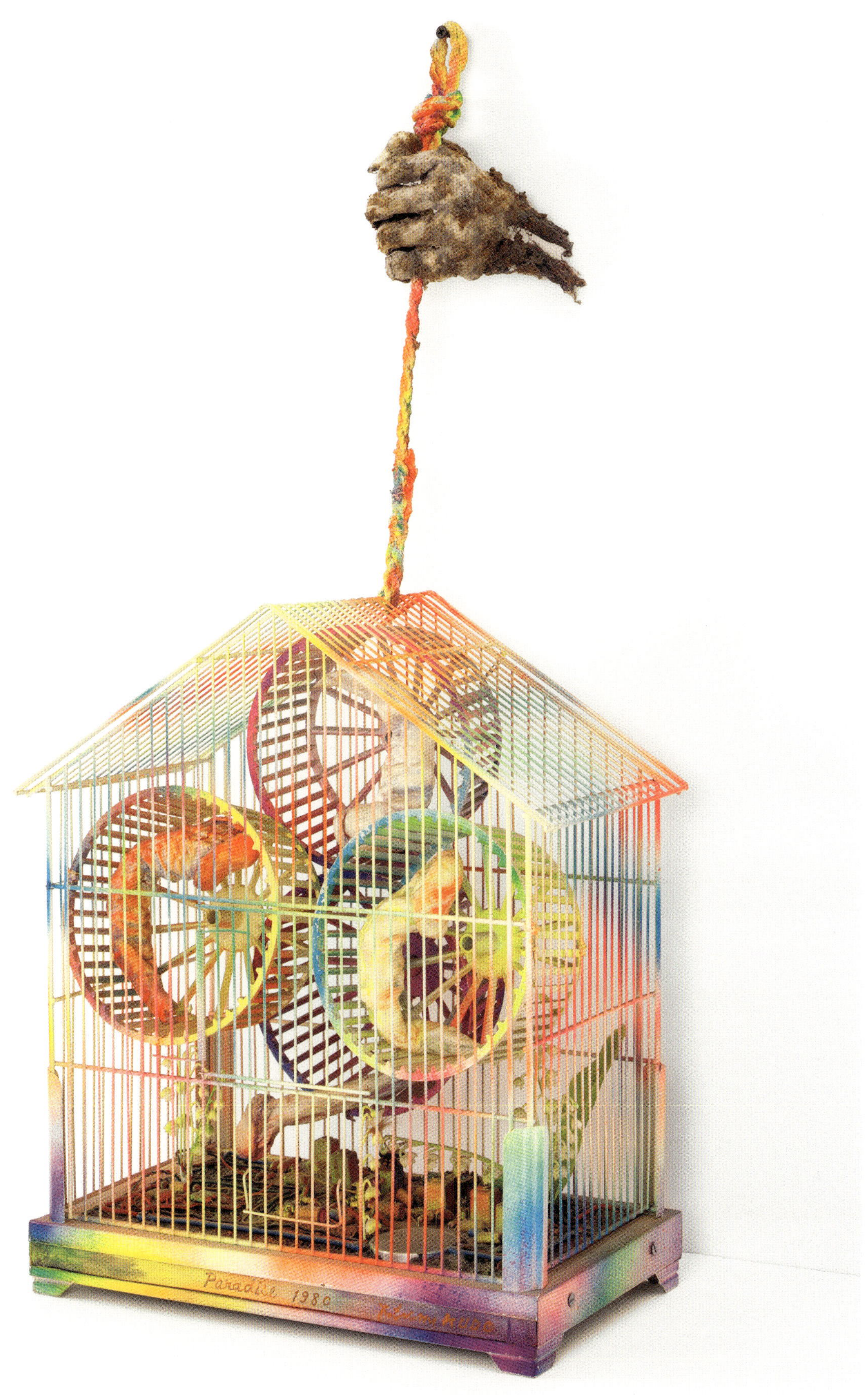


*aradise*, 1980

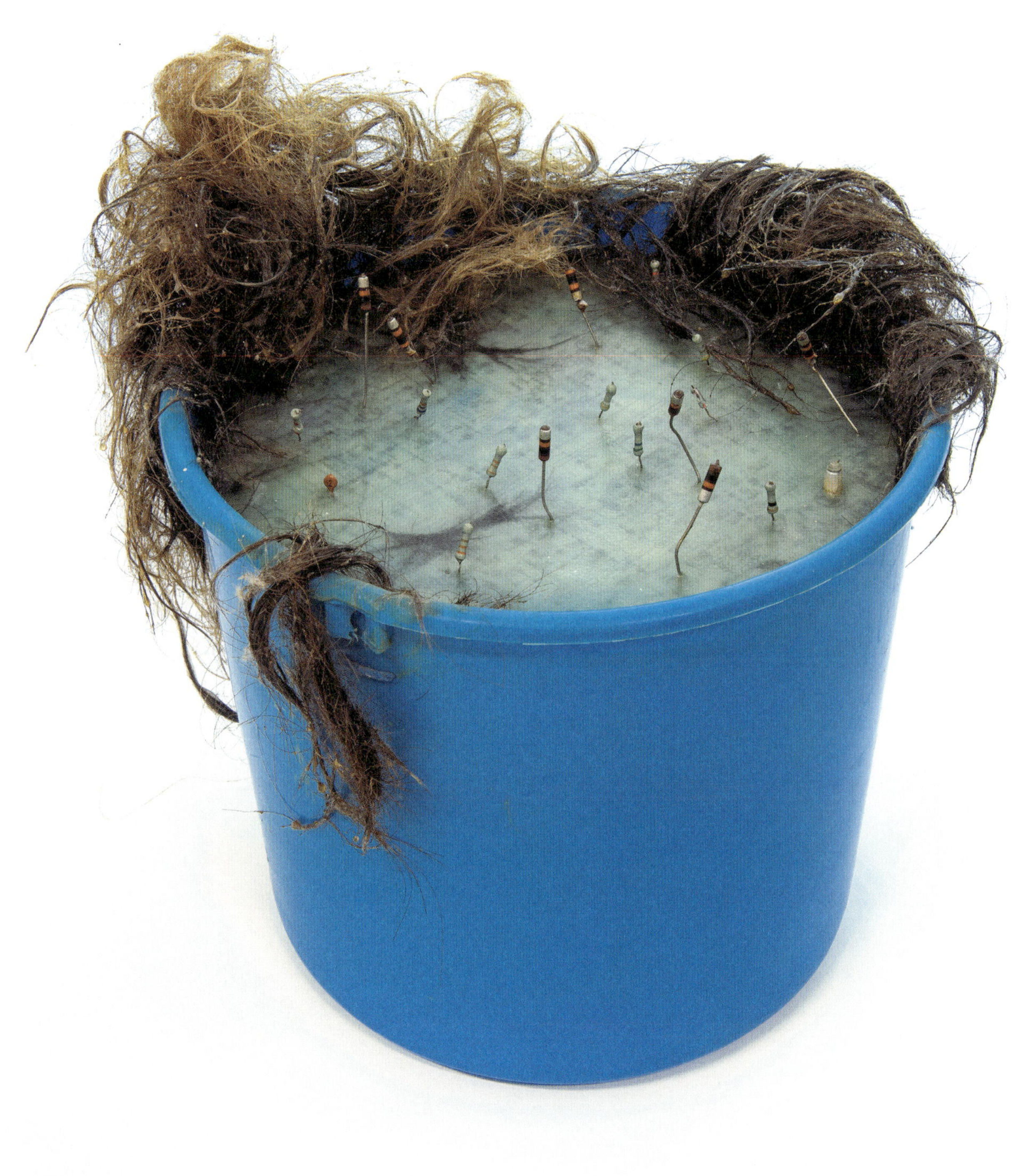

*Cultivation of Nature & People Who Are Looking at It*, 1970

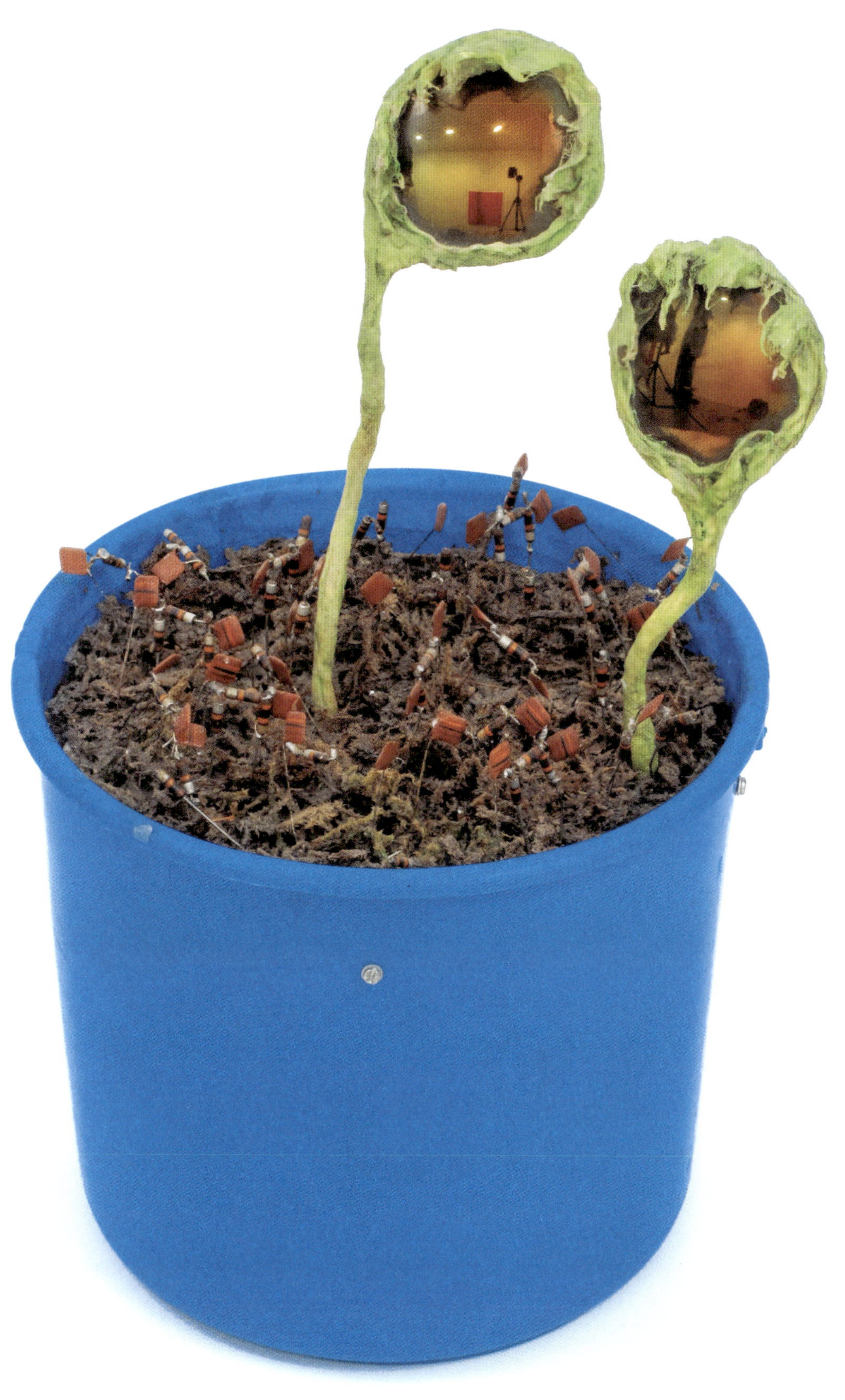

*ltivation of Nature & People Who Are Looking at It*, 1970-71

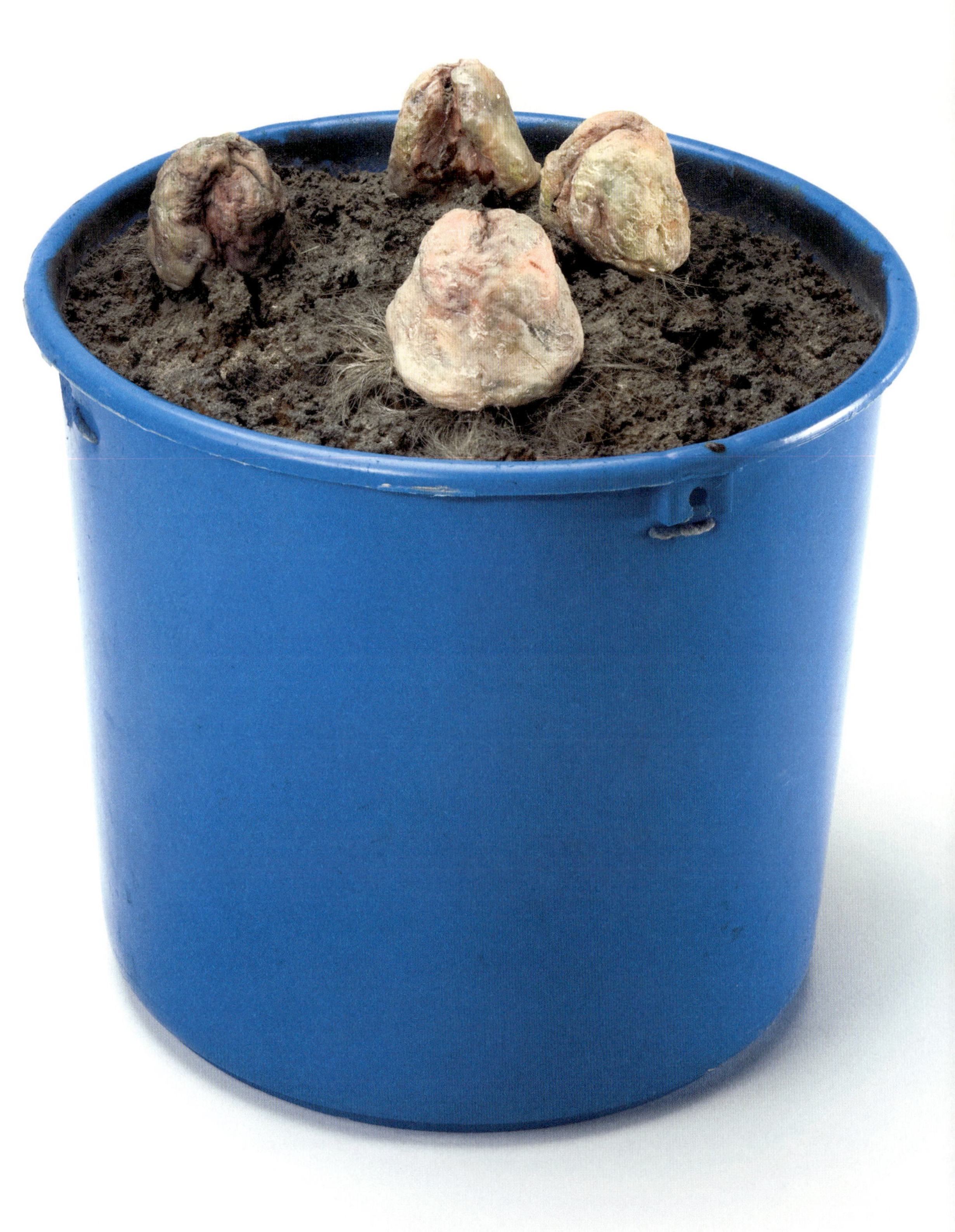

*Cultivation of Nature & People Who Are Looking at It*, 1970

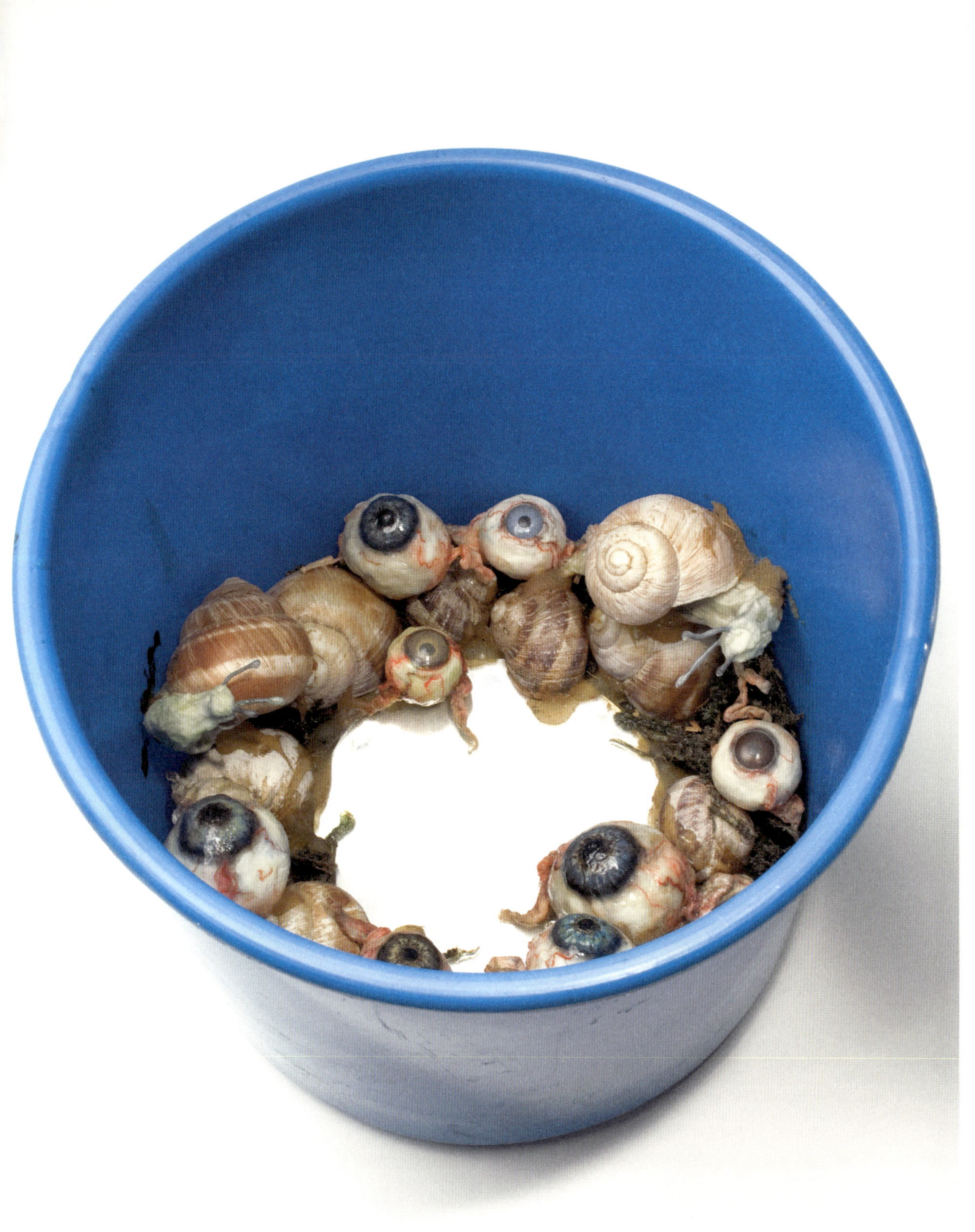

*ultivation of Nature & People Who Are Looking at It*, 1970

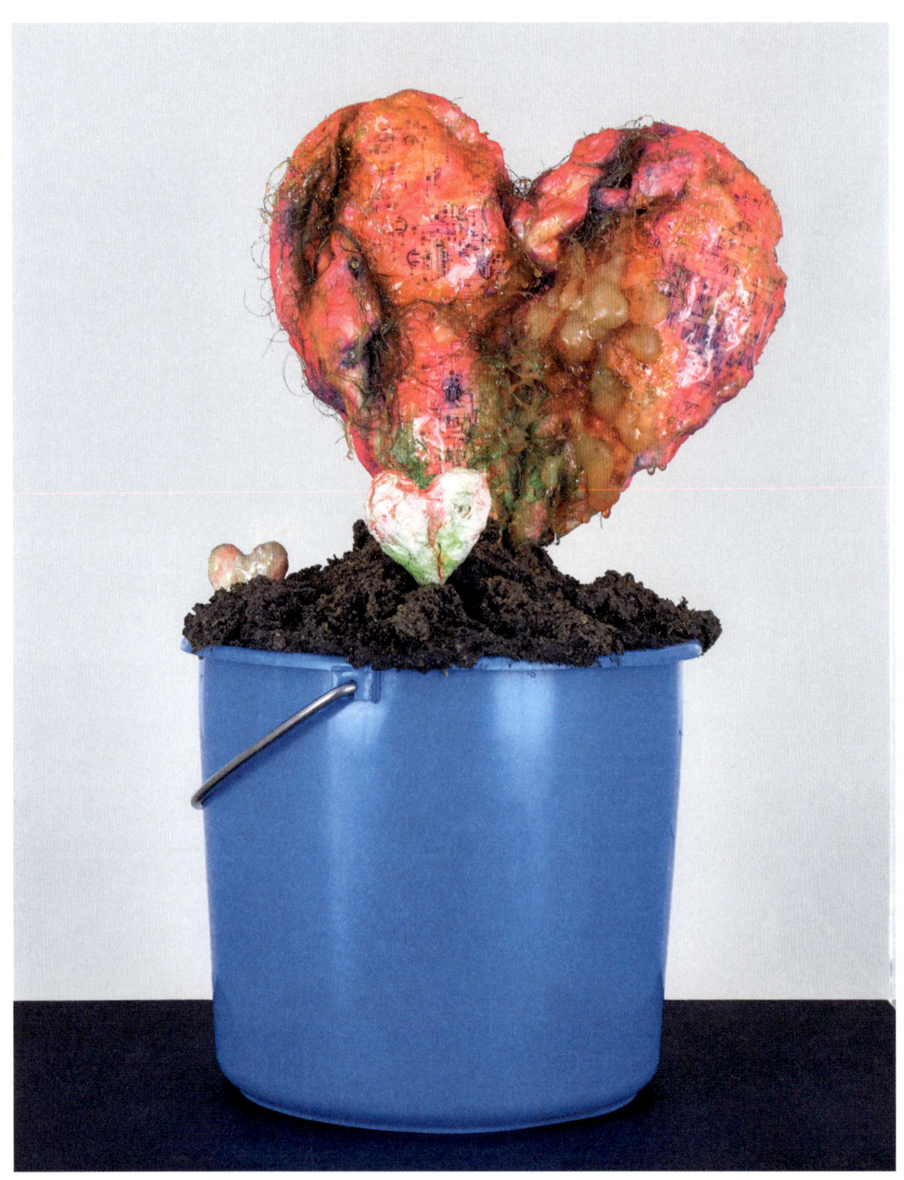

*Cultivation of Nature & People Who Are Looking at It*, c. 1970

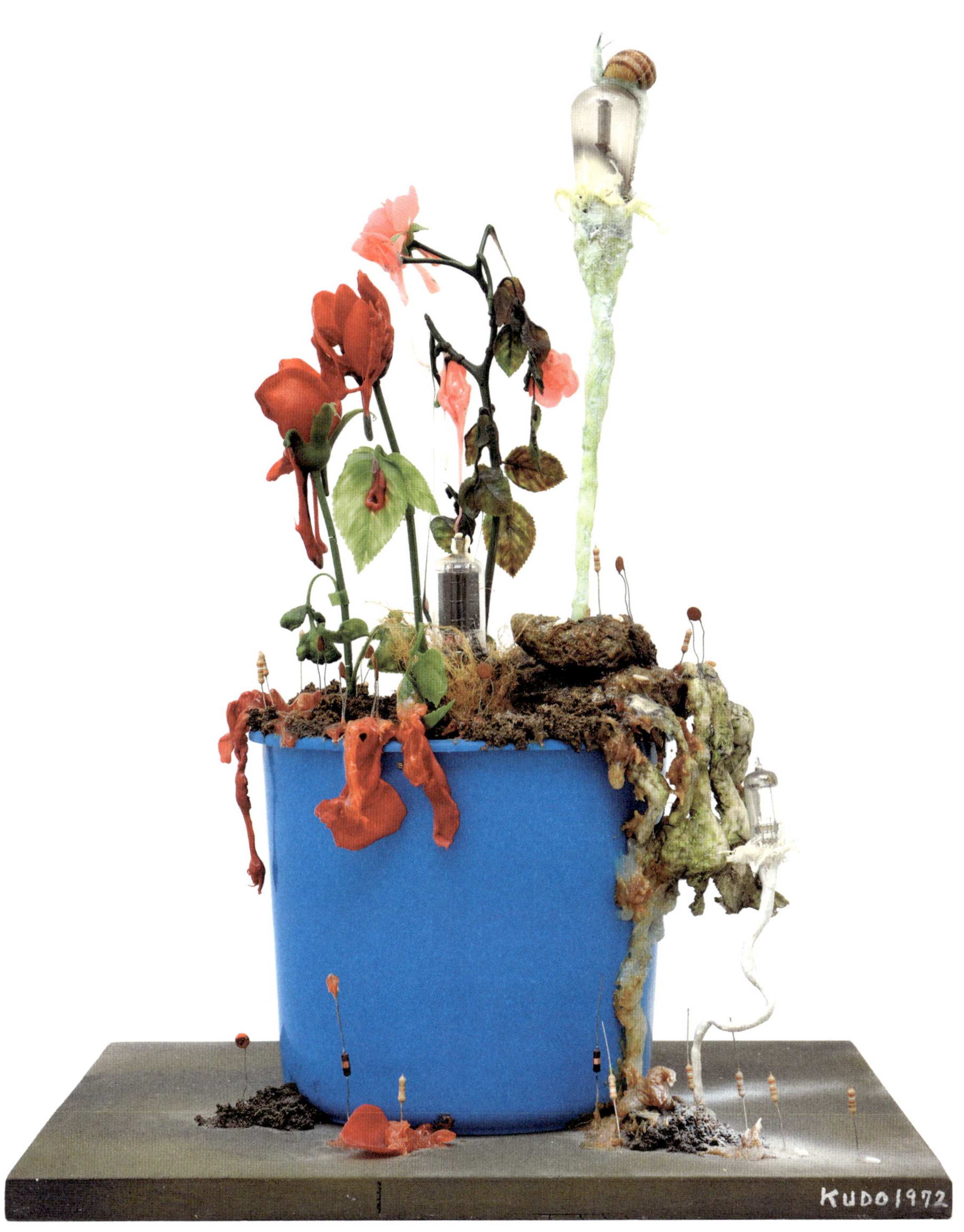


*ans titre*, 1972

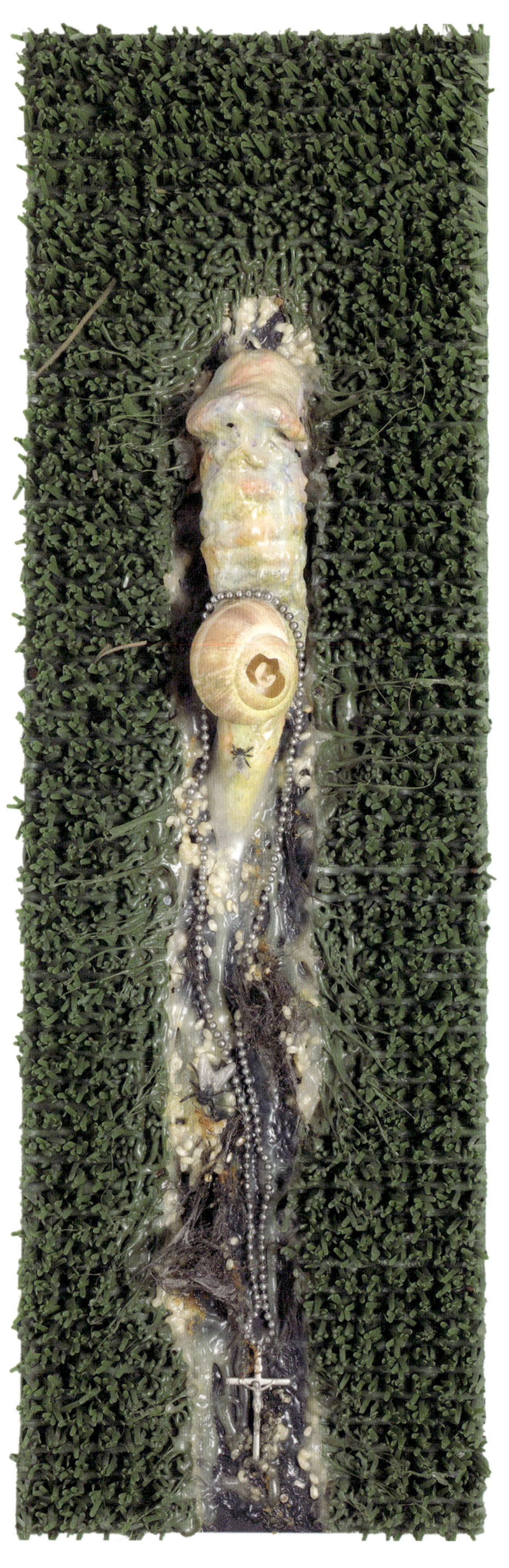

*Origine de la pollution*, 1972-7

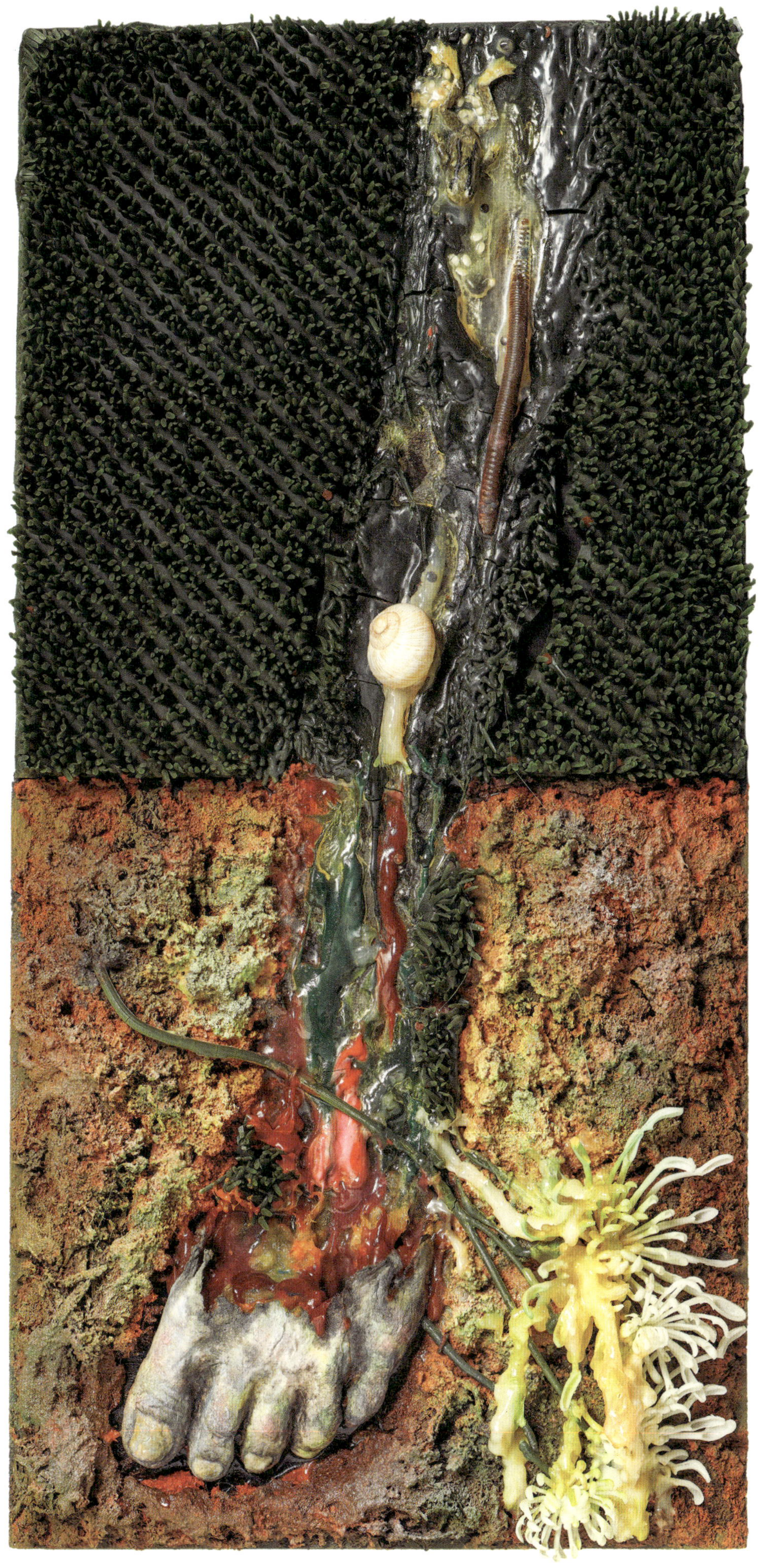

*ollution*, 1971-73

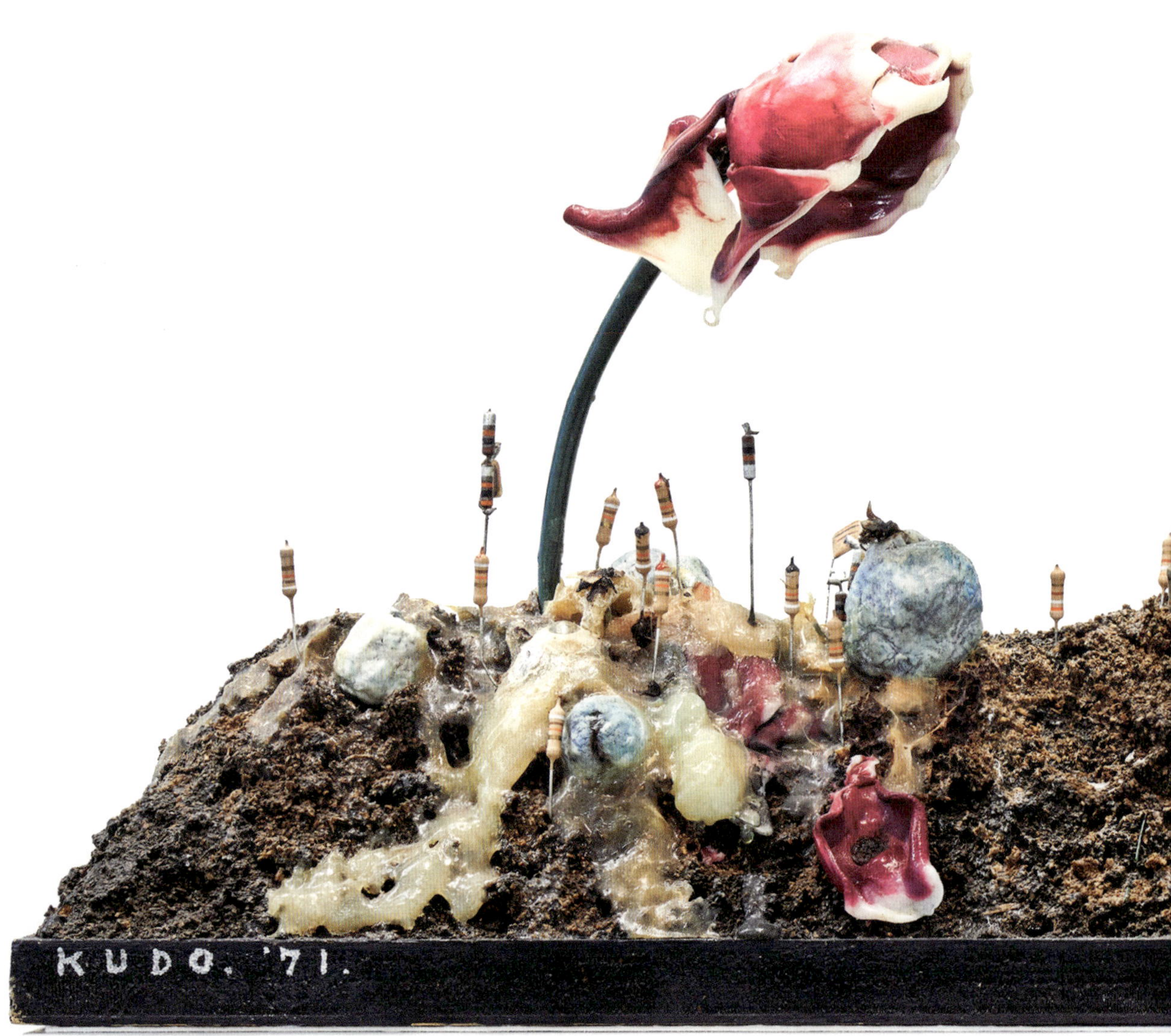


*Pollution – cultivation – nouvelle écologie (B)*, 1971

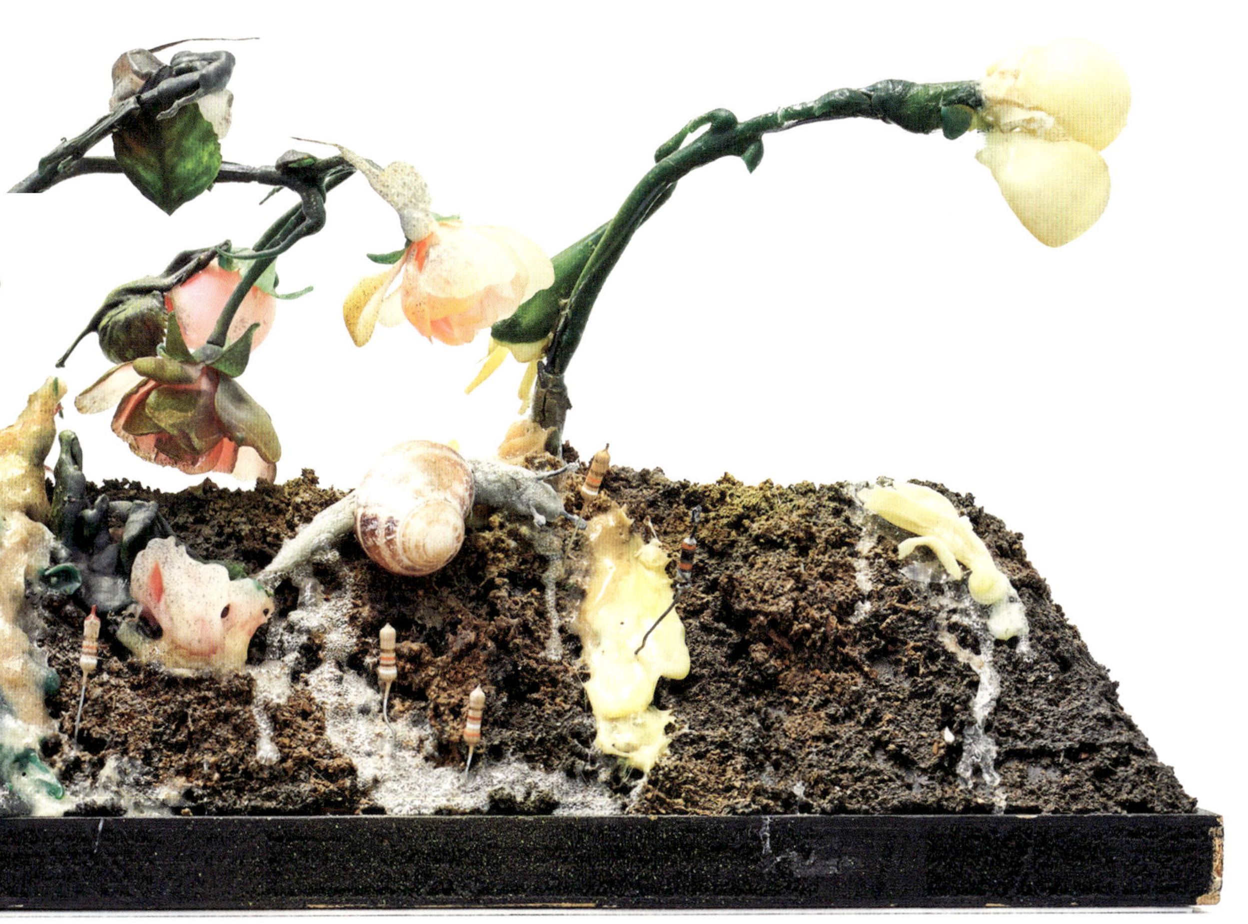

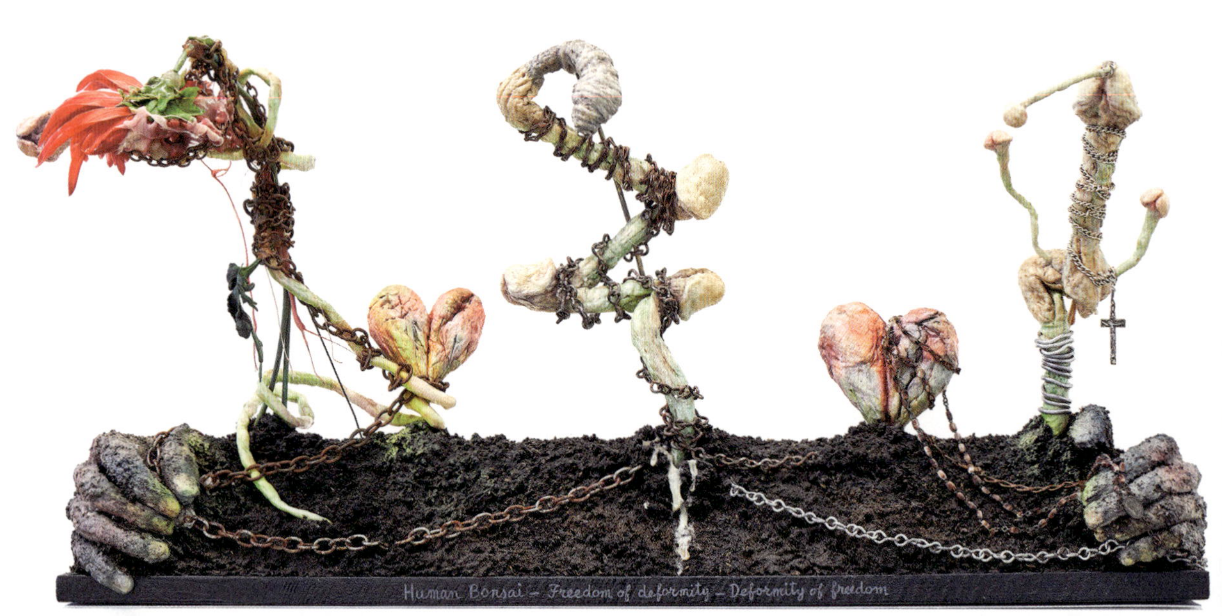


*Human Bonsai – Freedom of Deformity – Deformity of Freedom* (detail opposite page), 1979

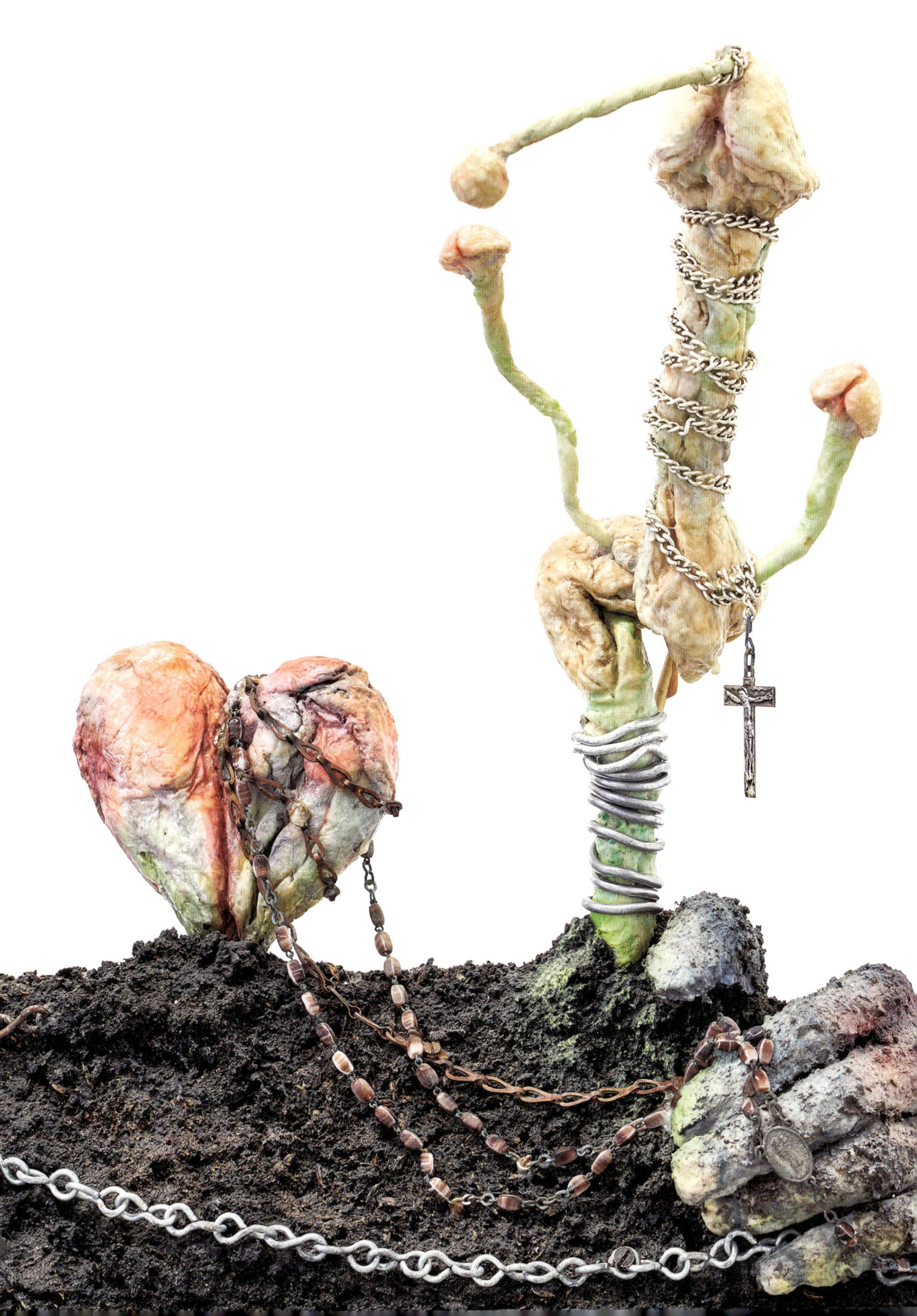

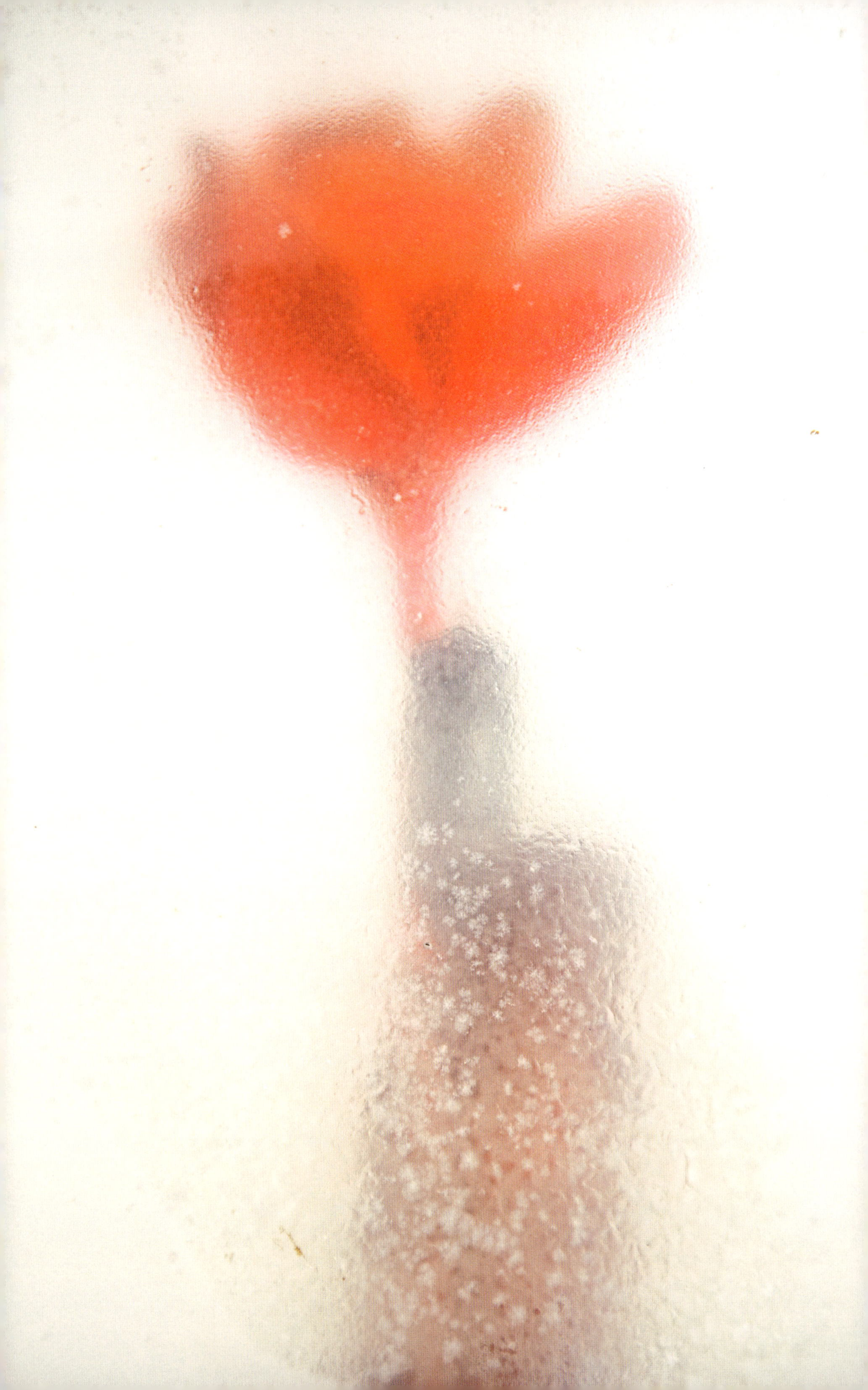

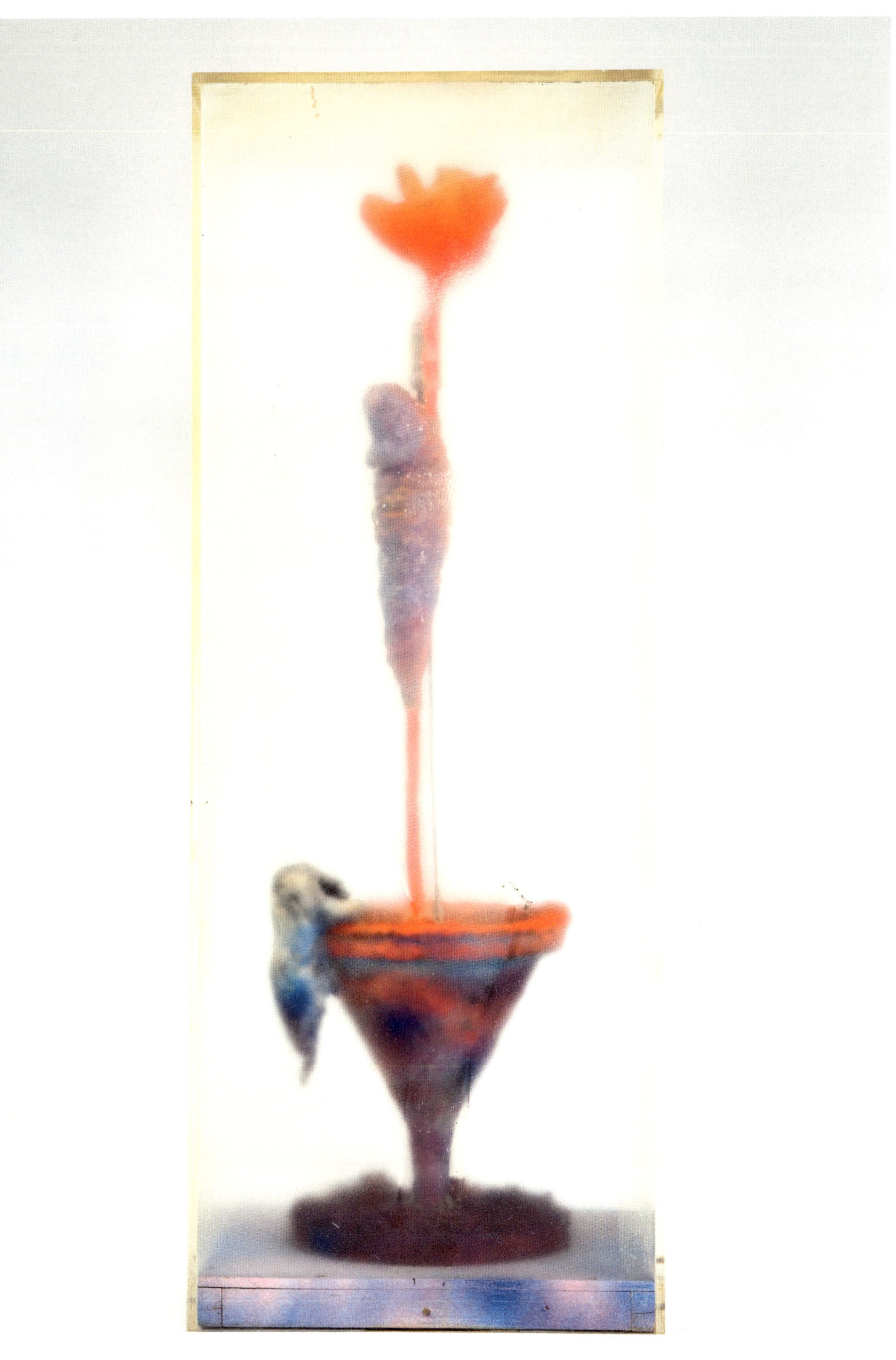

*ultivation by Radioactivity in the Electronic Circuit (Pink Flower)* (detail opposite page), 1968

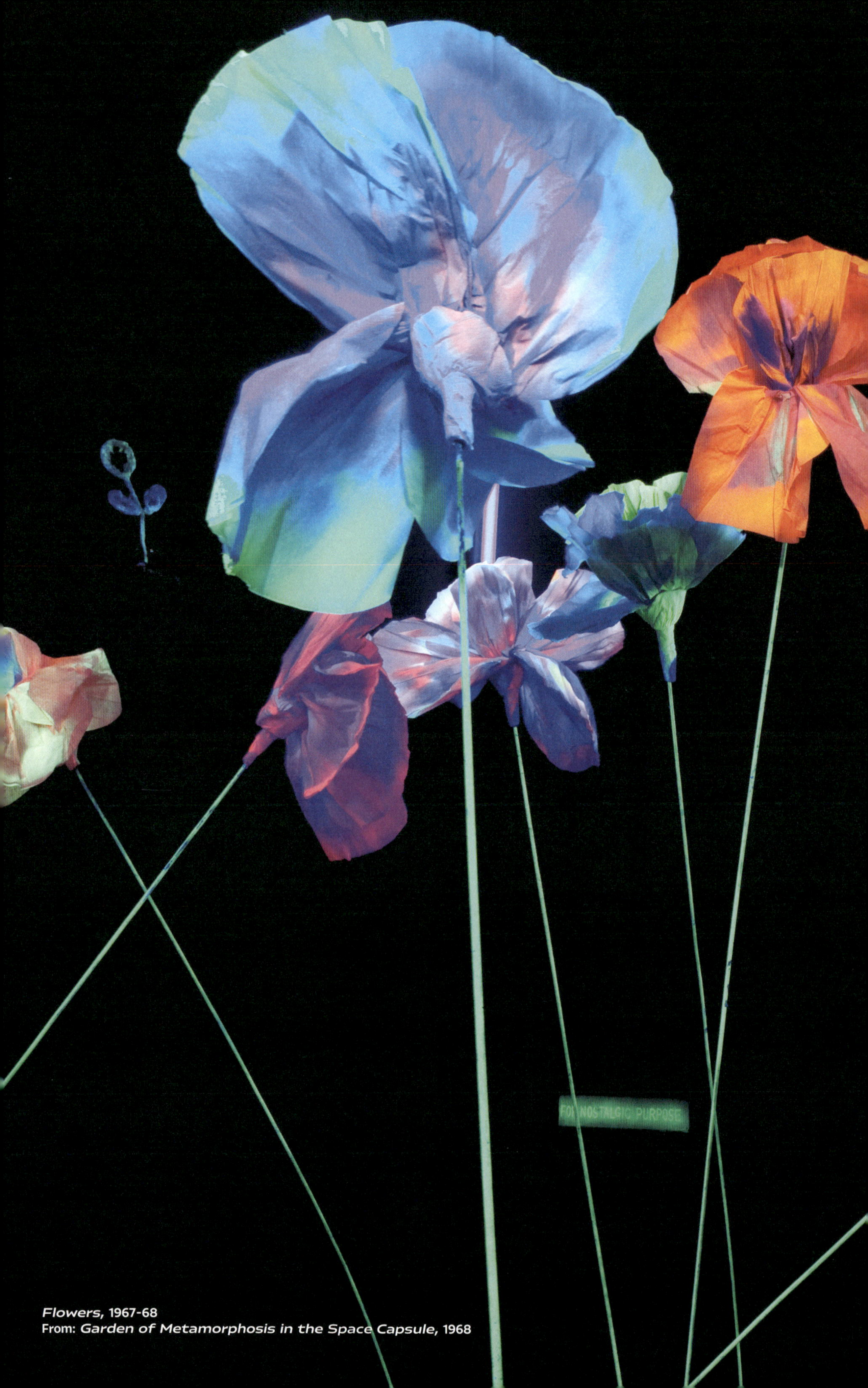


*Flowers*, 1967-68
From: *Garden of Metamorphosis in the Space Capsule*, 1968

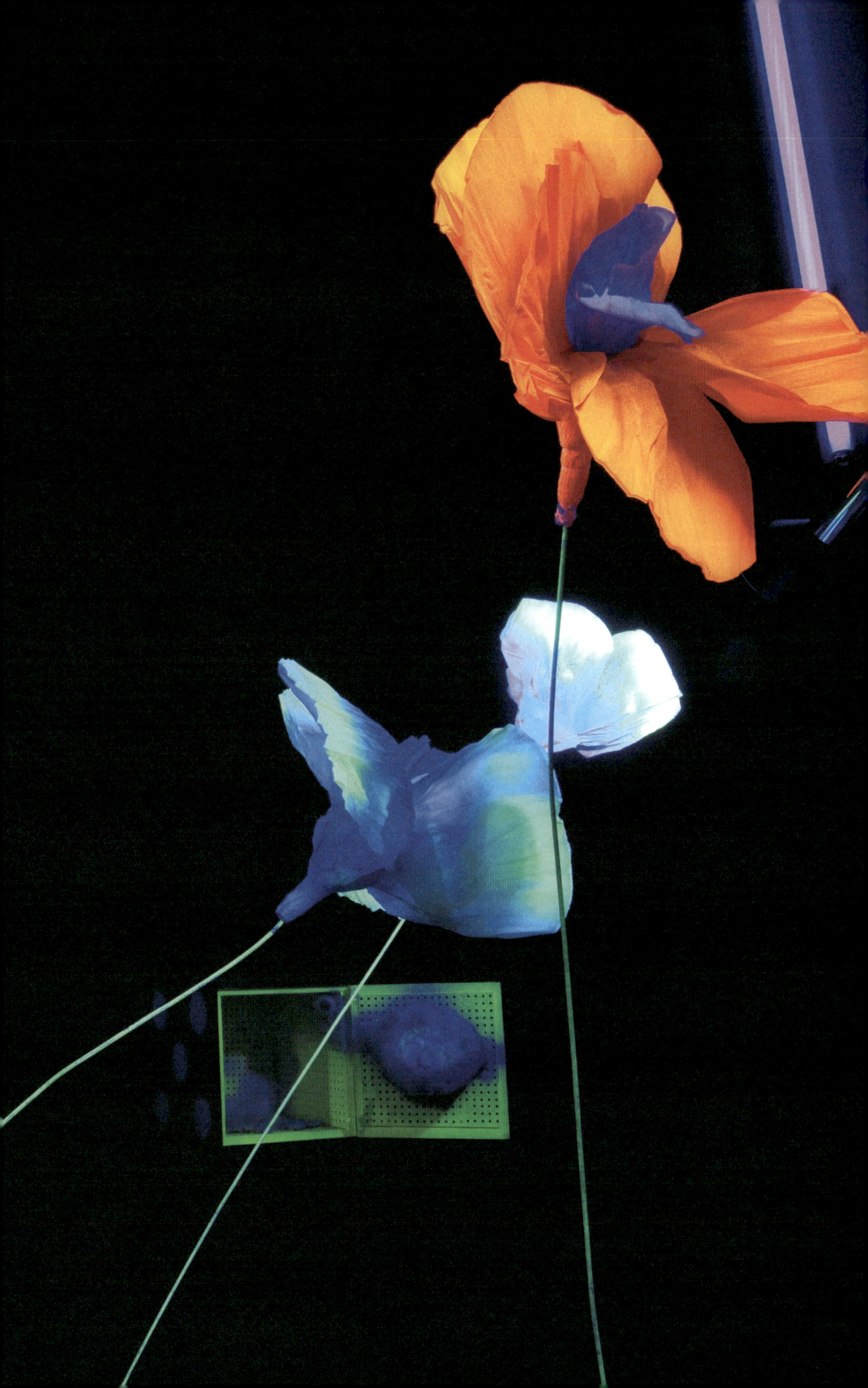

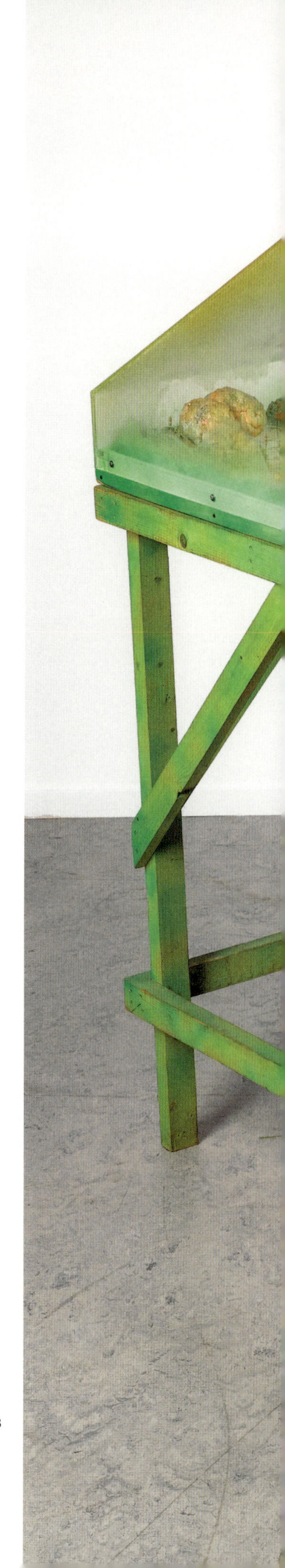

*Cultivation by Radioactivity in the Electronic Circuit*, 1968

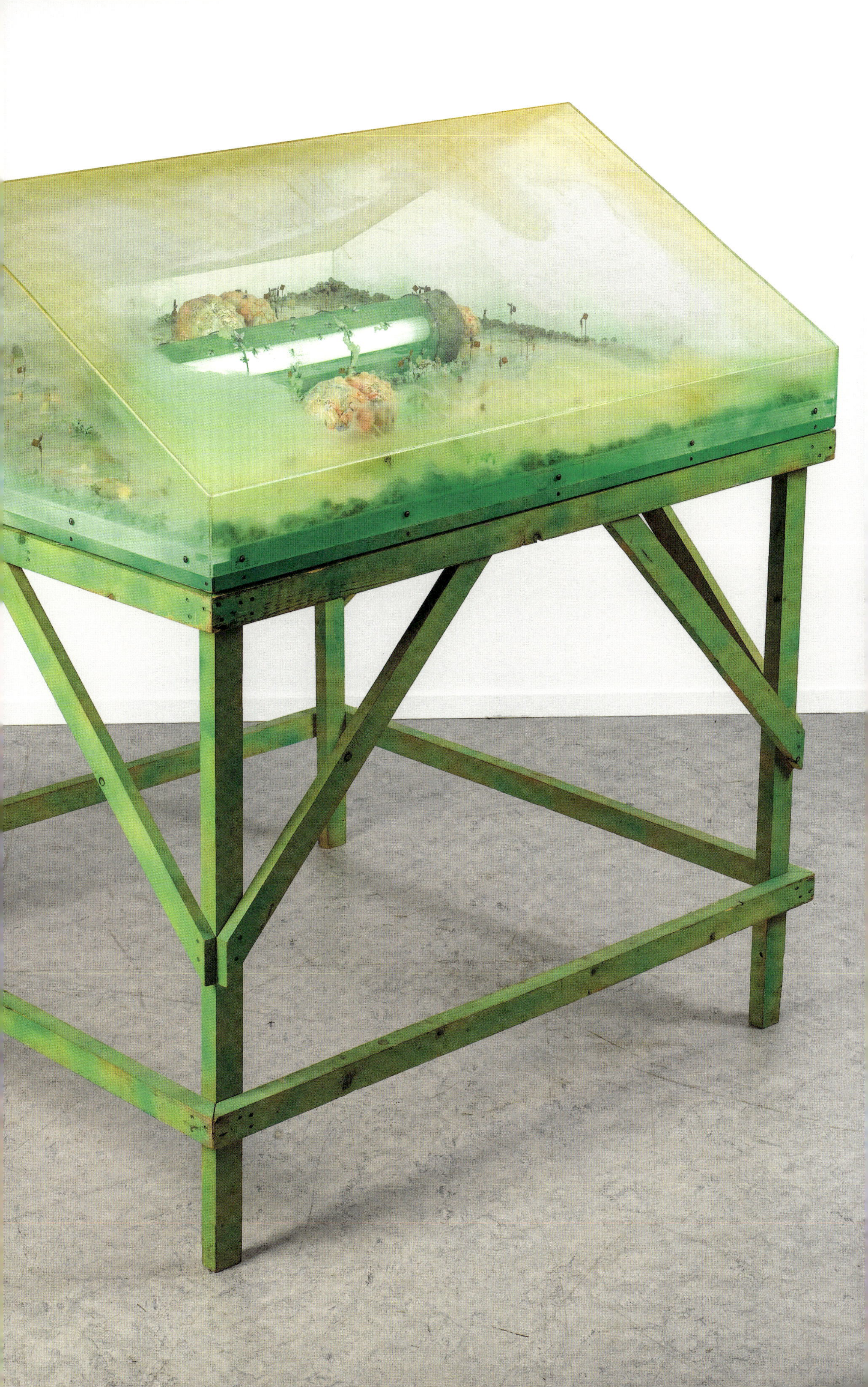

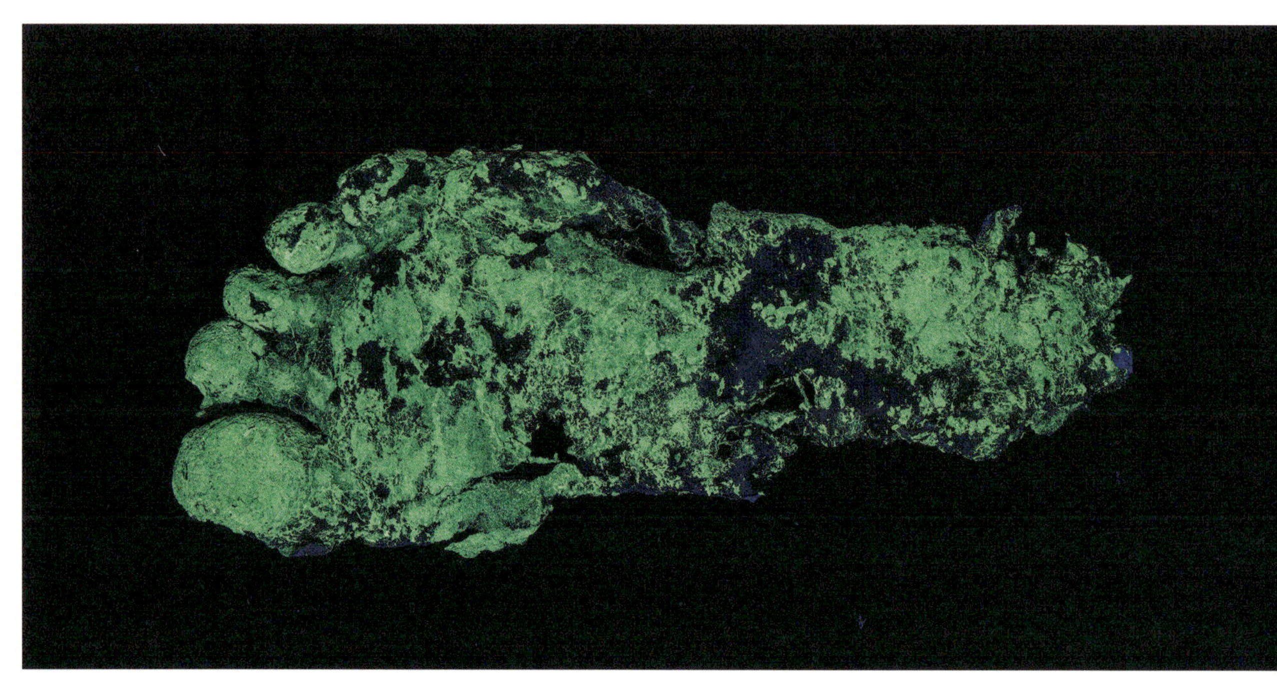

*Souvenir la Mue — 1965 Homo sapiens*, 1965
Opposite page: *CULTIVATION*, 1967

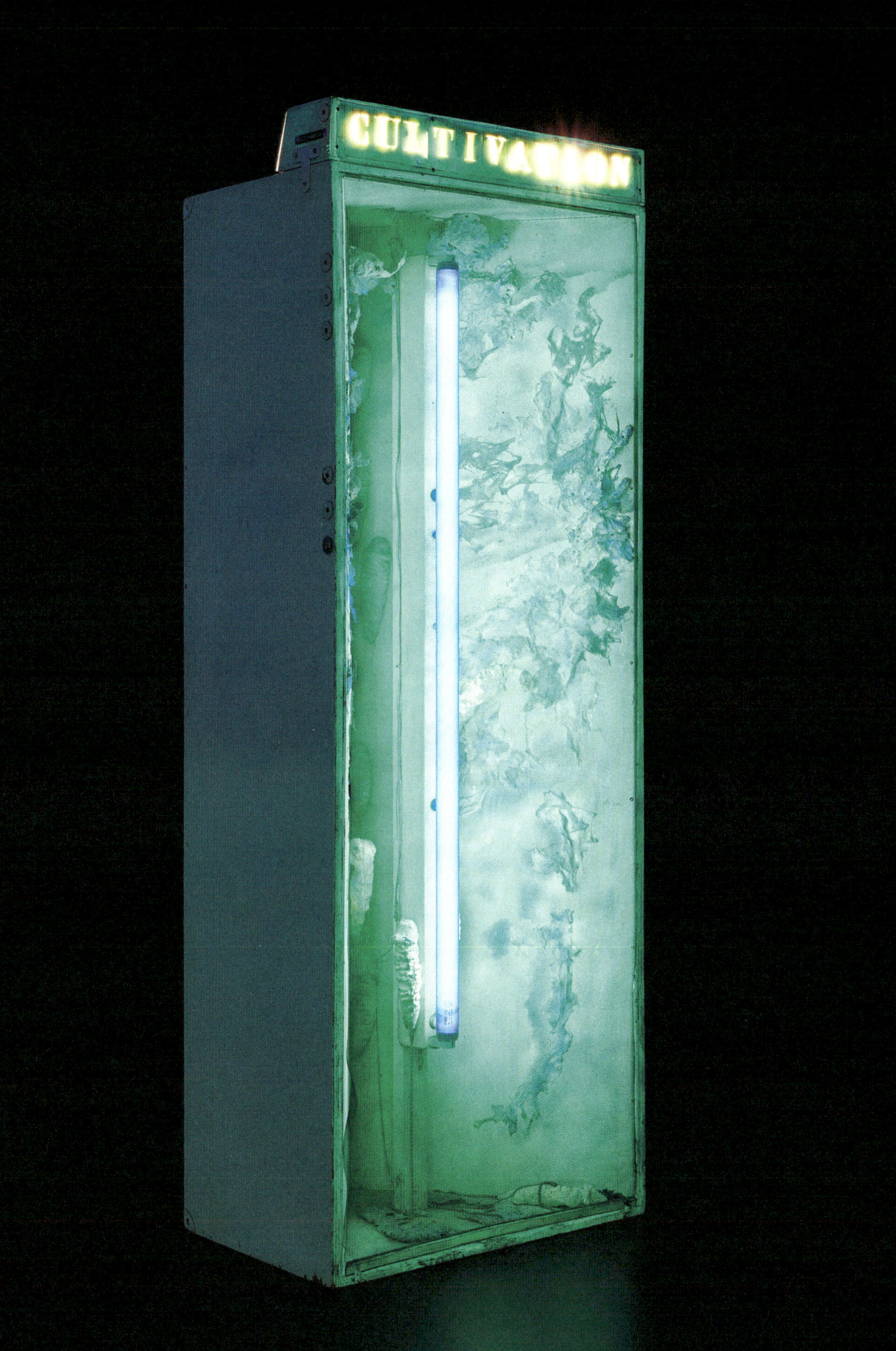
CULTIVATION

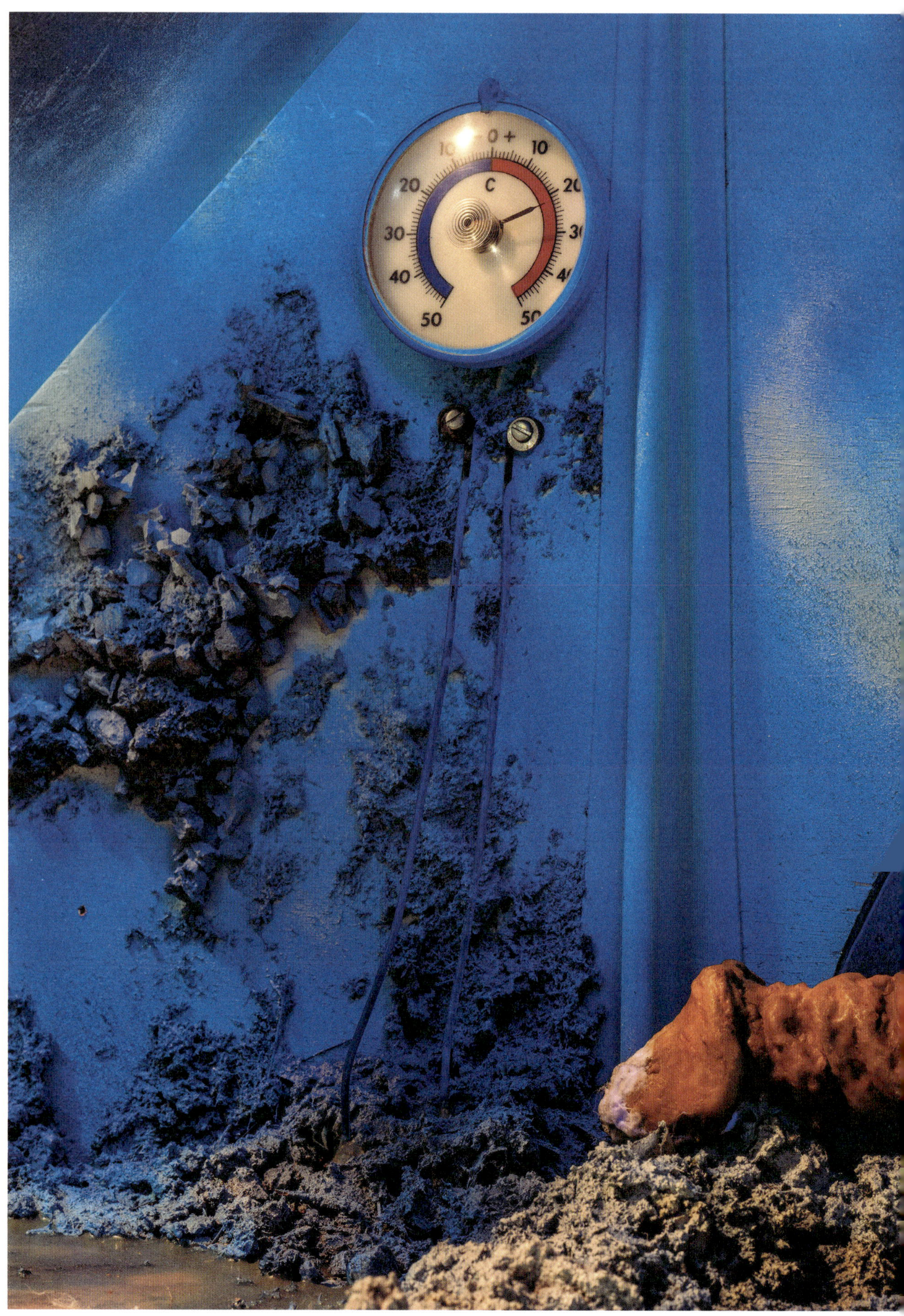


*Cultivation by Radioactivity in the Electronic Circuit* (details this page and next spread), 1968

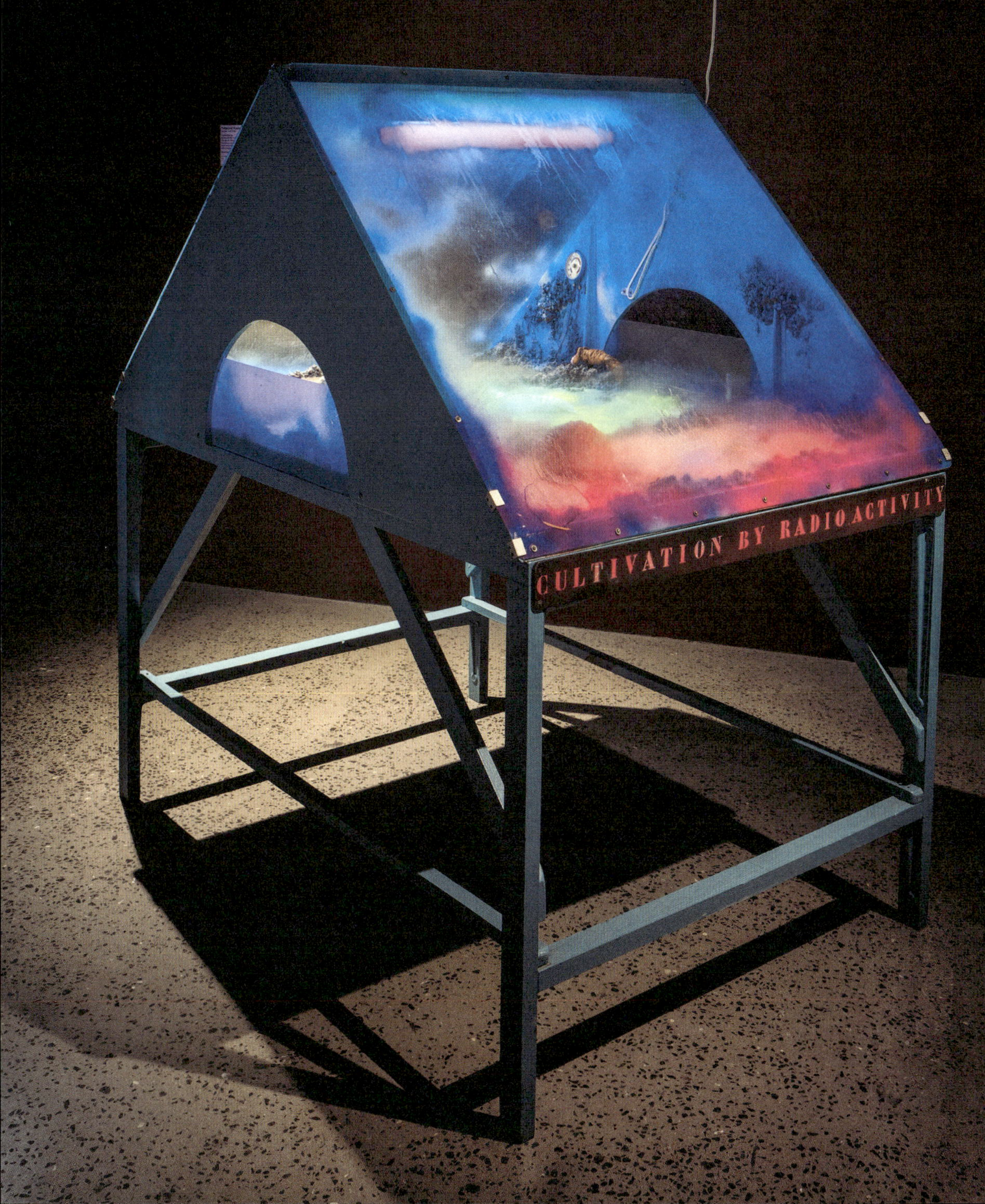
CULTIVATION BY RADIOACTIVITY

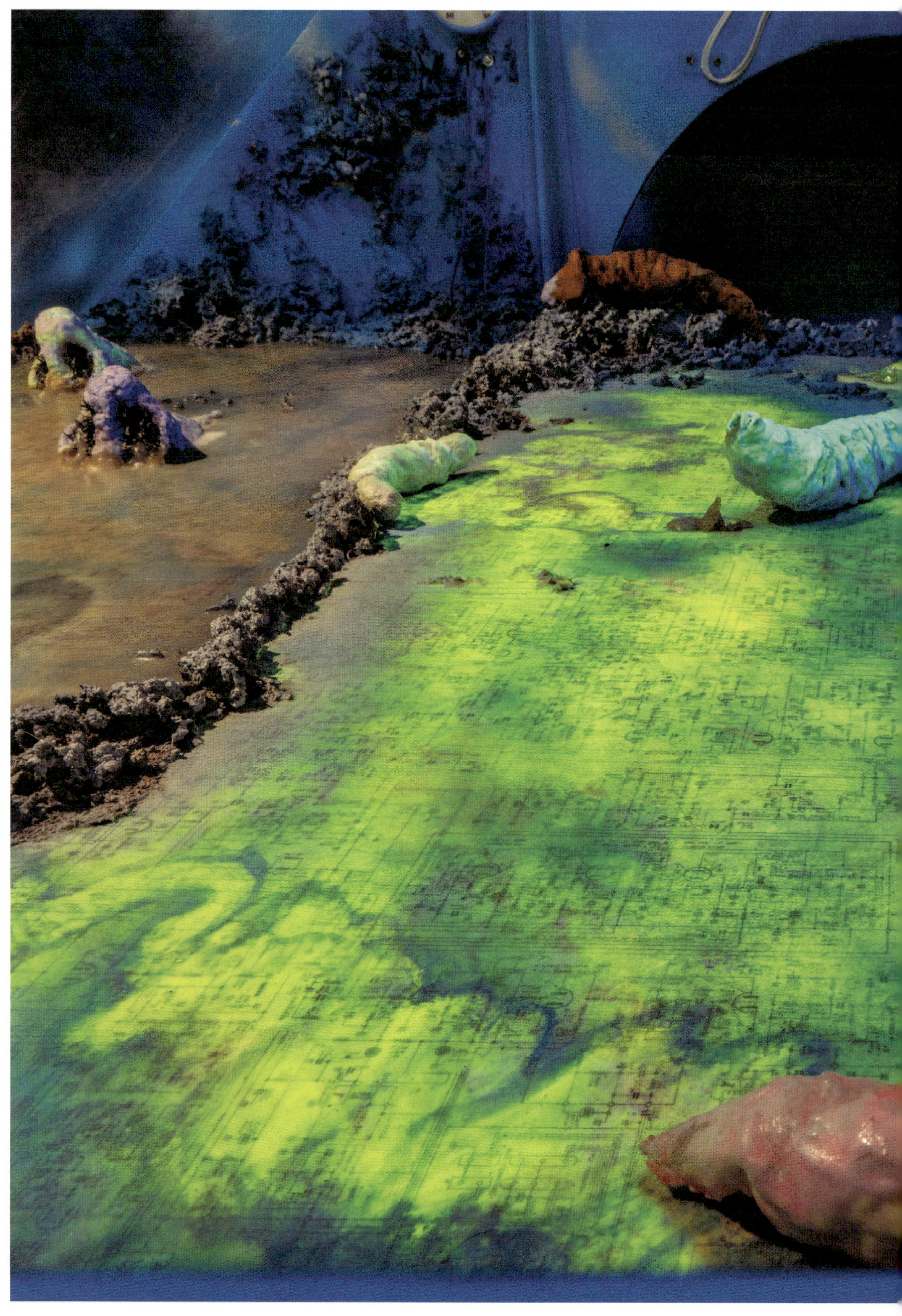

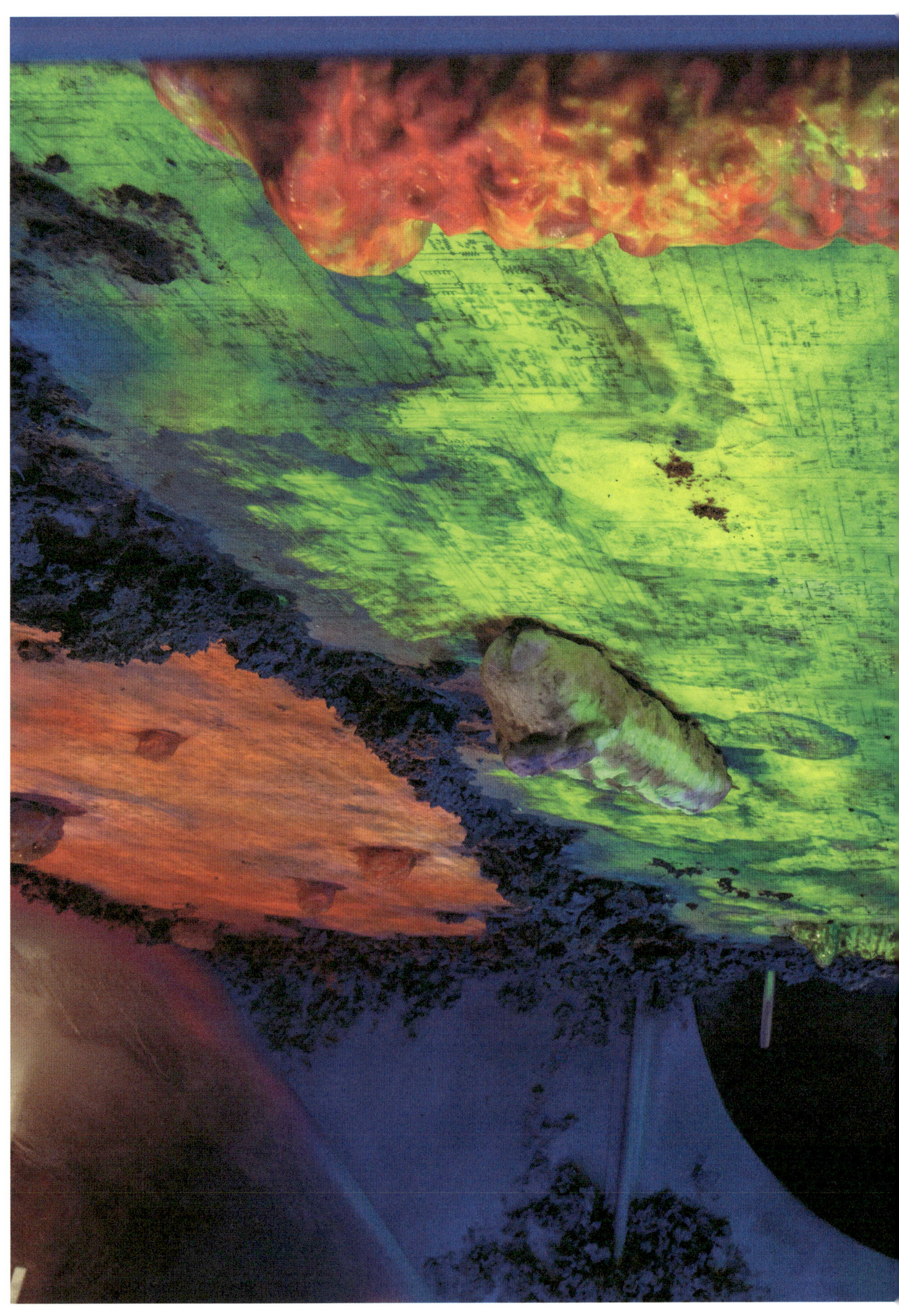

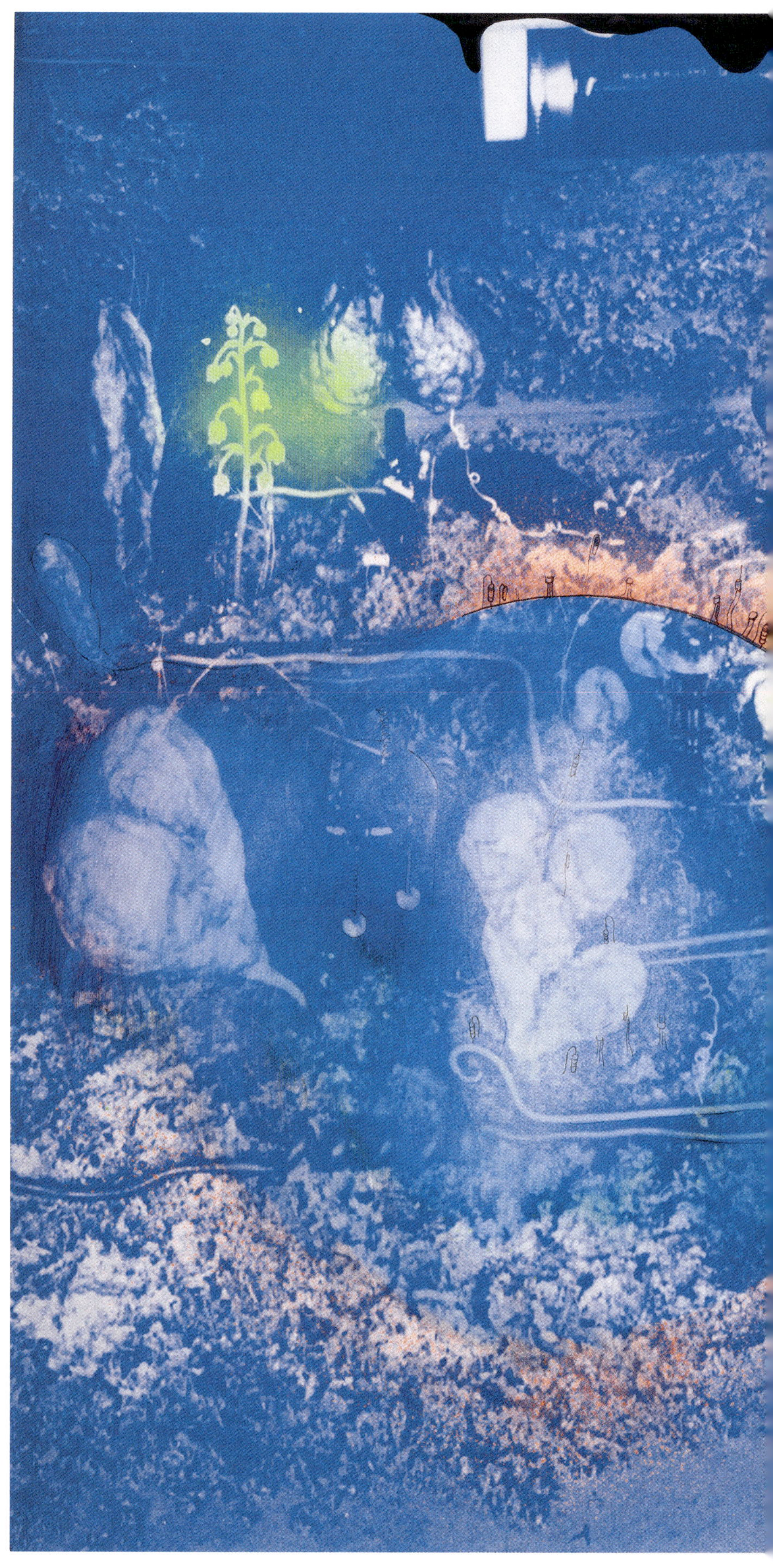

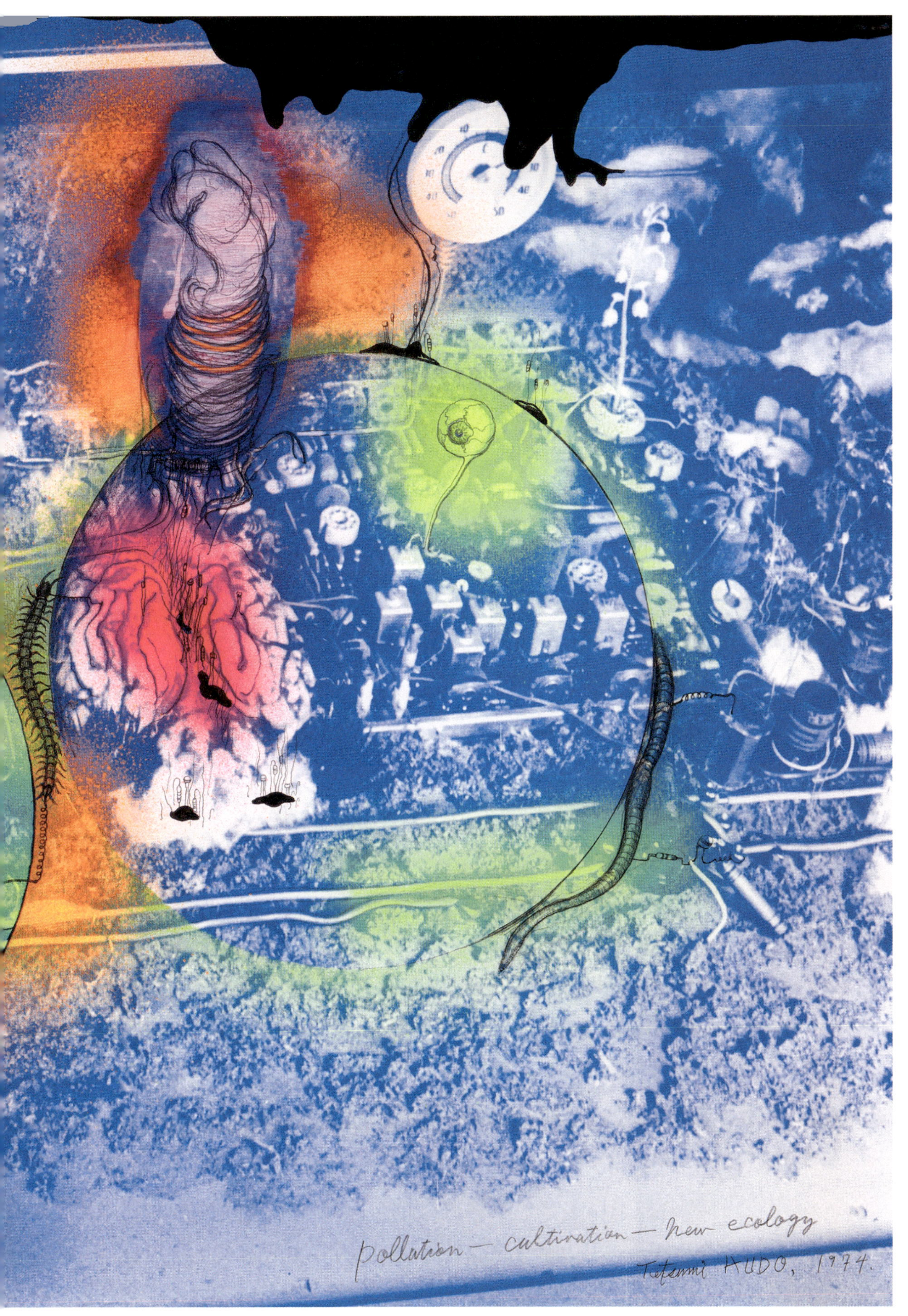


*Pollution Cultivation New Ecology*, 1974

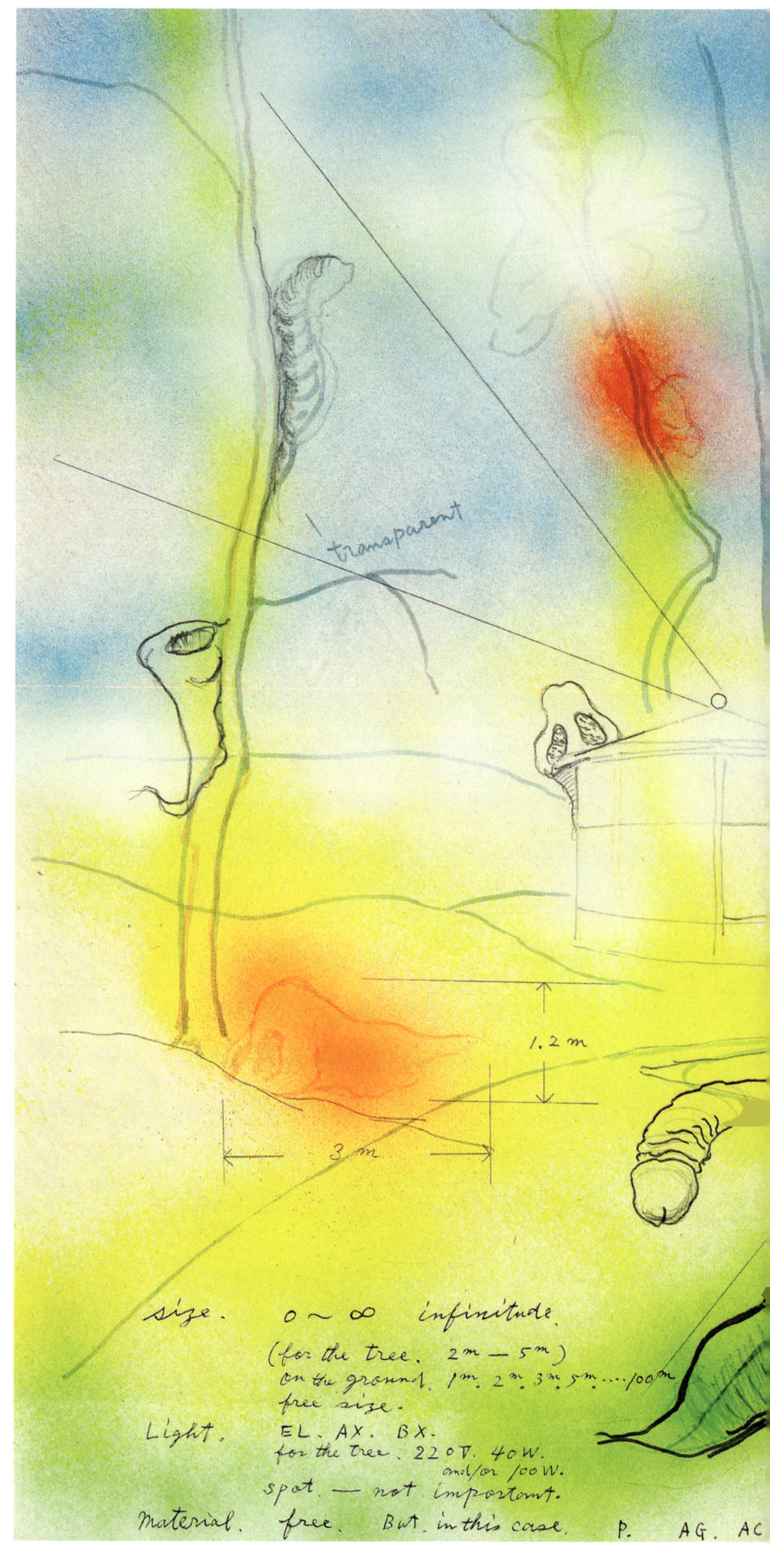

transparent
1.2 m
3 m
size. 0 ~ ∞ infinitude.
(for the tree. 2m — 5m)
on the ground. 1m. 2m. 3m. 5m. ....100m
free size.
Light. EL. AX. BX.
for the tree. 220V. 40W.
and/or 100W.
spot. — not important.
Material. free. But in this case. P. AG. AC

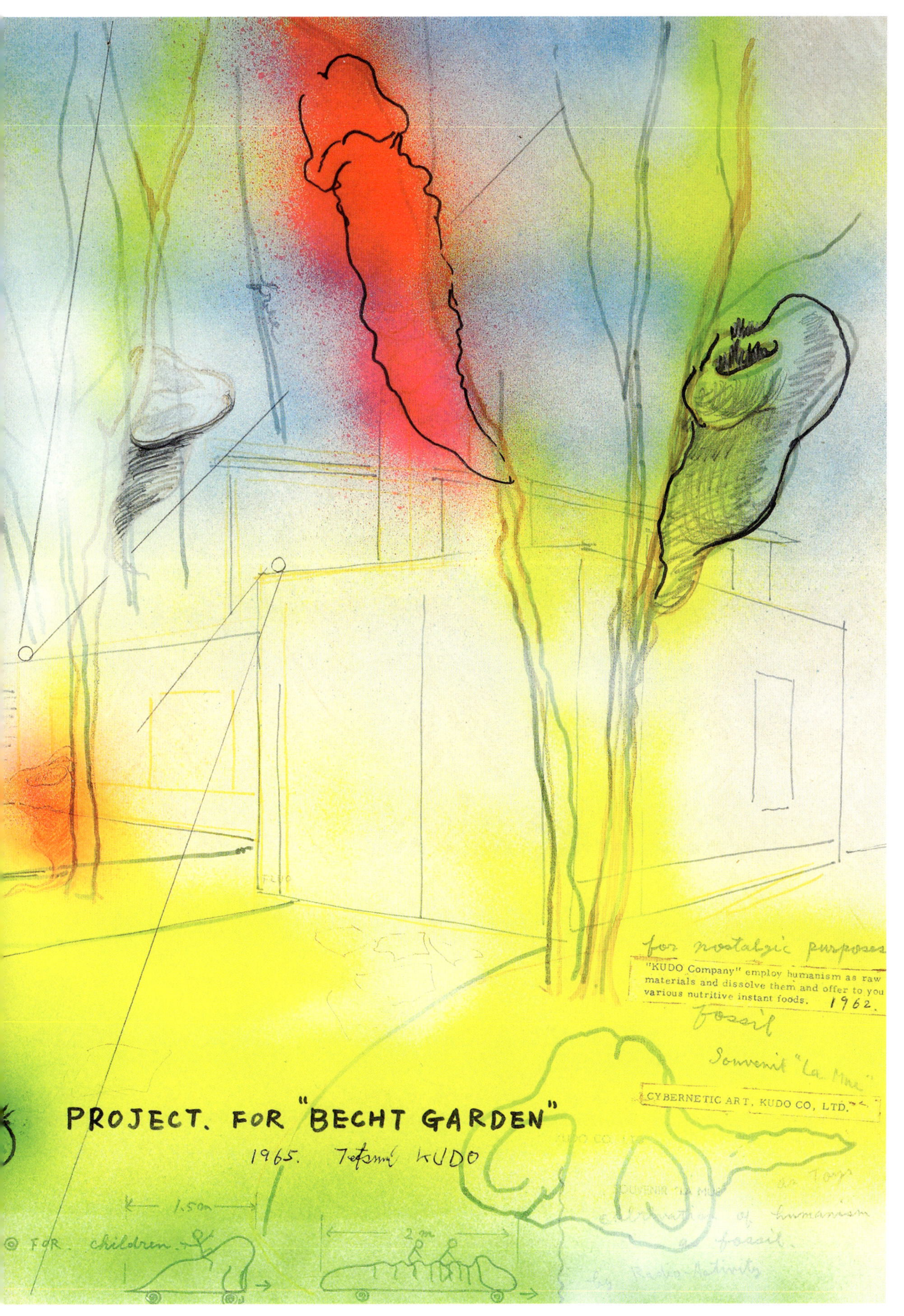


*Project for "Becht Garden"*, 1965

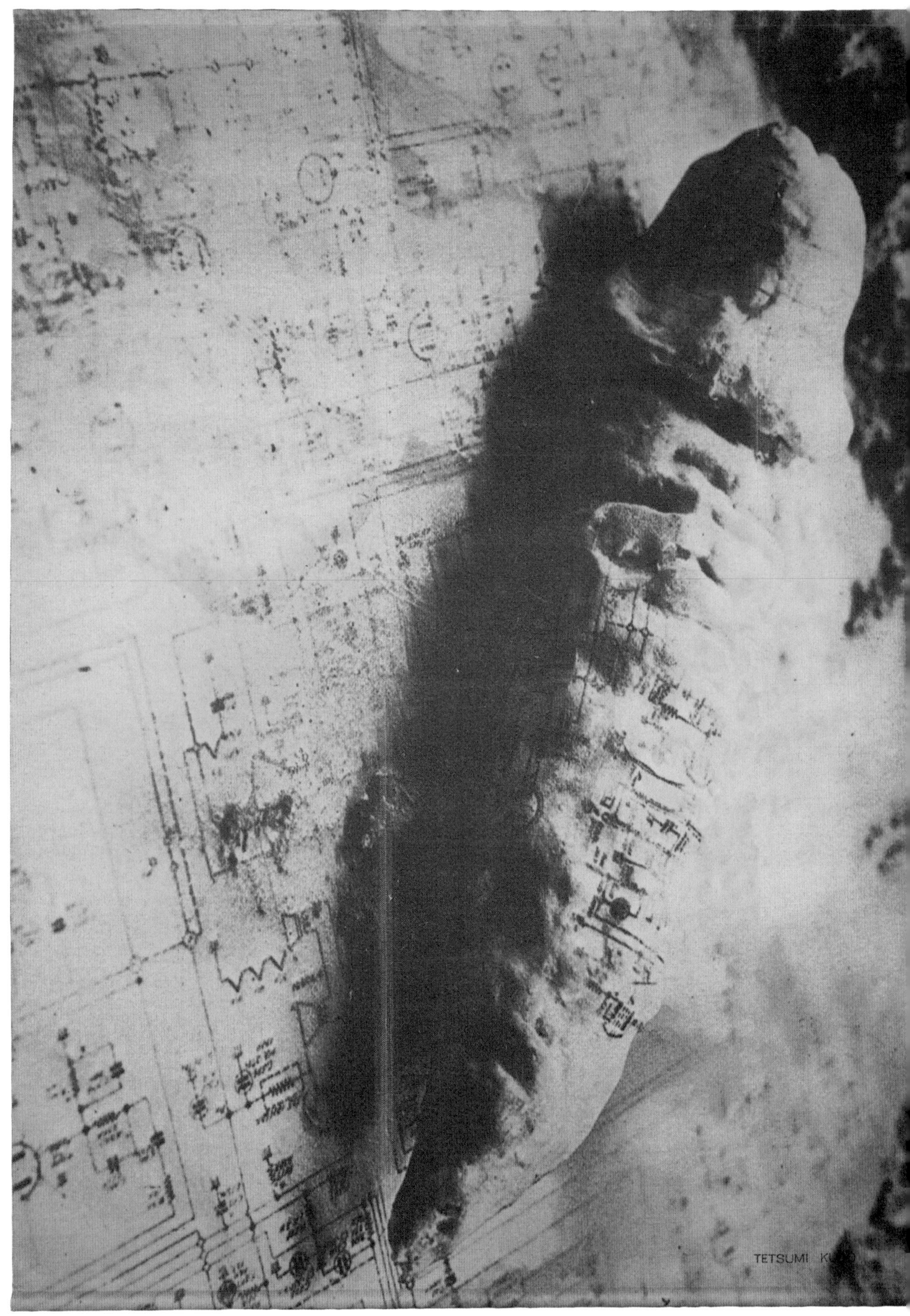


*Translation Painting by Computer B*, 1971

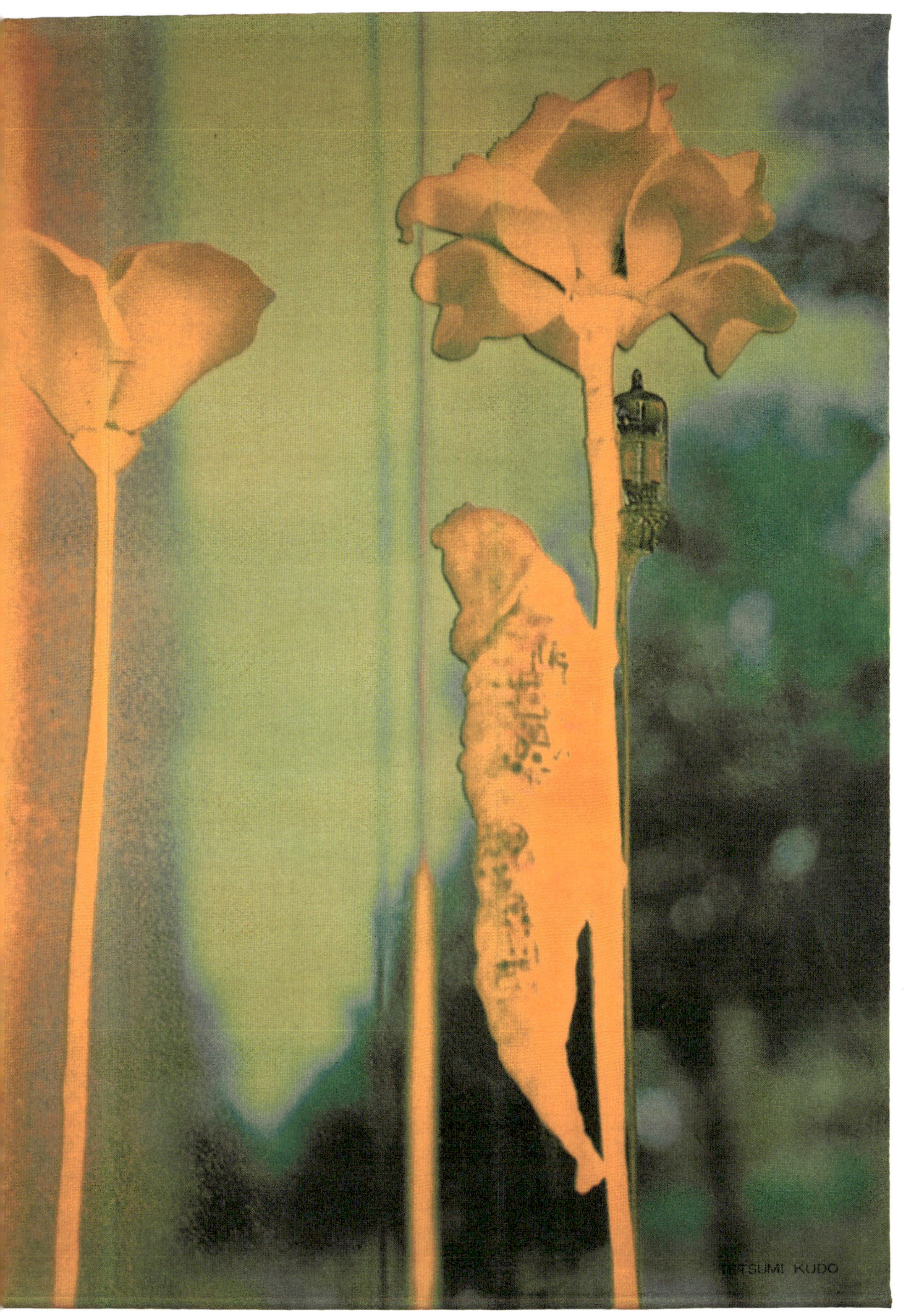


*ranslation Painting by Computer A*, 1971

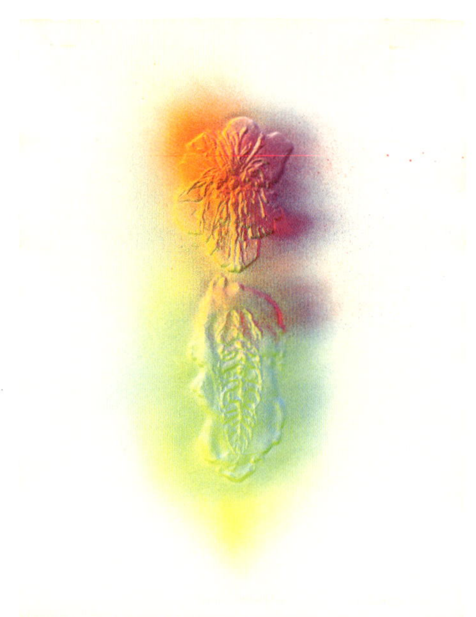

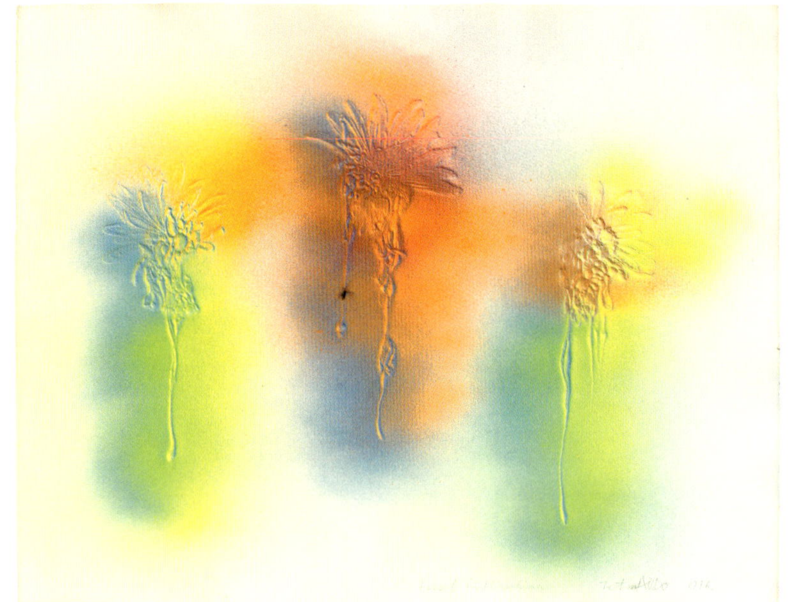

*Fossil in Hiroshima*, 1976

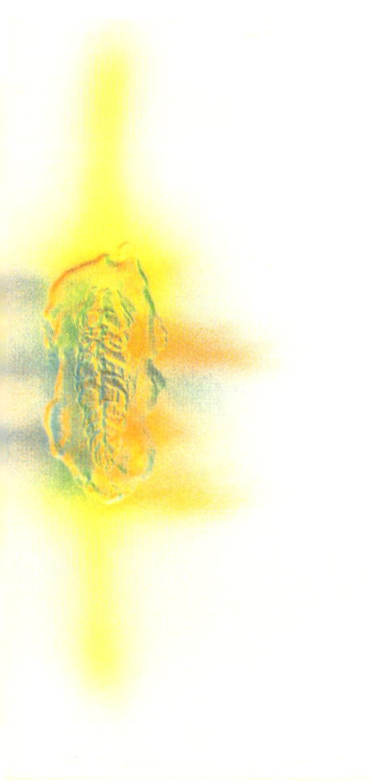

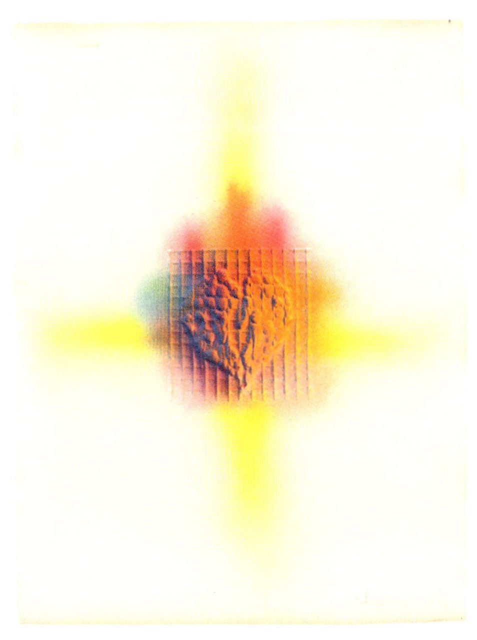

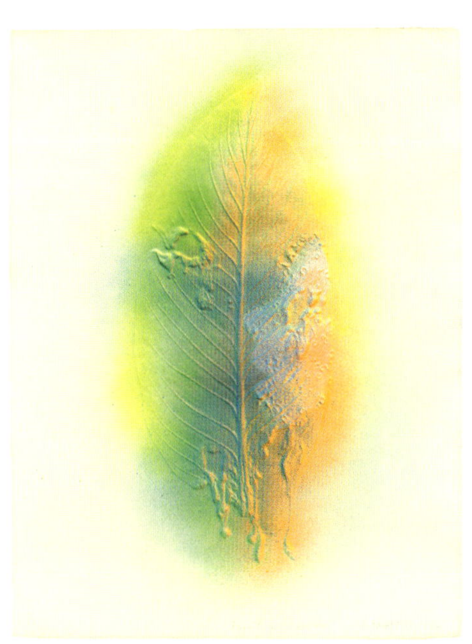

*Votre Portrait*, 1974

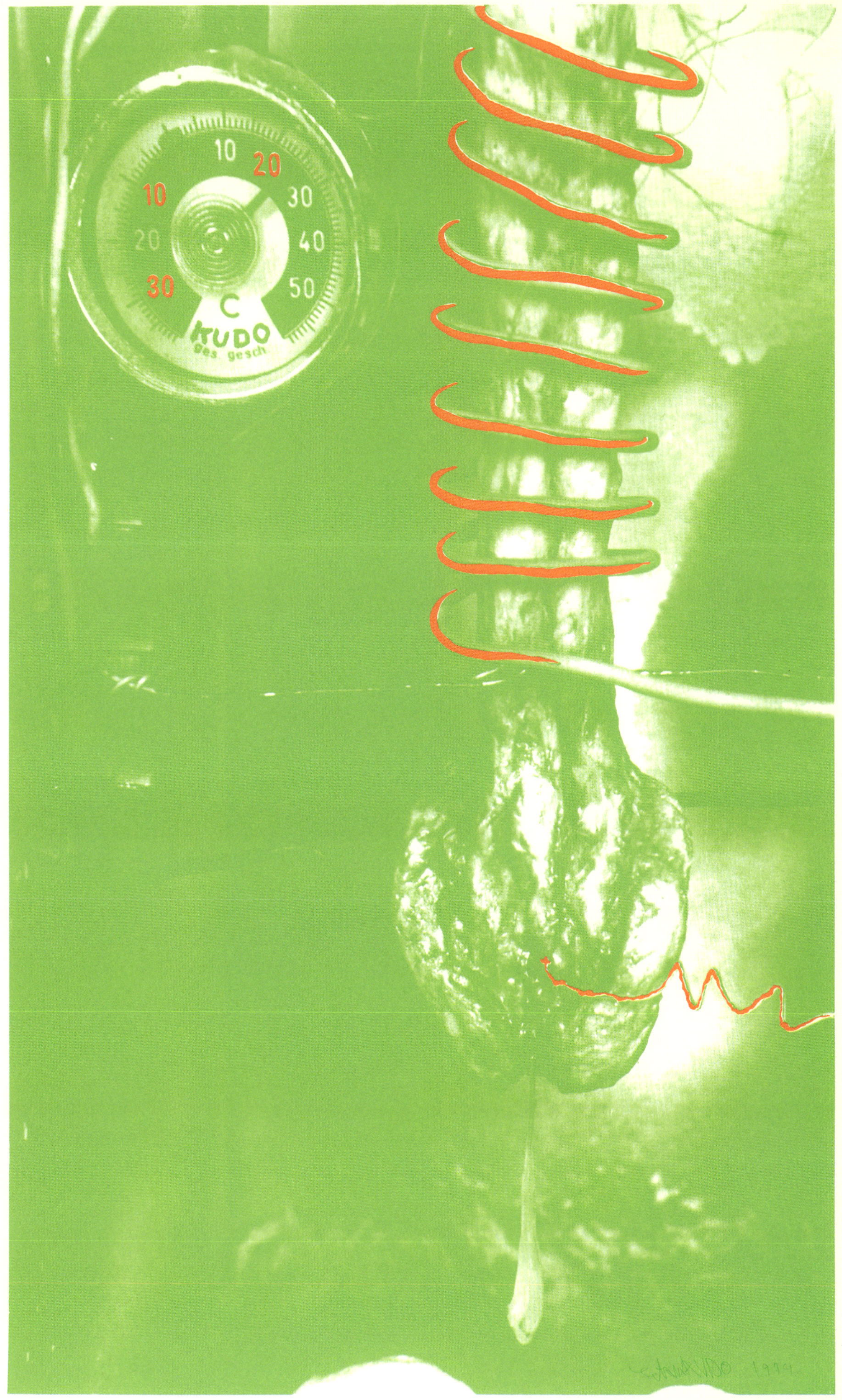
10
20
10
30
20
40
30
50
C
KUDO
ges gesch

WORKS

TETSUMI KUDO